Critical Rationalism and the Theory of Society

Investigating Karl Popper's philosophy of critical rationalism, *Critical Rationalism and the Theory of Society*, Volume 1, explores a non-justificationist conception of critical reason and its fundamental outcomes for the theory of society.

Through a set of fundamental contributions to epistemology, the theory of rationality and sociology, this volume (a) situates the idea of critical rationalism in its true epistemological context, (b) uses non-justificationist epistemology to reinvent critical rationalism and (c) applies its revised concept of rationality to show how people's access to critical reason enables them to agree on the common values and social institutions necessary for a peaceful and just social order. These contributions lead the reader to a new epistemological understanding of the idea of critical rationalism and recognition of how a non-justificational concept of reason changes the content of the theory of society.

The reader also learns how thinkers, movements and masses apply their critical reason to replace an established social order with an ideal one through activating five types of driving forces of social change: metaphysical, moral, legal, political and economic. Written for philosophers and sociologists, this book will appeal to social scientists such as moral philosophers, legal scholars, political scientists and economists.

Masoud Mohammadi Alamuti is a sociologist and faculty member at the Institute for Management and Planning Studies (IMPS) in Tehran, Iran. His research interests include epistemology, sociological theory, sociology of modernity and development, and globalization studies.

Routledge Studies in Social and Political Thought

152 Stupidity in Politics
Its Unavoidability and Potential
Nobutaka Otobe

153 Political Correctness: A Sociocultural Black Hole
Thomas Tsakalakis

154 The Individual After Modernity: A Sociological Perspective
Mira Marody

155 The Politics of Well-Being
Towards a More Ethical World
Anthony M. Clohesy

156 From Hitler to Codreanu
The Ideology of Fascist Leaders
Carlos Manuel Martins

157 The Fascist Temptation
Creating a Political Community of Experience
David Ohana

158 Accumulating Capital Today
Contemporary Strategies of Profit and Dispossessive Policies
Marlène Benquet and Théo Bourgeron

159 Critical Rationalism and the Theory of Society
Critical Rationalism and the Open Society Volume I
Masoud Mohammadi Alamuti

For a full list of titles in this series, please visit www.routledge.com/series/RSSPT

Critical Rationalism and the Theory of Society

Critical Rationalism and the Open Society Volume 1

Masoud Mohammadi Alamuti

LONDON AND NEW YORK

First published 2021
by Routledge
2 Park Square, Milton Park, Abingdon, Oxon OX14 4RN

and by Routledge
52 Vanderbilt Avenue, New York, NY 10017

Routledge is an imprint of the Taylor & Francis Group, an informa business

© 2021 Masoud Mohammadi Alamuti

The right of Masoud Mohammadi Alamuti to be identified as
author of this work has been asserted by him in accordance with
sections 77 and 78 of the Copyright, Designs and Patents Act 1988.

All rights reserved. No part of this book may be reprinted
or reproduced or utilised in any form or by any electronic,
mechanical, or other means, now known or hereafter invented,
including photocopying and recording, or in any information
storage or retrieval system, without permission in writing from
the publishers.

Trademark notice: Product or corporate names may be trademarks
or registered trademarks, and are used only for identification and
explanation without intent to infringe.

British Library Cataloguing-in-Publication Data
A catalogue record for this book is available from the British Library

Library of Congress Cataloging-in-Publication Data
Names: Alamuti, Masoud Mohammadi, author.
Title: Critical rationalism and the theory of society / Masoud
    Mohammadi Alamuti.
Description: Abingdon, Oxon ; New York, NY : Routledge, 2021. |
    Series: Routledge studies in social and political thought ; 159 |
    Includes bibliographical references and index. | Contents:
    volume 1. Critical rationalism and the open society
Identifiers: LCCN 2020044009 (print) | LCCN 2020044010
    (ebook) | ISBN 9780367461317 (hardback) | ISBN
    9781003027102 (ebook)
Subjects: LCSH: Critical theory. | Rationalism. |
    Sociology—Philosophy.
Classification: LCC HM480 .A434 2021 (print) | LCC HM480
    (ebook) | DDC 301.01—dc23
LC record available at https://lccn.loc.gov/2020044009
LC ebook record available at https://lccn.loc.gov/2020044010

ISBN: 978-0-367-46131-7 (hbk)
ISBN: 978-1-003-02710-2 (ebk)

Typeset in Times New Roman
by Apex CoVantage, LLC

To Thomas Gutmann

Contents

Preface	x
Acknowledgements	xii

Introduction   1

1 Epistemology and the problem of objective knowledge   9
Section I: knowledge as justified true belief 9
Section II: the dogmatic epistemology of justified true belief 12
Section III: the sceptic epistemology and objective knowledge 20
Section IV: justificationism and the problem of objective knowledge 24

2 Karl Popper's critical rationalism: an epistemological critique   27
Introduction 27
Section I: Popper's epistemology: problem situation 27
Section II: Popper's theory of knowledge 33
Section III: Popper's philosophy of critical rationalism 38

3 William Bartley's pancritical rationalism   46
Introduction 46
Section I: Bartley's non-justificationist epistemology 46
Section II: rationality as a moral attitude: Bartley's critique 51
Section III: Bartley's pancritical rationalism 55

4 Towards a non-justificationist epistemology   66
Introduction 66
Section I: objective knowledge: the failure of justificationist solutions 66
Section II: objective knowledge as 'unfalsified conjecture' 70

viii Contents

Section III: deductive logic: a non-justificational theory 73
Section IV: towards a non-justificational theory of
knowledge 82

5 Unfalsified conjecture and critical rationality: towards a new theory of rationality

87

Introduction 87
Section I: from justification to criticism: the unfinished project
of critical rationalism 88
Section II: unfalsified conjecture and the unfinished project
of critical rationalism 91
Section III: towards a new theory of the growth of critical
rationality 95
Section IV: critical rationality and moral dialogue for common
values 103

6 Justificationism and the theory of society

107

Introduction 107
Section I: Emile Durkheim: social epistemology and social
order 107
Section II: Max Weber: Kantian epistemology and social
order 112
Section III: Talcott Parsons: epistemology and social order 120
Section IV: Jürgen Habermas: epistemology and the theory
of society 130

7 Critical rationalism and the theory of human action

143

Introduction 143
Section I: non-justificationism and the rationality of action 143
Section II: the problem situation in action theory 146
Section III: critical rationalism, moral philosophy and human
action 148
Section IV: the theory of human action: a critical rationalist
formulation 150
Section V: from human action to social order: the
rationalization of society 155

8 The theory of social order: a critical rationalist understanding

161

Introduction 161
Section I: the problem of social order: a reformulation 161

Contents ix

*Section II: emancipatory actions and the five mechanisms
of social ordering 165*
*Section III: ordinary actions and stabilization of social
order 178*

9 Towards a critical rationalist theory of social change 181
Introduction 181
*Section I: emancipatory action and the problem of social
change 181*
*Section II: critical rationalism and the cultural mechanism
of social change 182*
*Section III: governance and social change: a critical rationalist
approach 189*
*Section IV: critical rationalism and the economic mechanism
of social change 192*
Section V: critical rationalism and the evolution of society 193

10 Critical rationalism and the theory of society: a summary 198
Introduction 198
*Section I: non-justificationism: rationality and human
action 198*
Section II: critical rationalist sociology: an overview 203
Section III: towards a sociology of the open society 206

Index 207

Preface

This is a radical book – radical in the sense that it pertains to the common roots shared by sociological theory and theories of knowledge and to the basic nature of society. It is also radical in the sense that it favours fundamental change, change at the root of social matters and that it provides a thoroughgoing and far-reaching analysis of how to accomplish this significant shift.

How we think is what we are. This book explores the role of human reason in the formation of social order and its change. It shows that an adequate theory of society and social development depends on an appropriate theory of knowledge and that rising to the challenge of converting social structures and institutions has to start with epistemology.

This book is radical in that it has fundamental merits with revolutionary conclusions for the way we should conceive objective knowledge, critical reason and social order. It is radical in that it reveals that our very conceptions of objective knowledge, critical reason and social order have a common root and that understanding this root might result in changing all three areas. In doing so, this book makes three main contributions: the introduction of a non-justificational theory of knowledge liberated from the justified true belief account of knowledge, the offer of a radically new philosophy of critical rationalism on the basis of this non-justificational epistemology and, finally, the application of this new concept of critical reason to reformulate the sociological theory of society.

In the process of offering its non-justificational theories of knowledge and rationality, the book firstly provides an entirely new critique of Popper's critical and Bartley's pancritical rationalism with significant results for the philosophy of science, thereby truly situating the idea of critical rationalism in its epistemological context. Secondly, through critical reviews of Durkheim's, Weber's, Parsons's and Habermas's theories of society, it explores, for the first time, the impacts of justificationism on the theory of society in order to show how justificational concepts of reason have prevented sociologists from addressing the role of human reason in the formation of social order and its change. It thirdly offers a "critical rationalist theory of society" by using its theory of critical rationalism to reformulate the theory of human action, showing that not only the means of action, but also the goals of action can be rationalized via conjecture and refutation. In doing so, it enables us to explore the epistemology of rational dialogue and mechanisms of transition from a closed to an open, more rational, freer, more just and peaceful society. This book hereby demonstrates that a reinvented critical rationalism is an indispensable part of Critical Theory, a relationship that has been blurred since the so-called (and wrongly labelled) *positivism dispute* between critical rationalists (Karl Popper, Hans Albert) and the Frankfurt School (Theodor W. Adorno, Jürgen Habermas) in 1961. Masoud Mohammadi Alamuti establishes a necessary connection between non-justificationism and emancipatory action: it is due to their access to critical reason that human actors can change the social order they have previously and unconsciously created.

This book aims to achieve no less a goal than to alter the very meaning of critical thinking on the basis of its new concept of critical reason and to demonstrate how a non-justificational concept of reason changes the content of the theory of society. As a result, the book fundamentally challenges mainstream sociological analyses of social order and social transformation: how we will think is what we will be, individually and as a society which has, in the course of time, become a world society.

Thomas Gutmann
University of Muenster

Acknowledgements

The ideas for this book project have been a work in progress for a long time, and I owe great thanks to a few individuals and a number of different institutions. To Professor Thomas Gutmann, a true colleague and friend, I owe perhaps the greatest debt of all for devoting his valuable time to support my project intellectually and administratively. In his capacity as Principal Investigator at the University of Münster's Cluster of Excellence 'Religion and Politics' and within his affiliated research project on the 'Dynamics of Modernization in the Relations between Politics, Law, and Religion', Professor Gutmann provided me with the facilities required for my concentration on the questions of how to reinvent the philosophy of critical rationalism and how to integrate this reinvention into a sociological theory of society. I also express my gratitude to his administrative staff, in particular to Petra Wedeking and Ruth Langer, whose support in completing this book was essential.

It would have been impossible to bring this book to fruition had I not been awarded the Georg Forster Research Fellowship by the Alexander von Humboldt Foundation in 2017. From 2017 to 2020, this Fellowship allowed me to complete this book for submission to the publisher. I hereby express my special thanks to the members of the Humboldt Foundation and their campaign for international understanding, scientific progress and development.

Having written this book while a visiting scholar at the Cluster of Excellence 'Religion and Politics' at the University of Münster, I am especially grateful to the staff of the Cluster for their support. I wish to thank Judith Grubel, Coordinator of Visiting Scholars, Viola van Melis, Head of the Centre for Research Communication, and Katharina Mennemann and Mareike König from the administrative staff. Moreover, I extend my thanks to the University of Münster, which has not only facilitated my writing of this first volume, but has also provided me with a research agreement to allow me to write a follow-up second volume to be entitled 'Towards a Sociology of the Open Society'. I am very grateful to Audrey Busch for her efforts in making this research agreement possible.

My special thanks go to Professor Peter Jones at Newcastle University, UK, whose promotion of my book proposal was very important in convincing the Routledge Group to publish this book.

I am very grateful to Nancy Kuehler, whose invaluable editorial assistance in preparing the manuscript has made my book much more readable for international audiences.

Finally, I would like to express my gratitude to the Institute for Management and Planning Studies (IMPS) in Tehran, Iran, for allowing me to take a leave of absence to write this book in Germany.

Masoud Mohammadi Alamuti
IMPS, September 2020

Introduction

Masoud Mohammadi Alamuti

This is the first volume of a collection entitled 'Critical Rationalism and the Open Society'. Its purpose is to reinvent the philosophy of critical rationalism and introduce it to the theory of society. The second volume applies the critical-rationalist theory of society to present a sociology of the open society. Through these two volumes, I aim to show that a non-justificationist understanding of rationality enables us to explore mechanisms of transition from a closed to an open society. It can be said that these volumes are the first systematic attempt to apply critical rationalism as a theory of rationality for a fundamental reformulation of sociological theory in general and as well as its application for understanding of closed and open societies in particular.

The question of how critical rationalism gives rise to the ideas of closed and open societies has received notable attention in epistemology and social philosophy. Karl Popper was the champion of the two ideas of critical rationalism and the open society. While I respect his valuable contributions to these ideas, I intend to criticize the way Popper has defined critical rationalism in terms of an irrational faith in reason. Later, in the second volume, I argue that Popper's definition of critical rationalism as irrational faith in reason has prevented him from a sociological understanding of the open society.

My intention to integrate critical rationalism in the theory of society in order to establish the idea of an open society upon a sound sociological theory directed me to the deeper question of whether or not critical rationalism itself has been understood correctly. These queries lead to the realization that Popper's critical rationalism cannot be used to formulate s sociology of the open society due to his definition of critical rationalism an *irrational* faith in reason or *a moral attitude* of openness to criticism. These observations result in two major insights: (i) the philosophy of critical rationalism ought to be reinvented in order to achieve liberation from irrational faith in reason and (ii) before addressing the question of how critical rationalism can be introduced to the sociology of the open society, we need to explore how it may be introduced to the sociological theory itself.

Therefore, the strategy of my two-volume book is as follows: the first volume has two purposes, one, to liberate the philosophy of critical rationalism from an

2 Introduction

irrational faith in reason, a task already been taken on seriously by one of Popper's students, William Bartley, but has not accomplished satisfactorily, the another, to use a new philosophy of critical rationalism to develop a sociological theory of society. Thus, the second volume has two tasks: the first of which is to show that Popper has not succeeded in presenting a social theory of the open society due to the lack of a theory of society; the second to provide a sociological analysis of the open society.

During my investigations for liberating critical rationalism from an irrational faith in reason, it became clear that Popper's defence of critical rationalism is justificationist. Popper argues that (a) although a rational belief requires justification in order to be regarded as true, (b) the rationalist cannot justify critical rationalism itself as a rational belief. Therefore, Popper concludes that the rationalist should accept critical rationalism with an irrational faith. Thus, Popper's justificationism forces him to define critical rationalism as an irrational faith in reason.

In his philosophy of science, however, Popper argues that a hypothesis cannot be proved, but rather only refuted. Surprisingly, when it comes to defining critical rationalism, Popper claims that critical rationalism which cannot be proved by argument makes our faith in reason an irrational faith. This irrational faith in reason cannot be an accurate definition for critical rationalism because the inability to *prove* any claim prevents the proof of an irrational faith in reason. This observation by Bartley led me to look for a sound non-justificationist theory of critical rationalism, which I found in Bartley's pancritical rationalism.

Bartley considers Popper's philosophy of critical rationalism unpersuasive and openly criticizes it. If critical rationalism is itself an irrational faith, what differentiates it from irrationalism? Bartley realizes that Popper admits an epistemological position of sceptic irrationalism by sharing with the sceptic the view that the rationalist cannot justify his claims of rationality by argument. Hence, Popper's critical rationalism and irrationalism agree that a justified rational belief does not exist; both result in any faith in reason being an irrational faith. Thus, Bartley correctly concludes that irrational faith in reason cannot demark the boundary between the rationalist and the irrationalist.

With these considerations in mind, I realized that Bartley seeks the origin of Popper's irrational faith in reason in justificationism, but does not base his theory of pancritical rationalism on a non-justificational epistemology; instead, he situates it within the context of Popper's philosophy of science. Hence, the lack of such a non-justificationist epistemology leads pancritical rationalism to another type of justificationism, as will be discussed. Bartley asks why the rationalist should justify all his beliefs by argument or experience. If justification is untenable, the rationalist is not required to justify his own belief in reason. This argument is persuasive. Bartley simply argues that a hypothesis which cannot be proven can only be refuted, which means the same as saying that a rational belief that cannot be proved can only be refuted. Just as Popper offers a non-justificational solution to the induction problem in science, Bartley suggests a non-justificationist solution to the problem of rationality, arguing that our faith in critical reason is actually a *rational* faith.

The question of whether or not Bartley's pancritical rationalism enables redefinition of the conception of rationality in sociological theory remains unanswered, however, and has led me to the justificatory nature of pancritical rationalism. Bartley's theory of rationality implies that the pancritical-rationalist holds all his beliefs open to criticism, including the belief in critical rationalism, and accepts only beliefs that pass a severe test. However, this theory does not tell the pancritical-rationalist how to refute his claims of holding rational beliefs open to criticism. Hence, I understand that Bartley's theory of rationality cannot address the question of how critical reason operates because the pancritical-rationalist cannot refute his claims of rational belief, so his openness to criticism does not put him in a better position than the irrationalist who argues that a claim of rational belief is not at all possible.

An important question regarding critical rationalism is whether Popper and Bartley establish their critical rationalism upon a sound epistemological foundation. In response, I realize that they have not. While Popper rejects a justified true belief account of knowledge, he fails to create a link between his idea of conjectural knowledge and the theory of rationality. What Bartley does is to expand the separation of justification and criticism from the theory of science to the theory of rationality. These observations shape my strategy for reinventing critical rationalism: I comprehend that a theory of rationality aiming to tell us whether or not our claims of rationality are true requires a theory of knowledge for addressing a general question of whether or not our claims of knowledge, metaphysical as well as empirical, may be judged true.

Since the justified true belief account of knowledge suffers from the problem of infinite regress, I establish my project for the integration of critical rationalism into the theory of society on an entirely new epistemological foundation. Thus, this volume is divided into two main parts: Part I 'Epistemology and Critical Rationalism' and Part II 'Towards a Critical-Rationalist Theory of Society'.

The first part of the book consists of five chapters. In order to show why Popper's 'critical' and Bartley's 'pancritical' rationalism have not liberated themselves from the justified true belief account of knowledge, Chapter 1 studies two major schools of epistemology, dogmatist and scepticist, arguing that their lack of success in addressing the problem of objective knowledge is to be found in the definition of knowledge in terms of justified true belief. If the process of knowing is modelled to show justification of the conclusion of rational argument, not only the premises of such an argument should be justified by argument or experience, but also the inference forms of such an argument should be considered undisputable. However, if neither premises nor inferences are infallible, the dogmatist theory of knowledge, whether the intellectualist or the empiricist, cannot address the question of objective knowledge, for, if the premises are not justifiable, neither is the conclusion. The main problem with dogmatist epistemology is the infinite

4   Introduction

regress imposed on it by the assumption of infallible premises and inferences. Chapter 1 concludes that sceptic epistemology recognizes this infinite regress and argues that objective knowledge is untenable with the justified true belief account of knowledge. However, the sceptic is wrong in saying that knowledge is untenable since the premise of justified true belief upon which the sceptic's argument is based is itself a wrong premise.

Before proposing my non-justificationist epistemology as an alternative to justified true belief account of knowledge in Chapter 4, I situate Popper's critical rationalism in its epistemological context in Chapter 2 and criticize irrational faith in reason due to its justificationist origin. Chapter 2 argues that, while correctly realizing that the justificational account of knowledge does not correspond to the conjectural logic of empirical science, Popper focuses his epistemology mainly on the logic of science. Popper offers an innovative solution to the problem of induction, arguing that objective science can exist, not because our hypotheses can be justified, but because they can be refuted. While using classical logic; i.e. the modus tollens, to show how logic allows re-transmittal of the falsity of the conclusion to the premises, Popper does not deal with the question of whether logic allows transmission of falsity from the premises to the conclusion.

Without a logical standard to show us how a metaphysical theory, e.g. the theory of rationality may be refuted by argument, Popper is not equipped with an epistemology to show that a claim of rationality is actually examinable to reveal its truth or falsity. Hence, when defining critical rationalism, Popper claims that critical rationalism not justifiable by argument should be accepted by an irrational faith. Chapter 2 shows that it is Popper's epistemology that leads him to an irrational faith in reason, rather than to critical rationalism as a theory of rationality.

Chapter 3 offers a similar epistemological critique of Bartley's pancritical rationalism, demonstrating that Bartley's critique of irrational faith in reason originates from the general separation he creates between justification and criticism. Bartley argues correctly that Popper is the first philosopher to offer a non-justificational concept of criticism, arguing that a scientific hypothesis cannot be justified by experience, but rather only falsified by it. Popper realizes the separation of justification and criticism through his philosophy of science, while Bartley wonders why Popper does not expand this separation to the philosophy of critical rationalism.

Bartley then attempts to find a solution for the unfinished project of critical rationalism. Chapter 3 situates Bartley's pancritical rationalism in its epistemological background, arguing that he uses the separation of justification and criticism to show that critical rationalism need not have a justification, but need only be held open to criticism. However, my critique of Bartley is that a metaphysical theory, like a theory of rationality, would not be refutable by argument without a non-justificationist theory of knowledge. My position is that Bartley uses the idea of the problem-solving ability of a theory, i.e. judging whether or not the theory solves the problem posed, to argue that pancritical rationalism can solve the problem of the rationalist identity.

In Chapter 4, the first systematic attempt to realize the ideal of separation between justification and criticism at the level of the theory of knowledge is revealed. Until now, No one has previously presented a non-justificational epistemology to help the philosophy of critical rationalism show how logic lets us refute a claim of rational belief and liberate critical rationalism from justificationism.

Chapter 4 addresses the question of how a claim of knowledge, whether metaphysical or empirical, may be refuted in order to prepare the epistemological ground for logical judgment regarding a rational belief. My epistemological inquiries into the aforementioned question lead me to an unintended, but far-reaching novel solution to the problem of objective knowledge, namely the proposal to use the separation of justification and criticism to replace the justified true belief account of knowledge with a non-justificational account, i.e. the consideration of objective knowledge as *unfalsified conjecture*. This concept of unfalsified conjecture is then used to introduce a non-justificationist theory of knowledge, which means that the conclusion of a rational argument defined as unfalsified conjecture does not permit premises or inferences to be considered infallible. A non-justificationist model of deduction is proposed through which the conclusion of a rational argument can be refuted by one of its premises when shown to be false by argument or experience. The novelty of my theory of knowledge lies in the deductive inference in its non-justificationist model.

Chapter 5 is now in a good position to use the non-justificationist epistemology to reinvent the philosophy of critical rationalism. Inspired by the general theory of knowledge, I argue that a claim of rationality which is *itself* a knowledge claim allows us to infer that rational belief is belief resting on objective knowledge. Chapter 5 argues that a claim of rationality can be judged true if and only if its premises and inference forms are not shown to be refuted by argument. In sum, a rational belief is an *unfalsified belief*. This non-justificationist concept of rationality offers an alternative for the justified true belief account of rationality.

The second part of the volume applies the non-justificational account of rationality to integrate critical rationalism in the theory of society. Why should critical rationalism be important for sociological theory? I contribute to this question by saying that that the integration of critical rationalism in the theory of society is not an *option*, but a *necessity* because, due to their infinite regress, justificational concepts of rationality cannot explain the function of reason itself; hence they cannot aid the sociologist to develop an accurate model of rational action. Seen from this perspective, the general theory of critical rationalism offers the theory of society that it seriously requires: a *non-justificational understanding of rationality*.

Chapter 6 illustrates how four classical and modern sociologists, namely Emile Durkheim, Max Weber, Talcott Parsons and Jürgen Habermas, have based their theories of society on justificationist accounts of rationality. I confess that my selection of these four sociologists may not be regarded as sufficient coverage. I argue, however, that these four major sociologists are the most relevant scholars in view of their theories of society in the context of my purposes in this book.

6 Introduction

In this way, Chapter 6 illustrates how justificationism has affected the theory of society through the concepts of reason it proposes in regard to the ideal types of rational action. If a rational belief cannot be justified due to infinite regress, it is not possible for the ideal type of rational action to show that it is human reason that guides action, whereby the word 'reason' is not used correctly in this respect, as discussed below.

Chapter 6 aims to explain why justificationism has fundamentally prevented the theory of society from addressing the role of reason in shaping the goals and means of action and, subsequently, the role of reason in the creation of the common values necessary for peaceful social order. Perhaps Chapter 6 is the first systematic effort to explore how justificationism has contributed to sociological theory. It will do so by connecting Durkheim's, Weber's, Parsons's and Habermas's epistemologies to their theories of society.

Using the ensuing observations, Chapter 7 attempts to establish the theory of human action upon an accurate reading of rationality, beginning with the important assumption that it is the theory of action that integrates critical rationalism into sociological theory. This chapter argues that the main claim of a theory of critical rationalism is that the rationalist can have rational beliefs, that is, beliefs which have not been refuted by argument or experience. However, the problem of rational action refers to the question of whether it is reason or passion that drives human action. Chapter 7 addresses the question of rational action in an innovative way: the main reason the two major theories of action, utilitarian and normative, are not successful in showing that it is actually reason, not passion, that drives action because they apply justificational accounts of rationality.

In the utilitarian model of action, utilitarians argue that action goals are subjective and cannot be rationalized for the epistemological reason that they want to justify moral claims regarding the goals of action. When their claims cannot be proved by argument, utilitarians deduce that it is only the means of action that needs to be rationalized. They forget, however, that goals of action which cannot be justified as true have as a consequence that the same follows for the means of action. Chapter 7 concludes that justificationism prevents the utilitarian model from seeing reason as the driving force of action. In the normative model of action, justificationism plays a similar role, but in a different manner.

Inspired by Kantian practical reason, the normative model of action argues in Chapter 7 that goals of action can be rationalized because the actors apply reason to justify their orientation towards a system of values in society. However, due to the assumption in the normative model that the ultimate values have to be *justified* in order to be seen as true, the actors are unable to rationalize the goals of action without creating values by basing their moral beliefs on unfalsified conjectures.

The novelty of the critical-rationalist action theory lies in showing that not only the means of action, but also the goals of action can be rationalized via conjecture and refutation. Chapter 7 expands its critical-rationalist model of action from the individual to the social level by introducing a three-level mechanism of *thinkers-social movements-masses* through which individuals shape a dialogue for using critical reason to determine action-goals.

This book recognizes two main problems of the theory of society as those of 'social order' and 'social change'. What links the philosophy of critical rationalism with these problems is to be understood in terms of (a) how rational beings apply critical reason to agree on a system of values necessary for controlling egoistic behaviour and (b) how rational beings use critical reason to revise the established values in order to advance social organization, thus enabling them to prevent conflicts of interest while promoting cooperative actions for the social good.

Chapter 8 applies the critical-rationalist models of action to show that rational actors initiate social dialogue and institutional measures to agree on a system of values to be turned into institutions of law, polity and economy. From this departure-point, the critical-rationalist theory of social order distinguishes its explanation of social order from justificationist theories. The novelty of the critical-rationality theory lies in the usage of the non-justificationist action model to address the problem of social order. Unlike Parsons's theory of social order, for example, the critical-rationalist theory shows that the actors give themselves their value system, which not only prevents them from conflicts of interest, but also leads to social cooperation. Hence, the actors are socialized persons who respect a given system of values and who, more importantly, create the value system itself as independent persons.

Chapter 8 argues that it is critical rationalism – in terms of unfalsified belief – that allows the theory of social order to connect action and social order: with its non-justificationist concept of reason, critical rationalism can address the meaning of rationality correctly. The critical-rationalist theory of society argues that the actor's beliefs regarding the universe and the place of man's good life within it can be refuted by argument even though they can never be proved by argument. Thus, critical rationality in terms of unfalsified conjecture with regard to the meaning of the universe and man's place in it enables the actors to reach a moral consensus on the values of the good life. Chapter 8 starts with the metaphysical aspect of social ordering and continues with the actors using their theories of the universe to explore the meaning of the good life, according to which the goals of action are coordinated. With the help of these cultural forces of social order, the actors apply critical reason to draw conclusions regarding such a normative agreement for social institutions. Chapter 8 argues that the actors create social order not only by using critical reason to agree on a system of unfalsified beliefs regarding the universe and good life but also by using it to create social institutions for human-rights, legitimate governance and efficient economy.

Chapter 9 advances the book's theory of society by dealing with the question of social change, arguing that social order originating in common values and social institutions given to the individual actors by themselves due to their access to reason implies the actors can also change the social order that they have previously

8 Introduction

created. The importance of the philosophy of critical rationalism for the sociology of social change is detected in its ability to show that the actors' critical reason allows them to subject their established beliefs regarding the universe and the place of man in it to rational criticism once they have realized that the premises or inferences are shown to be false. Without this cognitive capacity, the actors may not be accounted as agents of social change. In order to see how their understanding of the universe and the good life is able to be changed and how their reshaped understanding is employed to revise the social institutions of law, governance and market, these actors are to be regarded as agents with the cognitive capacity of learning from criticism.

Chapter 9 argues that it is the actors' evolving accounts of critical reason that enable them to divine new beliefs regarding the universe, the good life, human rights, legitimate governance and an efficient economy. Critical reason is used to judge whether these beliefs are rational due to the truth or falsity of their premises and inferences. However, the justificationist concept of rationality does not allow for knowledge of how the actors revise their previous concepts of reason and the implications for transition from an old social order to a new one. Chapter 9 argues that the question of the evolution of human society finds a new answer on the basis of the philosophy of critical rationalism: societies evolve as individuals open the premises of their beliefs to rational criticism and learn from mistaken premises.

Chapter 10 brings the book to an end by summarizing the integration of critical rationalism into the theory of society, concluding that the critical-rationalist theory of society, the final product of the first volume, has presented a sociological theory for the second volume, enabling it to argue for a sociology of the open society aimed at addressing the transition from a closed to an open society.

Chapter 1

Epistemology and the problem of objective knowledge

Masoud Mohammadi Alamuti

Section I: knowledge as justified true belief

What is the main task of epistemology? One short answer is that epistemology reveals the legitimacy of our concept of knowledge by explaining how achieving knowledge is possible. As Laurence BonJour (2010: 4) argues, the main epistemological question concerns the standards that must be satisfied for a claim of knowledge to be true. According to traditional epistemology, knowledge is *justified true belief*. In a different sense, knowledge is a special kind of *belief* that can be *justified*. As Alan Musgrave (1974: 561) points out, the idea of knowledge as justified true belief can be defined briefly in the following way: "... to say 'I know *X*' means something like 'I believe, *X*, and I can justify my belief in *X*, and *X* is true'". The history of epistemology is, in fact, the history of a great debate about the truth or falsity of this central idea.

In short, one party in this debate, the dogmatists, assert that their belief in *X* is true because it can be justified. The opposing party, the sceptics, try to show that there can be no justification for the belief in *X* to be true. Hence, our theory of knowledge depends mainly on our answer to the question of whether our knowledge claims can be justified. In this chapter, I emphasize the central point that it is justificationism that has directed the focus in the main debate between dogmatists and the sceptics towards the wrong problem in their theories of knowledge: the question of whether or not argument or experience can justify a claim of knowledge.

It is worth noting that defining knowledge as justified true belief leads us to a theory of knowledge that formulates the *knowing process* through which objective knowledge in terms of justified true belief would be the result or conclusion. The next section will show that both the dogmatist and sceptic epistemologies offer justificationist solutions to the problem of objective knowledge that assume, from very beginning, that the knowing process must lead to justified true belief if it aims at creating objective knowledge. However, while the dogmatist claims that this process is capable of leading us to justified true belief at its conclusion, the sceptic argues that justified true belief would not be the result of such process and that objective knowledge is hence untenable.

10 Epistemology and the problem of objective knowledge

In order to clarify the idea of knowledge as justified true belief, we need to refer to its three main conditions. As pointed out by Alan Musgrave (1993: 2),

> . . . the first condition for the truth of a statement of the form "*A* knows that *P*" (where *A* is a person and *P* a proposition) is that *A* genuinely believes that *P*. But clearly belief is not enough: I may genuinely believe that someone is outside the door, but if in fact there is no one there I will not be said to know it. Belief is, as the philosophers say, a necessary condition for knowledge but not a sufficient condition. What else is required?

Musgrave (1993: 2) replies that a second condition is that 'P is true'.

> If I am to know that there is someone outside the door, then there really must be someone outside the door. Before the belief is entitled to be called "knowledge", what is believed must be true. If I say "I know that *P*" and then find out that *P* is false, I will withdraw my claim to knowledge: I will say that I thought I knew that *P* but did not really know it.

Musgrave then asks if anything else is required and answers with:

> A third condition for knowledge will be apparent in what has already been said. For me to know something it is not enough that I believe it and that it happens to be true; I must also be able to give reasons for my belief, or justify it . . . Only if I can justify my claim and show that it was not a lucky guess, will I be said to know it.
>
> (Musgrave 1993: 3)

With these three conditions in mind, for a statement of the form '*A* knows that *P*' to be correct, it must be the case that:

(1) *A* believes that *P*.
(2) *P* is true.
(3) *A* can justify his belief in that *P*.

We have now arrived at the traditional philosophical distinction between genuine knowledge and mere belief or opinion: "genuine knowledge is justified true belief" (Musgrave 1993: 3). The three conditions for knowledge incorporated into the traditional view (belief, truth and justification) are meant to be individually necessary and jointly sufficient conditions.

In 1963, Edmund L. Gettier wrote a short paper which generated a great deal of interest and has had enormous influence on subsequent developments in epistemology. Gettier (1963: 121–123) devises rather bizarre cases according to which a person has a justified true belief although we would not say that the person knew the proposition in question. Gettier's cases actually refute the idea of knowledge as justified true belief. Gettier argues that, keeping in mind (a) as defined below, we can show that it does not state a *sufficient* condition for someone knowing a given proposition:

(a) S knows that P IFF (i) P is true.

  (ii) S believes that P.
  (iii) S is justified in believing that P.

Gettier (1963: 121) argues:

> I shall begin by noting two points. First, in the sense of "justified" in which S's being justified in believing P is a necessary condition of S's knowing that P, it is possible for a person to be justified in believing a proposition that is in fact false. Secondly, for any proposition P, if S is justified in believing P, and P entails Q, and S deduces Q from P and accepts Q as a result of this deduction, then S is justified in believing Q.

Against this background, Musgrave (1993: 5) asks us to suppose that

> Smith has a friend, Jones, who he knows has in the past always owned a Ford and who has just offered Smith a lift in a Ford. Smith justifiably believes (a) Jones owns a Ford. Smith has another friend, Brown, of whose whereabouts he is totally ignorant. However, Smith deduces from "Jones owns a Ford" the proposition (b) "Either Jones owns a Ford or Brown is in Barcelona", and so comes to believe this proposition too. Now suppose that Jones does not in fact own a Ford (the car he is driving is a rental car), but that by lucky chance Brown is in fact in Barcelona. Does Smith know (b)? Not intuitively not. Yet he believes (b), (b) is true, and he is justified in believing (b) since he deduced it from (a) which he justifiably believes.

This quotation presents an example indicating that the idea of objective knowledge as justified true belief is untenable (Gettier 1963: 122–123).

Defenders of the justified true belief account of knowledge must either bite the bullet and say that, contrary to intuition, Smith does know (b) or argue that he does not because one of the three conditions for knowledge is not satisfied, after all. The only plausible candidate for the unsatisfied condition is the third: Smith is not justified in believing (b). Gettier's example has an importance consequence for justificationist epistemology: without *conclusive reasons* for justifying the truth of a claim of knowledge, objective knowledge would be untenable. In this sense, we should give the third condition for knowledge a *strong interpretation*, whereby justifying a belief means having conclusive reasons for it, reasons that *do prove* it. Therefore, it is not unfair to argue that a belief might not be entitled to be called 'knowledge' if the reasons are less than conclusive. It is in this sense that traditional epistemology equalizes *knowledge* with *justification*. In regard to the

12 Epistemology and the problem of objective knowledge

Gettier's objection, it is the third condition, which has not been met, that makes Smith's belief in the proposition (b) true.

It is worthy of note that justification, by its very nature, has some kind of connection with truth. This can be seen by considering how the *process* of *justifying a belief*, conceived as showing that the belief has the *property* of being justified, is always used to provide the grounds required for considering the belief true. Having said that, the standards we use for determining justification are responsive to our considered judgments about which internal sources tend to produce true beliefs. The way we comprehend justification therefore helps us to understand how our claim of knowledge is actually true.

Dogmatists and sceptics agree that knowledge, if it exists, is justified true belief. They disagree only about whether knowledge is attainable. They agree, in other words, that talk of absolute or objective truth makes sense only if that truth can be known – that a belief is 'objective' only if it is true and known to be true. They disagree only about whether anything can be *known to be true* and hence about whether any belief can be 'objective'. Given the notion of knowledge as 'justified true belief', I shall now review the dogmatic and sceptic epistemologies to see how they deal with the problem of objective knowledge.

Section II: the dogmatic epistemology of justified true belief

As noted earlier, the history of epistemology is, in large measure, the history of a great debate about whether man can know anything. This section briefly describes the theories of knowledge that dogmatism and scepticism offer to explain the process of knowledge formation beginning with premises and ending to conclusion. It is important to note that these theories of knowledge assume the conclusion of such a process of knowledge formation as justified true belief and then attempt to address the logical process through which the truth of the premises is transmitted to conclusion. In this context, the idea of knowledge as justified true belief plays a key role, for, if the conclusion of such a knowing process is defined from very beginning as a justified true belief, then the premises and the form of inference upon which such a justified true conclusion can be drawn must themselves be *infallible*. The dogmatists claim that the knower can reach objective knowledge through infallible premises and inference forms; the sceptics, however, argue that the claim of using unjustified premises to conclude objective knowledge in terms of justified true belief is baseless since the premises and inference forms are fallible.

Dogmatic epistemology

In order to see how dogmatic epistemology defends its theory of objective knowledge, we should know how it explains justification of conclusion through its premises. To prove that a statement X is true, we must produce additional statement(s)

Y, from which *X* logically follows: *Y* then establishes *X* in the sense that, given *Y* is true, *X* must also be true. Obviously, however, the truth of *Y* needs to be established in turn, and so on ad infinitum. Under this condition, the dogmatist requires a stop to the justification process at some point(s) in order to show that certain ultimate premises which do not need further justification build the foundations of our objective knowledge. This argument leads the dogmatic to claim that infallible premises *justify* conclusion by an infallible form of reasoning. In sum, if objective knowledge is defined as the final product of a rational argument starting with certain premises and if such a final product must be justified by its premises, then we should admit that objective knowledge can be produced if and only if: (a) the premises are infallible and (b) the inference forms are undisputable.

Hence, dogmatic epistemology faces a twofold challenge. First, it must show that infallible premises are stopping the infinite regress upon which an objective conclusion is drawn. Second, the very forms of inference through which premises transmit their truth to the conclusion should be regarded as infallible. In brief, a conclusion can be justified as indisputably true through its logical relation with the premises.

As observed by Musgrave (1993: 562),

> Dogmatists were the champions of "objectivity": they insisted that objective truth can be known, that we do have a means of proving it. Now the chief weapon in the sceptic's armoury was the infinite regress of proofs, discovered already by the Greeks.

Whereas dogmatists and sceptics agree upon the premise that objective knowledge is justified true belief, they disagree about whether anything can be *known to be true*. The dogmatic theory of knowledge is called *dogmatic* because of its assumption that premises and form of inference can be taken into account as infallible. If, however, these assumptions actually are untenable, the dogmatist integrates infinite regress, arguing that the acceptance of certain premises of a valid argument must be admitted dogmatically or without justification.

Dogmatic epistemology uses the notions of *self-evident principles* or *sense experiences* in order to stop the infinite regress of proofs at 'first principles', whose truth is guaranteed. The justification of all other beliefs is then relative to these 'first principles'. Yet dogmatists disagree amongst themselves about what the 'first principles' are. Empiricism claims that our senses enable us to know the truth of certain observation statements immediately. Intellectualism believes that intellectual intuition enables us to see the truth of first principles immediately. Allow me to discuss these two major branches of dogmatist epistemology briefly.

The intellectualist theory of knowledge

The father of intellectualism, the French philosopher Rene Descartes, set out to find something which, by its very nature, would be impossible to doubt and by

14   Epistemology and the problem of objective knowledge

means of which the worth of other opinions might be assessed. Descartes argues that all our opinions are to be based on 'clear and distinct' ideas presented to the intellect; of these, the famous indubitable *cogito ergo sum* is the paradigm of such clear ideas requiring no justification because doubting them would be absurd. Yet what guarantee does Descartes have that a falsehood will not be self-evident and indubitable? Proof is needed to prove that self-evidence guarantees truth.

In *Rules for the Direction of the Mind*, Descartes argues that, by going over the proof again and again, we can come to see that axioms yield the theorem in a single act of intuition, just as we see that axioms are true in single acts of intuition. He argues that suspicion of an error in reasoning ought to lead to going through the reasoning repeatedly until we have direct certitude that our assumptions are correct, and thus so is the theorem derived from them. As Harold H. Joachim (1957: 29) reminds us, Descartes argues that

> The intellectual certainty with which I see the mutual implication of self-consciousness and existence is immediate, like sense-perception; but, in the case of sense-perception, my assurance fluctuates. . . . But the certainty of intellectual insight is steady, constant and absolute. To see a truth – that x implies y – is to see it absolutely and timelessly, once for all and unvaryingly.

Descartes claims that there is no special problem regarding the proofs if we can rely upon our intuition regarding the axioms. In his words,

> I noticed that while I was trying to think everything false, it was necessary that I, who was thinking this, was something. And observing that this truth " 'I am thinking, therefore I exist" was so firm and sure that all the *most* extravagant suppositions of the sceptics were incapable of shaking it, I decided that I could accept it without scruple as the first principle of the philosophy I was seeking.

Thus, Descartes arrives at the famous *Cogito, ergo sum*, i.e. 'I think, therefore I am'. Descartes's dogmatism originates from the claim that the idea of 'I think, therefore I am' cannot be fallible and that it is a true premise upon which objective knowledge can be justified since deductive logic makes no mistake in the transmission of the truth from the premises to the conclusion.

Descartes tries to establish other truths on the basis of the *Cogito* and finds the self-evident principle, which can stop the infinite regress of proofs. Descartes (1984: 127) states:

> After this I considered in general what is required of a proposition in order for it to be true and certain; for since I had just found one that I knew to be such, I thought that I ought to know what this certainty consists in. I observed that there is nothing at all in the proposition "I am thinking, therefore I exist"

Epistemology and the problem of objective knowledge 15

to assure me that I am speaking the truth, except that I see very clearly that in order to think it is necessary to exist. So I decided that I could take it as a general rule that the things we conceive very clearly and very distinctly are all true.

This quotation shows that Descartes thinks that the indisputability of his premise is also justification for the conclusion of such an infallible premise. It is important to see Descartes's theory of knowledge in connection with his theory of mind. As observed by Kim Jaegwon (1980: 589):

The Cartesian doctrine of the mind is the *private inner* stage, "the Inner Mirror", in which cognitive action takes place. The Platonic doctrine of knowledge as representation was transformed into the idea of knowledge as *inner representation* of outer reality. The Cartesian contribution was to *mentalize* the Platonic doctrine.

When Descartes argues '"I" am thinking, therefore I exist', he implies that there are self-evident principles upon which valid knowledge can be produced as the inner representation of outer reality. This understanding of knowledge is justificationist because it uses self-evident premises to justify an inner image corresponding to the outer reality.

However, as argued by Musgrave (1993: 201), Descartes cannot guarantee that he will never clearly conceive a falsehood. Can he rule out the possibility that A clearly conceives that P, while B clearly conceives that not-P? Hence, the self-evident principle aimed at stopping infinite regress faces the same problem. If this is so, Descartes's rationalist epistemology fails. Sceptical doubts about rationalism remain: that something is self-evident to you, that you clearly conceive it, that you cannot doubt it, does not establish that you know it. Yet, this failure does not mark the end of dogmatic rationalism.

Immanuel Kant introduces a new version of intellectualism. Like Descartes, he defines knowledge as justified true belief, suggesting, however, a different theory of objective knowledge. According to Kant, as stated by Douglas Burnham and Harvey Young (2007: 10),

. . . reason refers to a type of thinking that attempts to discover knowledge simply through reasoning and "pure" concepts; "pure" here meaning not empirical . . . Such pure reason seeks to reach conclusions purely, rather than through any empirical investigation of the world. This type of cognition is what is meant by "pure reason".

Kant seems to be the first philosopher to situate the epistemology of "pure" reason at the core of philosophy; neither Plato nor Descartes conduct a critique of pure reason. Kant believes that Hume also misses this opportunity. Kant recognizes

16 Epistemology and the problem of objective knowledge

Hume's critique of induction, which shows that no general law can be established as true on the basis of experience. Yet, he does not claim Hume's critique to be a failure of pure reason in defending objective knowledge and rationalism.

Kant asks how our certain knowledge of things can be reconciled with Humean criticism and replies that we know the fundamental laws of mathematics and of mathematical physics, laws that are synthetic rather than analytic. Our knowledge of them is either a priori or a posteriori. Hume shows that we cannot know these laws a posteriori. Therefore, we must know them a priori; that is, they must represent synthetic a priori knowledge. The Kantian revolution in epistemology refers to a reversal in the relation between the claim of knowledge and the object. Like Descartes and Hume, Kant is a justificationist who wants to justify a knowledge-claim as a true belief due to its correspondence to the object. However, unlike Descartes, Kant does not devote a central role to the self-evidence principles of pure reason. Moreover, Kant does not admit Hume's scepticism because epistemology can address the question of objective knowledge by 'pure' reason.

In his rationalist solution for the Humean problem of induction, Kant does not deny the demand for justification itself; hence, his critique of pure reason remains justificationist. In other words, Kant admits the justified true belief account of knowledge (Underwood 2003: 8). Without giving up justificationism, Kant applies the doctrine of pure reason to solve the problem of knowledge. In Kant's words (1956 [1787]: Xxvi–Xxviii): "Hitherto it has been assumed that all our knowledge must conform to objects". Instead, he continues, we must suppose that objects must conform to our knowledge. For "we can know *a priori* of things only what we ourselves put into them". Kant states that we must therefore perform trials to see whether we may not have more success in metaphysical tasks if we suppose that objects must conform to our knowledge.

Kant argues that the rational structure of pre-modern scientific inquiry involves the conception of science merely as a passive observer of things and an accumulation of experiences through inductive inference, whereas Kantian epistemology argues that an active role ought to be given to the observer in order to justify a claim of knowledge: instead of justifying a claim of knowledge by a limited number of sense experiences, such a claim of knowledge can be justified by the discovery of the conditions of the possibility of experience. As pointed out by Jaegwon (1980: 590), it is worthy of note that, from a Kantian perspective, "Philosophy, as epistemology, must set universal standards of rationality and objectivity for all actual and possible claims to knowledge". Hence, Kant offers a general theory of knowledge on the basis his own justificationism.

On these grounds, a critique of pure reason will have to first explore the condition of experience. In short, Kant's intellectualist theory of knowledge aims to show that it is the categories of the faculty of reason – as a priori justified categories – that lead us to the discovery of the conditions of the possibility of experience or objective knowledge. According to Kant (1956 [1787]), we impose a temporal structure on incoming stimuli, so that all our experiences are located in

Epistemology and the problem of objective knowledge   17

time, i.e. occurring before or after one another. We also impose a spatial structure, so that what we experience has a spatial location. In addition, we impose a causal structure, so that the things we experience stand in causal relations to one another. Nothing counts as an experience of the world if it is not structured in this way. This structuring of our experience proceeds according to certain laws: temporal structuring is governed by the laws of arithmetic, spatial structuring by the laws of geometry and causal structuring by the laws of mechanics. Kant claims that all experiences of the world conform to these laws and that no experience of the world can refute them.

In response to the question of 'how synthetic judgments are possible a priori', Kant reiterates that we can come to know a priori that these judgments are justified as true by studying the way in which we structure experience. Kant's intellectualist epistemology replaces Descartes's self-evident principles with a priori justified categories of thought which represent synthetic a priori knowledge. Kant insists that we do not find out how we experience the world from experience; instead, we engage in what he calls a 'transcendental analysis of human reason'.

If, however, the demand for justification itself involves infinite regress, then Kant's theory of knowledge faces the same problem. Kantian rationalism involves no pleas for self-evidence for a sceptic to attack. Kant does, however, claim that the categories of human thought are justified a priori. If justification is not possible, Kant does not show us how his critique of pure reason solves the problem of objective knowledge. In short, Kant, like Descartes, ought to admit certain premises dogmatically in order to argue that justified true belief would be the conclusion of such *a priori* true premises.

The empiricist theory of knowledge

While intellectualist epistemology claims that infallible premises in the intellect can be used to justify a claim of knowledge in terms of conclusion, the empiricist theory of knowledge claims that undisputable sense experiences play such a justifying role. Modern empiricism stemming primarily from the works of Bacon, Locke and Hume claims that a rationalist derives all his knowledge from sense observation. Rationalists attempt to stop the infinite regress of proofs with sense observations manifestly assumed to be true.

The main idea of empiricism is that we can use our senses to come to know the truth of certain propositions directly. The propositions in question are statements reporting what we observe and are the basic propositions in the light of which we can justify other beliefs. As argued by Musgrave (1993), the appeal to sense experience as a source of direct knowledge of observation statements is the central idea of empiricist epistemology. Naive empiricists regard sense-experience as a foundation for knowledge: our senses guarantee us the truth of observation-statements, and our other beliefs must be justified by an appeal to sense experience. We know, however, that our interests and our prior beliefs help to determine what sensory

18 Epistemology and the problem of objective knowledge

stimuli we pay attention to. In addition, we are also familiar with several examples of the way prior beliefs helping us to make sense of our experience actually lead us to perceptual error.

Francis Bacon is an empiricist who believes that genuine knowledge can be obtained by using our senses and tries to address the question of how to avoid this error. Bacon (1960 [1620]: 21–22) argues that the first step is to empty the mind of all prejudices in order to be able to observe the world as it really is. Bacon talks of purging the mind of prejudices in order to qualify it for dealing with the truth. Can, however, a person empty her mind of all her prejudices?

As a founder of English empiricism, John Locke's epistemology plays a key role in the formation of the empiricist epistemology. In *An Essay Concerning Human Understanding*, Locke (1960 [1659]) argues: what I know, that I am certain of; and what I am certain of, that I know. This certainty leads us to Locke's justified true belief account of knowledge, but how can the knower use infallible premises to achieve such an absolutely true belief? As an empiricist, Locke criticizes intellectualists like Descartes for their claim of the existence of self-evident premises. Locke develops his epistemology in the context of his critique of self-evident premises. He criticizes the notion of innate ideas, which is central to Descartes's dogmatic epistemology. As pointed out by Ake Petzall (1937: 11),

> At first he [Locke] wanted to make clear certain ideas to himself and to his friends, but very soon he discovers that he and most of his contemporaries to a frighteningly large extent uncritically accept unproved maxims, which turn out not only to be completely valueless but also directly obstructive to real knowledge. . . . . Dogmatism in the form of scholasticism and uncritical rationalism is, according to Locke, a real danger to the science of the time, because people in general are not yet aware of the fact that they accept unthinkingly "truths" which undermine both knowledge and action.

Locke's epistemology paves the way for the rise of a critical rationalist attitude; nevertheless, it remains justificationist because it replaces the self-evident principles with undisputable sense experience.

With this clarified, we can understand the reason why Locke argues that

> It is necessary to get rid of the self-assumed authority which with no vestige of right has ventured to act as "the dictator of principles and teacher of unquestionable truths"; for this authority cannot appeal to any other principle than "the principle of principles" . . . This must be considered destructive to all study of knowledge. There is nothing more dangerous than to base one's opinions uncritically upon unverified principles, "especially if they be such as concern morality, which influence men's lives, and give a bias to all their actions".
>
> (Petzall 1937: 12)

Epistemology and the problem of objective knowledge 19

While Locke rightly criticizes the dogmatism of Cartesian intellectualism, he appeals to sense experience in order to stop infinite regress.

Locke aims to show that the notion of innate ideas is to be replaced by the empirical source of objective knowledge. His critique of Cartesian epistemology does not reject the justified true belief account of knowledge. Locke's critique of the dogmatic intellectualism pursues different justifying premises, ones coming from experiences. Nevertheless, Locke is right in saying that we shall find that the natural faculty of reason includes what is necessary for the welfare of human beings if we free ourselves from the incorrect view uncritically held by dogmatism. In criticizing the innate ideas, Locke argues that universal consent, while generally stated to be the criterion of innate truth, is an unsatisfactory criterion. Since many human beings are not conscious of any universal truths, there cannot be any general consent. With that said, Locke does not, however, give up the idea of a self-evident premise. Locke finds it self-evident that man is equipped with natural reason, as this enablement to reach objective knowledge through experience is necessary for practical life.

Locke argues that criticism of the notion of innate ideas is intended to pave the way for seeing how *natural reason* uses *experience* to produce objective knowledge. As rightly expressed by Petzall (1937: 47),

> Locke was evidently of the opinion that he acted in the spirit of empirical observation, when he made the nature of these faculties appear only in the process acquiring knowledge, without trying to state what they really are. This, too, is an example of the ambiguousness of Locke's attitude to dogmatism . . . but still he presumes dogmatically that the notion of natural faculties is legitimate.

Locke claims that no idea is as agreeable to the commonality of natural reason as the idea of God. But is there universal consensus on this idea? If there is no such universal consensus, then experience cannot be utilized as an undisputable premise of justified true belief.

While Locke's solution to the problem of knowledge is based on natural reason as the last resort for all knowledge, he also argues that inductive logic can be used to generalize the origination of sense experiences from natural reason. Locke thus defines natural reason in terms of the faculty of combining such empirical evidence in order to reach a justified conclusion. He argues that people are endowed with natural reason, enabling them, firstly, to reach absolute true knowledge about the things for which such knowledge is necessary and, secondly, to reach satisfactory, if not absolutely true, knowledge about the things for which knowledge of this kind is necessary.

In brief, Descartes's and Locke's attempts to rescue epistemology from dogmatism, either by inborn ideas or by natural reason, take place within the justified true belief account of knowledge. Hence, in both cases, the theory of knowledge

20 Epistemology and the problem of objective knowledge

is still dogmatist because the premises are unquestionable. A critique of sense experience as self-evident premises is offered in the following. We experience a table and thereby come to know that the statement 'There is a table here' is true. However, this overlooks the gap that exists between the experiences we have when looking at a table and the statement we formulate on the basis of these experiences. We must formulate observation statements as ultimate premises from which other statements are to be proved because experiences themselves are just happenings and cannot be regarded as the premises of any argument.

However, as Musgrave (1993) observes, in absorbing sensory stimuli and incorporating them in a certain way in order to develop observation reports, we employ concepts which commit us to certain predictions in respect to our future experiences. Since any of these assumptions might turn out to be false, future experiences might lead us to reject a past observation report. This is why any observation report transcends the experience and could be a false report. If the argument is sound, the sense experience is to be read as the fallible report of an active observer. If all sense experiences might be mistaken reports, the idea of infallible experiences is untenable.

To sum it up, there are two major problems with the method of empiricist epistemology: (a) sense experiences in terms of observation reports are not unquestionable and (b) the inductive form of inference cannot bring conclusion to the truth of a limited number of such observation reports. These two problems show that the empiricist branch of dogmatist epistemology, just like the intellectualist one, is faced with the problem of infinite regress because the premises upon which the knowing subject can deduce a conclusion as justified true belief, whether logical or empirical, are not infallible.

Due to their justified true belief account of knowledge, we can regard the intellectualist and the empiricist theories of knowledge as justificational epistemology simply because both of them attempt to show that the truth of infallible premises can be concluded. Hence, justificationism in these dogmatic epistemologies is reflected in the demand for not only a justified true conclusion, but also for undisputable premises and inference forms. However, since neither the premises nor the inference forms can be considered infallible, the problem of objective knowledge has not been solved by either the intellectualist or the empiricist theories of knowledge.

Section III: the sceptic epistemology and objective knowledge

The main idea of sceptic epistemology is that knowledge defined as justified true belief is not objective knowledge because conclusion of a rational argument cannot be justified simply upon the basis of premises which are neither self-evident nor infallible experience. As observed by Harald Thorsrud (2009: 147) in *Ancient Scepticism*, "If the sceptic can systematically block all of our attempts at justification, we will be left in the troubling position of believing that we ought to do what we cannot". In this section, the subject of inquiry is the sceptic position with regard to objective knowledge. In one sense, the study of scepticism might be said to define epistemology by showing that the idea of knowledge as justified true belief is untenable. In order to address the problem of objective knowledge from the sceptic viewpoint, I begin with a brief history of sceptic epistemology.

Scepticism: historical origin

Academic scepticism and Pyrrhonism are two branches of scepticism in ancient Greece which are opposed to the Stoics, who maintain that knowledge is possible. Academics believe that this inability can be recognized although the knowledge claims cannot be justified. Pyrrhonians, on the other hand, claim that even this inability is not recognizable. Most of what we know about Pyrrhonian scepticism is based on its presentation by Sextus Empiricus. Pyrrhonians delineate their scepticism by reasoning that the search for justification leads to suspension of judgment, arguing that the lack of any legitimate way to decide which side of the disagreement is correct results in suspension of judgment or the conclusion that nothing can be known (Hazlett 2014).

Similarly, Chi-Ming Lam (2007: 2) describes the sceptics' major claim as follows:

> . . . the problem is that we are unable to verify or justify our beliefs rationally. In fact, this problem had been widely discussed by sceptical philosophers . . . For example, Pyrrho of Elis, regarded as the founder of the sceptical tradition, suggests suspending judgement in order to achieve tranquillity, since good grounds can be found not only for any belief but also against it.

According to Sextus (1994), there are at least three modes of suspension of judgement. The mode derived from infinite regress maintains that the argument itself that is brought forth as a source of belief for the matter proposed itself also needs such a source, which also needs a source, and so ad infinitum, so that there is no point from which to start to establish anything, resulting in suspension of judgement. Sextus also argues that the mode of hypothesis, in which the dogmatists, thrown back ad infinitum, begin with something which has not been established, but merely claimed as an assumption. The reciprocal mode occurs when what ought to confirm the object under study actually needs the object under examination to make it convincing. In this case, the inability to use either claim in order to establish the other leads to suspension of judgement about both claims.

Sceptics offer two major reasons for their critique of objective knowledge: firstly, that, likewise, neither the intellectualist nor the empiricist can prove the existence of infallible premises, whether in terms of self-evident principles or sense experiences, and secondly, that inductive inference is unable to transmit the

22 Epistemology and the problem of objective knowledge

truth of fallible premises to conclusion. Hence, even a dogmatist who can demonstrate undisputable premises may not argue that inductive inference enables justification of a universal knowledge claim on the basis of a limited number of empirical facts.

Scepticism and fallibility of the premises

In order to show that objective knowledge is untenable, sceptics should prove that not only self-evident principles but also sense experiences are disputable; hence, even a valid deduction which is used to conclude a knowledge claim would not result in a justified true belief. Let us examine how the sceptic argues that sense experiences are not infallible. Sceptics have long asserted that such observation statements as 'The boat is stationary' and 'The oar is straight' do not provide a secure basis for knowledge. The reason for this is that our senses often offer us conflicting appearances, for example, "The same boat appears from a distance small and stationary, but from close at hand large and in motion . . . The same oar appears bent in water but straight when out of it" (Sextus 1994: 31). As we can never determine whether the real world is actually as it appears to be, we can never assume that an observation statement is infallible.

As argued earlier, heeding sensory stimuli and reading these in a certain way in order to report observations always involves the use of words or concepts which commit us to certain predictions in regard to our future experiences. Since any of these presumptions might turn out to be false, future experiences might lead us to rejection of a past observation report. This is what we mean by saying that any observation report transcends the experience which causes it and is therefore fallible (Musgrave 1993). If empiricists argue that the senses give us immediate knowledge, not about external objects, but about ideas or sense data in our own minds, the sceptic might respond to this claim that, in the end, this new empirical basis for knowledge is not absolutely certain. If the basis for knowledge must consist of statements rather than experiences and is thus only a *statement* which can *justify* another *statement*, then the notion of sense data faces infinite regress.

It has been argued that empiricists seek to solve the problem of infinite regress by saying that the senses are a source of undisputable knowledge about the world. The intellectualists' reply to the aforementioned problem is structured in a similar way: by seeking to stop infinite regress with the concept that reason or intellect is a source of undisputable knowledge about the world. Despite Euclidean achievements, the sceptic's response to intellectualism remains negative. While intellectualists say that their axioms are true because they are self-evident, sceptics argue by questioning what guarantee the rationalist has that a falsehood will not be self-evident and clearly perceived. The sceptic, however, regards self-evidence as a psychological relation which certain propositions have for certain people. This is how the sceptic can suppose that a proposition might have a certain effect on one person and not on another. Something that seems self-evident to you, that you clearly and distinctly conceive, does not establish that you know it as a justified true belief.

As argued earlier, Kant says that he was aroused from this dogmatic slumber by David Hume (Dicker 2001). Hume's critique of induction shows that no general law can be established as true on the basis of experience. How can our certain knowledge of these things be reconciled with Humean scepticism? In response, Kant argues that Hume has shown that we cannot know things a posteriori. Therefore, we must know them a priori; that is, they must represent synthetic a priori knowledge. In short, as Musgrave (1993: 219) states: "Kant's question was 'How is synthetic a priori knowledge possible?' His answer . . . is that it is possible because it consists of laws which we impose upon sensory stimuli to create the world of experience". Kant argues that we cannot know the things-in-themselves, but only the world of experience upon which we can impose the law of mind.

However, the sceptic asks how Kant can prove that things-in-themselves and other minds exist and how Kant knows that all humans understand the world of appearances in the same way, so that they face a common 'world of appearance'. As observed by Musgrave (1993), Kant's epistemology can argue that there is synthetic a priori knowledge, but that it does not concern 'things-in-themselves'; instead, it concerns 'things-as-experienced-by-humans'. In addition, the success of Einstein's theory devastated all hopes of explaining the rationality of science in terms of a priori foundation. Now, if Kant could be wrong about the a priori certainty of Newtonian Mechanics, how could anyone ever claim to be certain a priori again?

In validating the sceptic critique of dogmatism, William Bartley (1984: 118) argues:

> Within a justificational approach, . . . We cannot go on justifying our beliefs forever since the question of the correctness of the conclusion shifts back to the question of the correctness of the premises; and if the premises are never established or justified, neither is the conclusion. Since we want to justify and cannot do so *rationally*, irrational justification or commitment seems the only resort. So, if rationality lies in justification, it is severely limited by the necessity for commitment.

Indeed, when the premises of a valid deduction are fallible and cannot be justified by experience or argument, conclusion of such a deduction also cannot be justified as true belief or objective knowledge.

In sum, sceptic epistemology implies that, if objective knowledge is to be defined as justified true belief since there are no infallible premises whose truth can be transmitted to conclusion, objective knowledge is untenable. In this argument, however, the sceptic epistemologist makes the following two mistakes: first, premises are to be justified in order to provide bases for objective knowledge.

24 Epistemology and the problem of objective knowledge

Second, deduction can infallibly transmit the truth of premises to conclusion. On the basis of these two false premises, sceptic epistemology rejects the possibility of objective knowledge. However, if the demand for justification is replaced by criticism, the sceptic's critique of objective knowledge becomes baseless. I explain this argument in Chapter 4 and explore its important consequence for the philosophy of critical rationalism in Chapter 5.

Section IV: justificationism and the problem of objective knowledge

Now, let us bring all of the proceeding arguments together to deduce an important conclusion: it is justificationism that prevents epistemology from overcoming the problem of objective knowledge. To sum it up, the dogmatist and the sceptic share the concept of knowledge as justified true belief. However, the dogmatist argues that infallible premises exist, either in terms of sense experience or in terms of self-evident principles and their truth that can indisputably be transmitted to conclusion. If the dogmatist models the process of knowing so that objective knowledge is the result of valid deduction of undisputable premises, the reason is because the model assumes that conclusion is justifiable by infallible premises.

The sceptic, on the other hand, argues that, if the premises of a conclusion are not justifiable, then neither can the conclusion be justified. Thus, the dogmatist, even with valid deductive reasoning, cannot say that objective knowledge is achievable, whereby the premises, either sense experience or principles of intellect, are also fallible. This is rather undisputable. Hence, the debate by the dogmatist and the sceptic with regard to objective knowledge originates deeply in the justified true belief account of knowledge.

Therefore, when defining knowledge as justified true belief in order to demonstrate that objective knowledge is tenable, the epistemologist should establish a logical model of knowing in which the knower starts with infallible premises, namely with sense experience or self-evident principles, and uses valid (infallible) forms of inference in order to draw conclusion. Objective knowledge as such justifies true conclusion by its premises. Hence, a notable part of the efforts made in dogmatic epistemology is devoted to showing the existence of undisputable bases for justification of the objectivity of our knowledge, on the one hand, and of valid deductive, or even inductive, forms of reasoning for transmitting the truth of premises to conclusion, on the other. Sceptic epistemology, however, attempts to show that undisputable premises do not exist and also that induction is unable to transmit the truth of premises to conclusion. Hence, it can be argued that it is the justificationist concept of knowledge that rules out dogmatist and sceptic epistemologies as a solution for the problem of objective knowledge.

If I understand this matter correctly, what would the consequence for a theory of objective knowledge be? Should one give up the idea of objective knowledge? Or, may another solution be offered on the basis of a new conception of objective knowledge? Allow me first to argue that it is not only the dogmatist who is

Epistemology and the problem of objective knowledge   25

at pain to meet his standard of objective knowledge as justified true belief, but so the sceptic who is unable to defend his argument against the dogmatist on the basis of the justified true belief account of knowledge. It seems that both schools of epistemology are handicapped by a common origin: a *justificational concept of knowledge*.

The sceptic is right in saying that dogmatism is unable to defend objective knowledge. However, can the sceptic prove this refutation? My answer is negative. Since the sceptic starts from the premises of knowledge as justified true belief, the impossibility of objective knowledge cannot be the conclusion of such an incorrect premise. The reason for this is simple: the premise of such an argument, i.e. the justificational concept of knowledge, is incorrect. The sceptic has already shown that all premises are fallible. Hence, how can the sceptic justify his own main premise? If, like the dogmatist, the sceptic admits the demand for justification and, if this demand involves infinite regress, then the sceptic's critique of the dogmatist is untenable.

The conclusion I draw is that the reason neither dogmatists nor scepticists can defend their argument for or against objective knowledge is because their epistemologies are established upon a mistaken premise: *objective knowledge is justified true belief*. If the process of justification involves infinite regress in the proofs, why should a claim of knowledge be true for a knower who can not bring justifying proofs to prove his claim of knowledge? In short, insofar as objective knowledge is defined as justified true belief, the epistemologist cannot solve the problem of knowledge.

It is the concept of knowledge as justified true belief that shapes the battle between the dogmatic and the sceptic schools of epistemology. If one rejects the premise of 'knowledge as justified true belief' and admits that all premises are fallible, a fundamental shift from the *justificational* to a *non-justificational* theory of knowledge comes into the picture. In Chapter 2, I argue that Karl Popper opted for a non-justificational approach to the concept of knowledge and established his philosophy of critical rationalism on this approach.

Bibliography

Bacon, F. (1620) "Novum Organum". In: Anderson, F.H. (ed.) *The New Organon and Related Writings, 1960*. New York, Liberal Arts Press.

Bartley III, W. (1984) *The Retreat to Commitment*. Chicago, Open Court.

BonJour, L. (2010) *Epistemology: Classic Problems and Contemporary Response*. Lanham, Rowman & Littlefield.

Burnham, D. & Young, H. (2007) *Kant's Critique of Pure Reason*. Edinburg, Edinburg University Press.

Descartes, R. (1984) *The Philosophical Writings of Descartes, Vol. 1*, Cottingham, R.J., Stoothoff, R. & Murdoch, D. (trans.). Cambridge, Cambridge University Press.

Dicker, G. (2001) *Hume's Epistemology and Metaphysics: An Introduction*. London, Routledge.

Gettier, E.L. (1963) "Is Justified True Belief Knowledge?" In: *Analysis*, 23 (6), pp. 121–123.

Hazlett, Allan (2014) *A Critical Introduction to Skepticism*. London, Bloomsbury.

Jaegwon, K. (1980) "Rorty on the Possibility of Philosophy". In: *The Journal of Philosophy*, 77 (10), pp. 588–597.

Joachim, H.H. (1957) *Descartes's Rules for the Direction of the Mind*. London, George Allen & Unwin.

Kant, I. (1956 [1787]) *Critique of Practical Reason*, Smith, N.K. (trans.). New York, Palgrave Macmillan.

Lam, C. (2007) "A Justification for Popper's Non-Justificationism". In: *Diametros*, 12, pp. 1–24.

Locke, J. (1960 [1659]) *An Essay Concerning Human Understanding*, A.C. Fraser (collation and annotation). New York, Dover.

Musgrave, A.E. (1993) *Common Sense, Science and Scepticism. A Historical Introduction to the Theory of Knowledge*. Cambridge, Cambridge University Press.

Musgrave, A.E. (1974) "The Objectivism of Popper's Epistemology". In: Schilpp, P. (ed.) *The Philosophy of Karl Popper*, Book I. La Salle, Open Court, pp. 560–596.

Petzall, A. (1937) "Ethics and Epistemology in John Locke's Essay Concerning Human Understanding". In: *Goteborgs Hogskolas Arsskrift*, XLIII (2), pp. 1–83.

Sextus, E. (1994) *Outlines of Scepticism*, Annas, J. & Barnes, J. (eds.). Cambridge, Cambridge University Press.

Thorsrud, H. (2009) *Ancient Scepticism*. Stocksfield, Acumen.

Underwood, L.J. (2003) *Kant's Correspondence Theory of Truth, An Analysis and Critique of Anglo-American Alternative*. New York, Peter Lang.

Chapter 2

Karl Popper's critical rationalism

An epistemological critique

Masoud Mohammadi Alamuti

Introduction

As argued in Chapter 1, the main task of a theory of knowledge is to define *a process of knowing* which addresses how the knower uses a set of premises to infer a conclusion logically, i.e. achieve objective knowledge. The epistemology of justified true belief offers a *justificational theory of knowledge* arguing that 'objective knowledge' is attained when the knower uses infallible premises, either sense experiences or self-evident principles, to produce a justified true belief as its conclusion. Sceptic epistemology, on the other hand, argues that conclusion of such a knowing process is not justifiable by its premises since all premises and forms of reasoning are fallible; hence objective knowledge is unattainable.

Karl Popper recognizes that the dispute between the dogmatists and the sceptics and their error in addressing the question of objective knowledge originate in the definition of knowledge as justified true belief. Nevertheless, Popper's theory of science is mainly concerned with the demarcation between science and non-science. An understanding of the epistemological problem is a prerequisite for a discourse on Popper's critical rationalism. Hence, it is no wonder that I pay great attention to the epistemology of critical rationalism in Sections I and II. In short, this chapter argues that Popper uses a non-justificational approach to address the objectivity of scientific hypotheses, but does not extend the non-justificational logic of science to the philosophy of critical rationalism. Instead, Popper takes a *justificational approach*, defining critical rationalism as *moral faith in openness to criticism.*

Section I: Popper's epistemology: problem situation

To understand Popper's theory of knowledge, we first need to understand the problem it intends to solve. To this end, this section proceeds in three stages: (a) a brief review of the Humean problem of induction and of Kant's unsuccessful attempt at solving it, (b) Popper's reading of the epistemological problem and (c)

28 Karl Popper's critical rationalism

Popper's formulation of the problem of knowledge on the basis of his critique of the epistemology of justified true belief.

Hume's problem of induction and the Kantian solution

Popper's theory of science was considered to be a solution for Kant's unsuccessful attempt at solving the induction problem posed by Hume. In other words, Popper's epistemological problem was shaped according to the justificational origin he recognized in the dispute between Humean scepticism and Kantian dogmatism. Thus, to understand Popper's problem situation in epistemology, we have to briefly address the question of why Popper did not regard the Kantian solution for Humean problem as satisfactory. Popper's observations are fundamental for understanding his argument in defence of science and for rescuing rationalism from Humean attack.

Let us return to the issue of Popper's problem situation in epistemology. By the eighteenth century, many philosophers had grown sceptical of attempts to ground objective knowledge upon a priori intuition. Epistemologists like Bacon and Locke were dissatisfied with the intuition basis of human knowledge and tried to establish objective knowledge on the basis of sense experience, claiming that universal laws of science can be inferred inductively from sense experiences. Hume, however, realized that any attempt to ground scientific knowledge on sense experiences leads to irrationalism due to the problem of induction. Hume's critique of empiricism targets inductive reasoning, arguing that, even if all sense experiences are infallible, any number of verifying experiences cannot justify a universal empirical law. Hume shows that scientific law cannot be justified through induction and also that metaphysical laws, such as the law of causality, i.e. 'every event has a cause', cannot be justified through any number of verifying experiences. Hence, the Humean problem of induction is a significant challenge, not only for science but also for philosophy.

Kant offers his theory of knowledge in terms of a *critique of pure reason* in order to defend the objectivity of natural science as well as that of metaphysics. To overcome the problem of induction, Kant does not reject the argument that a limited number of justifying sense experiences as premises cannot prove a universal law in science conclusively. He does, however, claim that inductive reasoning using a limited number of experiences need not be used for justification of such a universal law; instead of looking for a correspondence of scientific conjectures with the external world, categories of thought should be imposed upon that world. Kant asserts that there must be a priori knowledge upon which the objectivity of science rests and points to Euclidean Geometry and Newtonian Mechanics as examples of a priori synthetic knowledge. Kant argues that the only thing we can know about *a priori* is what we ourselves interpolate. So why then is it not possible for the mind to make a mistake when imposing its laws upon nature? Can Kant prove that our understanding of such imposed laws must be self-evident or infallible? We know that the answer is negative.

Stating that "The question whether inductive inferences are justified, or under what condition, is known as *the problem of induction*", Popper (1992 [1959]: 4) realizes that Kant's solution to the problem is not successful; otherwise, the sceptic's rejection of objective knowledge and rationalism would have to be taken seriously. According to Popper (1992 [1959]: 5),

> ... (T)he principle of induction must be a universal statement ... Thus if we try to regard its truth as known from experience, then the very same problems which accessioned its introduction will arise all over again. To justify it, we should have to employ an inductive inference ...

If, however, the principle of induction cannot be justified by a limited number of experiences, it is through argument that it must be justified instead. Arguing that Kant attempts to follow this line of reasoning, Popper (1992 [1959]: 5–6) writes:

> Kant tried to force his way out of this difficulty by taking the principle of induction ... to be "*a priori* valid". But I do not think that his ingenious attempt to provide an a *priori* justification for synthetic statements was successful.

As argued in Chapter 1, Kant's justificationism draws him into infinite regress. Since a priori true categories of mind do not exist, the principle of induction cannot be justified by such undisputable premises.

As argued by Christine M. Korsgaard (2000: 9):

> ... Kant's deduction only licenses our use of the principles of pure understanding for objects as we *experience them*, that is, as "phenomena". It does not provide us with a justification for applying them to things as they are in themselves – to "noumena". In this way, Kant rescues the metaphysical basis of natural science from Humean scepticism. But he does so at great cost to speculative metaphysics, for the traditional proofs of God, immorality and freedom are undermined.

However, the reason why Kant cannot rescue philosophy from Humean scepticism is that his notion of *a priori* true categories of thought is untenable. Not only our sense experiences, but also our categories of thought are merely fallible conjectures rather than a priori true. Hence, even Kant's solution to the induction problem is unsatisfactory.

The problem of objective knowledge: a Popperian perspective

Keeping in mind the Kantian attempt to rescue science and metaphysics from scepticism, Popper realizes that the problem of induction confronts the justified

30　Karl Popper's critical rationalism

true belief account of knowledge with a serious challenge and tries to find a new solution. Hans Albert (1999: 36) describes Popper's epistemological problem and the consequences for his critical rationalism as follows:

> In the field of the natural sciences, Albert Einstein drew epistemological conclusions that were irreconcilable with Kant's views. And in regard to mathematics, Bertrand Russell, whom we must thank for the above mentioned discovery, drew from this the conclusion that the last area of certainty had thereby disappeared from human knowledge. Both of these conclusions amount to a critique of the classical rationalism that was still present in Kant's thought.
>
> This *problem situation is the starting point for the critical rationalism developed by Karl Popper*. It started with Kant's question of the conditions for the possibility of knowledge, but Popper's answer took into account the scientific discoveries of the last century that are irreconcilable with Kant's views, and the development of philosophical thought during this period. In it the ideal of knowledge formulated by Aristotle and, thereby, the search for an absolutely certain foundation of knowledge, is given up and replaced by a consistent fallibilism and a methodological rationalism in which the *idea of critical examination* takes the place of the demand for a *final foundation* (emphasis added).

If scientific discoveries make Kant's epistemology unacceptable, then Popper is faced with the serious question of whether or not objective knowledge is possible at all. The validity of scientific beliefs is questioned by the Humean problem of induction, so can any other rational beliefs be defensible? In 'Optimist, Pessimist and Pragmatist Views of Scientific Knowledge', Popper (1963: 3) points out:

> Broadly speaking, there have been since antiquity two main schools in the theory of knowledge: one is the school of the pessimist, the sceptics (or the agnostics) who deny the possibility of justification, and with it, of any established knowledge; the other is the school of those who believe in the possibility of justification; of giving a justification of our claim to know, to be able to attain knowledge.

Popper attempts to situate his epistemology in the middle ground between these two major epistemological schools.

In Popper's (1963: 7) words,

> I shall now try to formulate the position I am taking up towards scepticism and optimism: Both pessimists and optimists at least agreed that the central problem of the theory of knowledge was the problem . . . of the rational justification of the claim that certain of our beliefs or theories are true. This

Karl Popper's critical rationalism   31

> formulation seems to me mistaken. I hold that there may be purely theoretical scientific knowledge which is not justifiable in this sense . . . The very best we can do – and we cannot do it always – is this. We may point out that, in the light of searching critical discussion, the theory in question appears to be preferable to all competing theories in the sense that it seems, so far, to be nearer to the truth . . .

If justification of a claim of knowledge is impossible, Popper is confronted with the question of how criticism of such a claim may overcome the problem of inductive reasoning. Thereby, Popper ignores a more fundamental epistemological problem, namely how criticism of a claim of knowledge may overcome the problem of objective knowledge.

Popper knows that Hume faced the problem of inductive reasoning when attempting to justify a universal law through it, i.e. by using a limited amount of verifying evidence for justification. If, however, the demand for justification is rejected from the very beginning, then the problem of induction does not arise at all. Without inductive usage of empirical evidence to justify a universal theory, however, the problem of the role of empirical evidence in the examination of a scientific theory emerges.

Nevertheless, Popper knows that the Kantian solution, which establishes the objectivity of science on a priori knowledge, does not give any role to external fact in the examination of subjective conjectures, assuming that mental laws are used for shaping our understanding of the external world. Popper realizes that the justified true belief account of knowledge advocated by Hume and Kant forced them to define an incorrect role to empirical evidence in the evaluation of a scientific theory, which made them incapable of defending the objectivity of human knowledge and rationality. Hume's justificationism led to giving induction an impossible logical task, thus directing him to scepticism and irrationalism. Kant's justificationism, on the other hand, forced him to impose the laws of intellect on our scientific understanding of the world and thus eliminated the need for any reference to empirical evidence for justification of a universal theory. It is under these conditions that Popper's epistemological problem is shaped: given the Humean problem of induction and the inefficiency of the Kantian solution, how can scientific logic allow a scientific hypothesis to be examined logically by empirical evidence?

As observed by Mark A. Notturno (2000: 99–100),

> Popper realized that the attempt to explain the rationality of science as a byproduct of its justification has failed. We cannot rationally ground science upon a priori cognition because a priori cognition is unreliable, and we cannot rationally ground science upon sense experience because inductive inference is invalid. If we want to avoid Hume's conclusion that science is irrationally grounded in custom and habit, then we have to explain how scientific knowledge can be rational given the fact that it cannot be rationally justified.

32   Karl Popper's critical rationalism

For this reason, Popper's epistemology addresses the question of objective knowledge in science.

Popper's critique of the justified true belief account of knowledge

In order to understand Popper's theory of scientific knowledge as a solution for the problem of induction, let us examine the pathway to his discovery that empirical science contradicts the justified true belief account of knowledge. Popper realizes that the justificational process of knowledge formation in which the knower uses undisputable premises in order to produce objective knowledge is not practicable in science because all premises are fallible and inductive inference cannot transmit the truth of the premises being true to conclusion. Popper recognizes that premises that are not infallible and induction as invalid inference point to the definition of a new model for creating scientific knowledge.

Popper criticizes the justified true belief account of science for its emphasis on the centrality of the source, arguing that the scientist uses conjecture rather than self-evident principles or sense experiences, as his starting point. Popper makes an important distinction between the *context of discovery* and the *context of justification*. In *Conjectures and Refutations*, Popper (1962: 27) argues:

> . . . (M)y answer to the questions "How do you know? What is the source or the basis of your assertion? What observations have led you to it?" would be: "I do *not* know: my assertion was merely a guess. Never mind the source, or the sources, from which it may spring – there are many possible sources . . . But if you are interested in the problem which I tried to solve by my tentative assertion, you may help me by criticizing it as severely as you can; and if you can design some experimental test which you think might refute my assertion, I shall gladly, and to the best of my powers, help you to refute it".

Popper knows that focusing on the sources of scientific knowledge leads to infinite regress since the sources are always disputable.

Popper emphasizes that scientific theories are not justified belief but rather guesswork. We do not know, we only take a guess. This leads Popper to an alternative concept of knowledge, *conjectural knowledge*. As observed by Alan Musgrave (1974: 561), ". . . Popper, whose first concern is with our scientific knowledge and its growth, begins by rejecting the conception of knowledge which lay at the heart of the traditional theory of knowledge". Musgrave (1974: 564–565) continues that

> Popper agrees with the sceptic, against the dogmatist, that we cannot infallibly know objective or absolute truth – but he agrees with the dogmatist, against the sceptic, that the notion of objective or absolute truth plays an important role as a regulative standard.

Popper tries to define his problem situation as if he can rescue epistemology from dogmatism without succumbing to scepticism.

In the same line of reasoning, John H. Sceski (2007: 63–64) writes,

> Popper rejects the belief epistemologies along with justificationism because both undermine the rationality of theoretical and practical inquiry. Concerning natural science, if we understand both the justification for belief in a universal theory and the content of the theory itself to be underwritten by an inductive inference from experience, then any such belief is irrational given the logical problem of induction.

Therefore, it is fair to say that Popper's emphasis on scientific statements as guesses is a radical epistemological shift from the justified true belief account of knowledge to a non-justificational one. However, Popper says openly, "Epistemology I take to be the theory of *scientific knowledge*" (Miller 1985: 60). Let us refer briefly to Popper's theory of knowledge.

Section II: Popper's theory of knowledge

In order to see how Popper's solution to the problem of knowledge prepares the ground for understanding his critical rationalism, I proceed by studying Popper's concept of conjectural knowledge and his solutions to the problem of objective knowledge, followed by a discussion of shortcomings in Popper's epistemology.

The idea of conjectural knowledge

Popper rightly argues that the practice of scientific theory does not fit well with the justified true belief account of knowledge. Therefore, a new concept of knowledge is needed to show how a scientific theory might be regarded as objective knowledge. Popper employs the concept of 'knowledge as unfalsified conjecture' to formulate his logic of science. As noted earlier, in response to the question of how one knows, Popper replies that he does not know, but only proposes a guess, inviting anyone interested in his problem to criticize his guess and offer counterproposals, which he, in turn, will try to criticize. This answer leads Popper to his alternative conception of knowledge: *conjectural knowledge*, which implies that scientific knowledge is just an empirical conjecture not yet refuted by evidence. Popper provides us with the logic of scientific discovery, thus enabling us to understand how empirical evidence can be used to refute a scientific hypothesis. This is not the case, however, for Popper's proposal regarding the critical evaluation of a non-empirical conjecture. In fact, Popper does not demonstrate a logical way of refuting metaphysical conjecture. Hence, the idea of conjectural knowledge is applicable mainly in Popper's philosophy of science.

34 Karl Popper's critical rationalism

Popper's solution for the problems of induction

The idea of conjectural knowledge leads Popper (1963: 7) to introduce his theory of science on the basis of a conjectural account of knowledge:

> In giving up the justification of claims to truth, we clearly side with the pessimists, the sceptics. But in contrast to both pessimists and optimists, we do not accept the view that the problem of justification is the same as the problem of knowledge. . . . (W)e insist that we cannot claim more for a theory than that it has been thoroughly criticized and tested, and that *so far* it has withstood all criticism and all tests.

In *The Two Fundamental Problems of the Theory of knowledge* (2009 [1979]), Popper defines the problem of induction as the question of whether a universal theory can be justified through particular experiences, and the problem of demarcation as the question of how can we decide whether a statement is scientific or 'only' metaphysical. In order to formulate a theory of science to address the problems of induction and demarcation, Popper assumes the following two major premises: (a) the scientist does not justify his hypothesis, hence eliminating the requirement for infallible premises and (b) the scientist does not use induction to justify a universal theory of science due to the invalidity of induction. Popper then goes on to find solutions for the problems of induction and demarcation at the core of his epistemology of science.

A simple formulation of the induction problem by Musgrave (2004: 20) provides a good starting point for a discussion of Popper's theory of science: if "(1) we reason, and must reason, inductively, [and if] (2) [i]nductive reasoning is logically invalid, [and if] (3) [t]o reason in a logically invalid way is irrational", we are, and must be, irrational. Musgrave then asks ". . . Can Hume's irrationalist conclusions be avoided?" It is worthy of note that Popper's real target is Hume's assumption that we must *reason* inductively. Popper admits that inductive inference is invalid, but he rejects the concept that a universal law is only true if it is justified. Hence, Popper reformulates the problem of induction to show that induction does not lead to scepticism if we reject the need for a scientific law to be justified in order to be objective and the need for inductive reasoning for justification.

According to Popper (1974: 1018), Hume's problem of induction asks,

> Are we rationally justified in reasoning from repeated instances of which we have had experience to instances of which we have had no experience? Hume's unrelenting answer is: No, we are not justified, however great the number of repetitions may be. And he added that it did not make the slightest difference if, in this problem, we ask for the justification not of certain belief, but of probable belief. Instances of which we have had experience do

Karl Popper's critical rationalism   35

not allow us to reason or argue about the probability of instances of which we have had no experience, any more than to the certainty of such instances.[1]

Popper (1974: 1020) then offers his reformulation of the induction problem:

Are we rationally justified in reasoning from instances or from counterinstances of which we have had experience to the truth or falsity of the corresponding laws, or to instances of which we have had no experience? . . . The answer to this problem is: as implied by Hume, we certainly are not justified in reasoning from an instance to the truth of the corresponding law. But to this negative result a second result, equally negative, may be added: we are justified in reasoning from a counterinstance to the falsity of the corresponding universal law . . .

By reformulating the problem of induction, Popper defines a new problem for his theory of science that shapes the very problem his epistemology intends to solve: how can a universal law be falsified by empirical evidence?

Popper introduces his theory of science as a solution to his reformulated problem of induction. As Sceski (2007: 62–63) writes:

(A)lthough Hume's logical critique argues it is impossible validly to establish universal theories from observations, Popper asserts Hume's criticism leaves "open the possibility that we may draw falsifying inferences: an inference from the truth of an observation statement ('This is a black swan') to the falsity of a theory ('All swans are white') can be deductively perfectly valid".

Thus, Popper's emphasis on scientific theories as guesses is a radical shift from traditional belief epistemologies because it provides a whole new approach to inquiry.[2]

Ian C. Jarvie (2001: 38) reminds us that

Popper's new solution to the problem of induction thus derives its impact from also being a solution to the problem of demarcation. . . . The solution to the demarcation problem that Popper poses and elaborates is that scientific statements be characterized as general statements which are in principle falsifiable.

Given the principle of falsification, a fundamental question for Popper's critical rationalism is how a theory of rationality can be objective in terms of its refutability if falsification is limited to an empirical test. As argued in Section III, Popper's epistemology does not provide us with a logical framework for refutation of a theory of rationality.

36 Karl Popper's critical rationalism

To better capture the essence of Popper's epistemology of science, let us examine the role of deductive logic in Popper's theory of science. As Hans Albert (1985: 16–17) points out,

A valid deductive argument – a logical inference – is a sequence of statements, of premises and conclusions, between which definite logical relationships exist; a conclusion, namely, is deducible from the premises in question with the aid of the rules of logic. . . . (T)he validity of a deductive argument only guarantees a. the *transfer* of the *positive* truth value – the *truth* – from the set of premises to the conclusion, and thus b. the *transfer* of the *negative* truth values – the *falseness* – from the conclusion back to the set of premises. An invalid deductive argument produces a wrong inference that affords no such guarantee.

By arguing for the use of a valid form of deduction, i.e. one allowing a negative truth value to be transferred backward from the conclusion to the premises, to test a scientific hypothesis, Popper discovered that the logic of science should have two main contexts: (a) discovery of a scientific hypothesis and (b) testing of the hypothesis deductively. Popper argues that even only *one* piece of falsifying evidence is enough for refutation of a universal hypothesis because it can transfer the negative truth value of the conclusion to the premises without involving the problem of induction.

In *The Logic of Scientific Discovery*, Popper (1992: 19) argues that

. . . it is possible by means of purely deductive inferences (with the help of the *modus tollens* of classical logic) to argue from the truth of singular statements to the falsity of universal statements. Such an argument to the falsity of universal statements is the only strictly deductive kind of inference that proceeds, as it were, in the "inductive direction"; that is, from singular to universal statements.

Hence, in his epistemology, Popper recognizes the role of the empirical test in terms of deductive inference through which the falsity of the conclusion is transferred back to the premises.

Popper was the first to demonstrate a clear logical contrast between justification and falsification. According to Popper's theory of science, the scientist does not use verifying evidence to justify a universal hypothesis but rather looks for only *one* piece of refuting evidence to show that a universal hypothesis is false. Popper does not explain why the hypothesis in question ought to be the conclusive premise for rendering the conclusion false.

Popper's logic of scientific knowledge leads to a new explanation of scientific knowledge. In *The Republic of Science*, Jarvie (2001: 98) argues:

An explanation is a description in the sense that the general theory or theories and the initial conditions from which it is deduced are descriptive statements.

"All men are mortal" describes men (or humanity), "Socrates is a man" describes Socrates, and together the two explain "Socrates is mortal".

Having said that, if the conclusion ('Socrates is mortal') is shown to be false by empirical evidence, then one of the premises, whether the general theory ('All men are mortal') or initial conditions ('Socrates is a man'), must be wrong.

As queried in Chapter 1, how may a fallible empirical statement reporting an experience be used to refute a general theory of science conclusively? Musgrave summarizes Popper's response:

> Popper's "empirical basis" does not . . . consist of statements whose truth is established by experiences. It consists rather of those easily testable experimental statements about whose truth or falsehood the community of scientists happens to agree at some time.
>
> (1974: 568)

Popper admits that this kind of agreement is open to revision, but insofar as the community of scientists does not find counterevidence, the agreement remains a valid empirical basis for refutation of a universal theory.

Some of Popper's defenders have attempted to spell out his notion of objectivity in terms of 'intersubjective criticism',[3] which Popper calls the 'intersubjective' testability of scientific claims. Although the notion of 'inter subjective' testability reinforces Popper's non-justificational solution to the problem of objective knowledge, it is, however, in his 'non-justificationism' that the origin of Popper's solution to the problem of objectivity is found. In sum, Popper's theory of science shows that objective knowledge is produced through conjecture and refutation, which is Popper's solution to the problem of objective knowledge.

Popper's epistemology and its shortcomings

A discussion of Popper's explanation of criticism demonstrates how his epistemology affects his philosophy of critical rationalism. Popper (1963: 7–8) writes

> . . . All criticism of a theory is an attempt to refute it; either by showing that it does not correspond to the facts, or by showing that it does solve the problems it claims to solve; or by showing that it is inferior to some of its competitors: for example, because it does not solve as many problems, or because it merely shifts some of the problems which its competitor can solve.

Although Popper clearly addresses falsification of an empirical theory by showing that it does not correspond to the facts, he does not clarify how to refute a metaphysical theory that does not solve the problem it claims to solve.

38 Karl Popper's critical rationalism

One important question Popper's epistemology faces is the use of deductive inference in transmitting the falsity of the conclusion of a metaphysical theory to its premises when there is no empirical evidence to imply the falsification of the conclusion. How can Popper claim that his principle of falsification, which is applicable for refuting a non-empirical theory, also demarcates science from metaphysics? The ability of a metaphysical theory to solve the problem it claims to solve does not demonstrate how the theory may be refuted *deductively* when transmission of the falsity from the premises to the conclusion is not possible, as in the case of a non-empirical theory. If this is the case, how can *deductive* inference be applied to criticism of a metaphysical theory such as the philosophical theory of rationality?

Popper (1963: 9–10) reminds us that

> . . . in fact deductive inference is formally valid if, and only if, no counter example exists. By "counter example" is here meant an inference of the same logical form as the inference in question, but with true premises and a false conclusion. The non-existence of a counter example ensures therefore the transmission of truth from the premises to the conclusion (provided the premises all are true) and the retransmission of falsity from the conclusion to at least one of the premises (provided the conclusion is false). This is the sole reason for the theoretical and practical significance of a valid deductive inference: it does not lie in a (more or less) arbitrary convention to regard certain inferences as valid . . .

With this quotation in mind, Popper's non-justificational concept of criticism can be said to be limited to the philosophy of science and does not include the philosophy of knowledge because Popper's logic of conjecture and refutation is designed to solve problems of induction and the demarcation of science from metaphysics.

I understand Popper's theory of knowledge as being unable to provide the rationalist with a *logical form* for refuting a philosophical theory of rationality to see whether or not it is false. This is because Popper's epistemology does not target the question of how a *claim of true knowledge can be differentiated from a false one*. On the contrary, Popper focuses on the question of how a scientific theory can be demarcated from a non-scientific one. Hence, Popper's philosophy of science has not provided his philosophy of critical rationalism with a non-justificational epistemological foundation.

Section III: Popper's philosophy of critical rationalism

In this section, I use the insights of the previous sections to offer a critical review of Popper's critical rationalism. First of all, it is important to keep in mind that a theory of rationality is itself a *claim of knowledge* aimed at addressing the question of what a 'rational belief' is. In this sense, the theory of rationality closely depends on the theory of knowledge. It can be argued, for instance, that the justified true account of knowledge leads to a justificationist concept of rationality and, when a conjectural account of knowledge is admitted, a non-justificational concept of rationality can also be suggested.

Mention of this linkage between the *theory of knowledge* and the *theory of rationality* leads to the question of whether Popper establishes critical rationalism on the basis of a theory of knowledge. As argued earlier, Popper's epistemology offers a philosophy of science, not a philosophy of knowledge. In his theory of science, Popper (1963: 7–8) argues: "All criticism of a theory is an attempt to refute it, either by showing that it does not correspond to the facts, or by showing that it does not solve the problems it claims to solve . . .". Popper refers to *modus tollens* as a deductive form through which an 'empirical' hypothesis can be shown to be false. *Modus tollens* cannot, however, be used for criticizing a metaphysical theory. Popper argues that a metaphysical theory may be evaluated according to its ability to solve the problems it claims to solve. He does not, however, introduce the logical form of such a critical evaluation. If Popper's epistemology does not offer an answer to the question of how a claim of rationality can be evaluated, then his epistemology is unable to serve his idea of critical rationalism. From perspective of this writer, the main reason for this shortcoming is that Popper does not apply the separation of justification and criticism for demarking a true claim of knowledge from a false one.

Critical rationalism: a moral commitment or a rational defence?

In *The Open Society and Its Enemies*, Popper (1994 [2013]: 435–436) defines *critical rationalism* in the following way:

> . . . I shall distinguish in what follows between two rationalist positions, which I label "critical rationalism" and "uncritical rationalism" or "comprehensive rationalism" . . . . Uncritical or comprehensive rationalism can be described as the attitude of the person who says "I am not prepared to accept anything that cannot be defended by means of argument or experience". We can express this also in the form of the principle that any assumption which cannot be supported either by argument or by experience is to be discarded. Now it is easy to see that this principle of an uncritical rationalism is inconsistent; for since it cannot, in its turn, be supported by argument or by experience, it implies that it should itself be discarded. . . . Uncritical rationalism is therefore logically untenable; and since a purely logical argument can show this, uncritical rationalism can be defeated by its own chosen weapon, argument. . . . The rationalist attitude is characterized by

40 Karl Popper's critical rationalism

the importance it attaches to argument and experience. But neither logical argument nor experience can establish the rationalist attitude; for only those who are ready to consider argument or experience, and who have therefore adopted this attitude already, will be impressed by them. This is to say, a rationalist attitude must be first adopted if any argument or experience is to be effective, and it cannot therefore be based upon argument or experience. . . . Thus a comprehensive rationalism is untenable. But this means that whoever adopts the rationalist attitude does so because he has adopted, consciously or unconsciously, some proposal, or decision, or belief, or behaviour; an adaptation which may be called "irrational". Whether this adoption is tentative or leads to a settled habit, we may describe it as an irrational *faith in reason*.

Upon closer inspection of the aforementioned quotation, it can be argued that Popper's defence of critical rationalism against uncritical rationalism is justificationist: since the uncritical rationalist cannot defend all his beliefs, including his belief in rationalism, by argument or experience, his position is logically untenable. By replacing the term 'defend' with 'justify', we realize that, if the demand for justification is invalid from a non-justificational perspective, then the uncritical rationalist need not meet this demand, and the lack of satisfying it renders comprehensive rationalism untenable. Unlike the scientist who need not justify his hypothesis by verifying evidence in Popper's theory of science, the rationalist, who cannot defend all his beliefs by argument and experience in Popper's definition of critical rationalism, should admit critical rationalism through an 'irrational' faith in reason. If critical rationalism is regarded as a claim of rational belief, why shouldn't the claim in question be refuted instead of justified? If justification involves infinite regress, what is the difference between justification of a scientific claim and justification of a claim of rational belief? Both claims are fallible conjectures which ought to be examined critically.

If the transition from justification to criticism is permitted in the theory of science, why shouldn't it be allowed in the theory of rationality? If the criterion of truth as justified belief is to be rejected in science, why should it be applied for demarcating uncritical rationalism from critical rationalism? Popper (1994 [2013]: 436) writes: ". . . a rationalist attitude must be first adopted if any argument or experience is to be effective, and it cannot therefore be based upon argument or experience". Popper views the adoption of such a rationalist attitude as necessary before any rational discussion, assuming that every argument has premises which are to be justified in order to provide a rational basis for argument. Since such justification involves infinite regress, an *irrational faith in reason* would be the only way out of such infinite regress. However, Popper's definition of critical rationalism as an irrational faith in reason stands on the mistaken assumption that a belief is rational if and only of it can be justified.

Gunnar Andersson (2009: 27) points out,

> For Popper, a critical rationalist is a person who is dogmatic only at one point: when he decides to accept the rationalist attitude. Such a person who understands the limits of reason Popper calls a critical rationalist. . . . According to Popper, a critical rationalist makes a minimum concession to irrationalism when he decides to adopt the rationalist attitude.

However, if we ask Popper why he says that a critical rationalist should make such a concession to irrationalism, the answer to this question on Popper's behalf is that the critical rationalist cannot defend his belief in reason by argument or experience. Andersson asks why Popper says that critical rationalism is not defendable by argument or experience and responds that ". . . he implicitly assumes the principle of sufficient reason in his discussion of rationalism. But why should we assume this principle as the ultimate principle when discussing rationalism?" (2009: 27). I argue that Popper's critical rationalism makes a justificational *return* when he says that uncritical rationalism is untenable because it cannot be *justified* by argument or experience, and this return occurs because his theory of knowledge does not provide him with a logical framework for showing how a theory of rationality can be refuted rather than justified.

In the same line of reasoning, Jarvie (2001: 207) points out:

> Popper maintains that since "all argument must proceed from assumptions, it is plainly impossible to demand that all assumptions should be based on argument" . . . . It follows that the decision to choose to listen and to give weight to arguments must precede argument. A choice not made on the basis of argument or experience is by definition an irrational choice.

However, it would be justificationist to argue that the assumptions from which our arguments proceed must be undisputable premises in order to be acceptable. Justificationism confronts Popper with the choice between offering justifiable premises and admitting an irrational choice. If, however, we replace the demand for justification by the demand for criticism, there is no reason to argue in favour of basing our faith in reason upon an irrational choice. Joseph Agassi (1987: 260) states: "As Popper presents critical rationalism, it is a commitment, a commitment to accept criticism of all of one's view but not of one's critical rationalism itself". However, an irrational commitment to accept this kind of criticism originates in justificationism and would thus be untenable.

It is noteworthy that Popper (1994 [2013]: 431) defines critical rationalism as an attitude of admitting that "I may be wrong and you may be right, and by an effort, we may get nearer to the truth". Popper claims that the rationalist attitude ". . . is very similar to the scientific attitude, to the belief that in the search for truth we need co-operation, and that, with the help of argument, we can in time attain something like objectivity". The preceding discussion of Popper's defence of critical rationalism reveals, however, that he does not extend the shift from justification to criticism found in the theory of science to the theory of rationality.

Critical rationalism and irrationalism

It is interesting to note how Popper (1994 [2013]: 437) describes his reasons for adopting of critical rationalism over irrationalism by asking:

> ... (W)hy not adopt irrationalism? Many who started as rationalists but were disillusioned by the discovery that a too comprehensive rationalism defeats itself have indeed practically capitulated to irrationalism. . . . But such panic action is entirely uncalled for. Although an uncritical and comprehensive rationalism is logically untenable, and although a comprehensive irrational- ism is logically tenable, this is no reason why we should adopt the latter. For there are other tenable attitudes, notably that of critical rationalism which rec- ognizes the fact that the fundamental rationalist attitude results from an . . . act of faith – from faith in reason. Accordingly, our choice is open. We may choose some form of irrationalism, even some radical or comprehensive form. But we are also free to choose a critical form of rationalism, one which frankly admits its origin in an irrational decision . . .

From an epistemological perspective, the quotation implies that Popper has estab- lished his reading of critical rationalism on the basis of the debate between the dogmatic epistemology of rationalism and the sceptic's rejection of rationalism. It should be noted that the sceptic's critique of dogmatic rationalism originates in its justificationism: since dogmatism cannot prove the premises, rationalism is untenable. After wrongly accepting the sceptic's critique of dogmatic rationalism as true, Popper establishes his philosophy of critical rationalism upon the justifi- cational critique that the sceptic levels at dogmatic rationalism and thus reaches irrational faith in reason rather than irrationalism.

Epistemology of critical rationalism

Although the relation between epistemology and the theory of rationality is made very clear in the debates among supporters of critical rationalism, David Miller (2017: 50) argues that ". . . the disappearance of the epistemological dimension of rationality is what is least understood about Popper's philosophy". Once the justificational origin of Popper's irrational faith in reason has been revealed, how- ever, the epistemological dimension of his critical rationalism becomes clear. It is important to distinguish critical rationalism as a hypothesis regarding rational beliefs and critical rationalism merely as a rationale for empirical science. It seems that Miller's attempt to put Popper's critical rationalism in its epistemological context does not pay enough attention to the aforementioned distinction between the two forms of critical rationalism. Miller (2017: 50–59) describes Popper's critical rationalism from an epistemological view by presenting it in three major aspects: (a) critical rationalism as the denial of certainty and reflection of fallibilism, (b) critical rationalism as the method of conjecture and refutation that demarcates fallibilism in critical rationalism from previous ones and (c) critical rationalism as "what is of central importance in the examination of any scientific theory is whether or not true. That it is true is indeed not something that we can recognize, but we can guess it . . ." (2017: 57). Hence, Miller's conclusion is that critical rationalism involves scepticism.

Miller's epistemology of critical rationalism reflects Popper's theory of science instead of pointing out how Popper's epistemology has contributed to his definition of critical rationalism as an irrational faith in reason. If Popper's epistemology does not allow him to base his philosophy of critical rationalism upon a non-justificational theory of knowledge, the origin of Popper's definition of critical rationalism as a moral attitude of openness to criticism is to be sought in his limitation of epistemology to the philosophy of science. As observed by Miller (1985: 60), Popper confesses that "Epistemology I take to be the theory of *scientific knowledge*". However, the epistemology of science deals with the question of 'How do I know science?' rather than with the general question of 'How do I know?'.

Hans Albert (1985: 10) provides a border view:

> . . . (C)ritical rationalism . . . cannot limit rationality to the sphere of science, nor to those technical and economic fields for which its usefulness is customarily conceded. It cannot consent to hold at boundaries of any kind – neither at those of scientific disciplines, nor at those of any social sphere that appears to be immunized against rational criticism by virtue of custom or tradition or conscious protective screening.

Validating this wider perspective, my intention in this chapter has been to show that the lack of a non-justificational theory of knowledge has led to a vital consequence for Popper's philosophy of critical rationalism in terms of a moral attitude of openness to criticism. As long as a critical rationalist does not know that how his openness to criticism enables him to be led logically to know whether or not his rational beliefs are true, his moral commitment to openness to criticism does not help him to be a critical rationalist simply because he does not know how to profit from error. Hence, there is no logical foundation for Popper's attempt to demarcate uncritical rationalism from critical rationalism on the basis of an irrational choice in favour of a moral attitude of openness to criticism.

In the same line of thought, Darrell P. Rowbottom (2011: 12) argues:

> . . . (T)he problem with comprehensive rationalism is the presumption of justificationism. The problem with critical rationalism, as espoused by Popper,

44 Karl Popper's critical rationalism

is the admission that trusting in experience and reason is irrational *because doing so is unjustified*.... Moving criticism to centre stage and decoupling criticism and justification – as Popper had already done in his treatment of science, long before Bartley pointed out that this could be extended to epistemology more generally – is the solution.

In the next chapter, I pursue the idea of the separation of justification and criticism in order to investigate William Bartley's theory of critical rationalism.

I close this chapter in agreement with Miller's (2017: 59) conclusion that:

> The great liberating force of critical rationalism is that it permits us to be logically rigorous without driving us along the road to irrationality. For the realization that this is possible we owe a great deal to one man: Karl Popper. It was he who first challenged the view that the role of argument is not to provide us with justification. By stressing the virtue of criticism, it was he who made it possible for rationalism to hold up its head in dignity again.

Nevertheless, in the course of my arguments it may become clear that the idea of critical rationalism is to be reinvented on the basis of a theory of knowledge that takes the shift from justification to criticism into account, thus enabling us to understand how a 'rational belief' can be examined logically without any need for irrational faith in reason. As long as critical rationalism is defined as a *moral commitment* to openness to criticism rather than as a *theory* of rational beliefs, it cannot contribute to the micro-foundation of the macro-theory of society.

Notes

1 Logical positivists such as Hans Reichenbach and Rudolf Carnap have argued that it is not possible to attain truth or falsity in regard to knowledge. In contrast, scientific statements can only attain continuous degrees of probability, the unattainable upper limit of which is truth. Popper rejects this solution, saying that nothing is gained if the principle of induction is accounted for as probable or if a certain degree of probability is to be attributed to statements based on inductive inference, for this then has to be justified by invoking a new principle on ad infinitum (Popper 1992 [1959]: 248–252).
2 It has been observed that Popper's deductive theory of science does not show how a scientific theory is falsified conclusively. As Deborah A. Redman (1994: 70) puts it: "Since the unit of appraisal is in practice not a simple statement, scientists cannot know which assumption of the theory is causing the problem; they can only conclude that at least one of the many assumptions is false. Hence, the theory can never be falsified conclusively. This difficulty is known to philosophers of science as the Duhem problem and was taken up in greater detail by Lakatos . . .". This difficulty, I suggest, originates from the nature of the modus tollens according to which the falsity of conclusion can refute at least one of premises.
3 Jarvie (2001: 29) writes: "The social content of Popper's philosophy of science was institutionalisation of the decision to maximize falsifiability. The form of institutionalization was methodological rules. These rules made possible intersubjective testability . . .".

However, with regard to the theory of rationality, Popper does not use intersubjective testability arguments, whereas critical rationalists open their rational beliefs to mutual criticism.

Bibliography

Agassi, J. (1987) "Theories of Rationality". In: Agassi, J. & Jarvie, I.C. (eds.) *Rationality: The Critical View*. Dordrecht, Martinus Nijhoff, pp. 249–263.

Albert, H. (1999) *Between Social Science, Religion and Politics*. Atlanta, Amsterdam.

Albert, H. (1985) *Treatise on Critical Reason*, Rorty, M.V. (trans.). Princeton, Princeton University Press.

Andersson, G. (2009) "Critical Rationalism and the Principle of Sufficient Reason". In: Parusnikowa & Cohen (eds.) *Rethinking Popper*. New York, Springer, pp. 21–30.

Jarvie, I.C. (2001) *The Republic of Science: The Emergence of Popper's Social View of Science 1935–1945*. Atlanta, Amsterdam.

Korsgaard, C.M. (2000) *The Creation of the Kingdom of Ends*. Cambridge, Cambridge University Press.

Miller, D. (2017) *Out of Error: Further Essays in Critical Rationalism*. London, Routledge.

Miller, D. (ed.) (1985) *Popper Selections*. Princeton, Princeton University Press.

Musgrave, A.E. (2004) "How Popper [Might Have] Solved the Problem of Induction". In: *Philosophy*, (01), pp. 19–31.

Musgrave, A.E. (1974) "The Objectivism of Popper's Epistemology". In: Schilpp, P.A. (ed.) *The Philosophy of Karl Popper*, Book I. La Salle, Open Court, pp. 560–596.

Notturno, M.A. (2000) *Science and the Open Society: The Future of Karl Popper's Philosophy*. Budapest, Central European University Press.

Popper, K.R. (1994 [2013]) *The Open Society and Its Enemies*. New One-Volume ed. Princeton, Princeton University Press.

Popper, K.R. (1992 [1959]) *The Logic of Scientific Discovery*. London, Routledge.

Popper, K.R. (1979) *The Two Fundamental Problems of the Theory of Knowledge,* English trans. (2009). London, Routledge.

Popper, K.R. (1974) "My Solution to Hume's Problem of Induction". In: Schilpp, P.A. (ed.) *The Philosophy of Karl Popper*, Book II. La Salle, Open Court, pp. 1013–1023.

Popper, K.R. (1963) "Optimist, Pessimist and Pragmatist Views of Scientific Knowledge". In: Shearmur, J. & Turner, P.N. (eds.) *Karl Popper, After The Open Society, Selected Social and Political Writings* (2012). London, Routledge, pp. 3–10.

Popper, K.R. (1962) *Conjectures and Refutations: The Growth of Scientific Knowledge*. New York, Basic Books.

Redman, D.R. (1994) "Karl Popper's Theory of Science and Econometrics: The Rise and Decline of Social Engineering". In: *Journal of Economic Issues*, 28 (1), pp. 67–99.

Rowbottom, D.P. (2011) *Popper's Critical Rationalism: A Philosophical Investigation*. New York, Routledge.

Sceski, J.H. (2007) *Popper, Objectivity and the Growth of Knowledge*. London, Continuum International.

Chapter 3

William Bartley's pancritical rationalism

Masoud Mohammadi Alamuti

Introduction

I have suggested that the lack of a non-justificational epistemology showing how a philosophical claim can be evaluated as true does not allow Popper to base his critical rationalism on argument. Instead, Popper takes a justificational turn: since uncritical rationalism is unable to be justified by argument or experience, the only remaining option is for the critical rationalist to defend his position by a moral choice in favour of reason rather than irrationalism, a logical result of uncritical rationalism.

The focus of inquiry in this chapter is upon William Bartley's pancritical rationalism as his critique of Popper's irrational faith in reason has special importance for my attempt in this book to integrate the philosophy of critical rationalism into the theory of society. Not only does Bartley criticize Popper for defining critical rationalism as a moral attitude, but he also speaks of critical rationalism as a theory of rationality. A theory of rationality allows critical rationalism to define *reason* as a faculty which is able to understand its function and let the actor govern his own behaviour. This chapter proceeds in three sections. Section I reviews Bartley's epistemology to show the basis on which he establishes his critique of Popper's critical rationalism and his own offer of pancritical rationalism. In Section II, Bartley's theory of rationality is presented, while Section III reflects my critique of Bartley's pancritical rationalism.

Section I: Bartley's non-justificationist epistemology

Bartley uses the idea of a non-justificational concept of criticism to introduce a theory of critical rationalism. To this end, he begins with a critique of what Popper calls uncritical rationalism "according to which *comprehensive* justification was a *necessary* condition of rationality" (Bartley 1984b: 238). Bartley's novel idea is that uncritical rationalism rests on the incorrect epistemological premise that a belief that can be justified is considered as true. This untenable premise makes comprehensive or uncritical rationalism an untenable position. However, Bartley does not aim to reach the same result as Popper, namely that it is the untenability of uncritical rationalism that leads the critical rationalist to defend his identity with an irrational faith in reason. Bartley attempts to suggest his theory of critical rationalism by finding a solution for the problem of the rationalist's identity. Bartley argues that, after discovering the existence of non-justificational criticism, he realized the impossibility and superfluity of the sort of justification demanded by uncritical rationalism. Bartley then argues that the non-justificational ability to criticize is a *sufficient* condition for rationality to make being a rationalist possible. In brief, Bartley applies the notion of non-justificational criticism to offer his theory of pancritical rationalism as a solution to the problem of the rationalist's identity.

From justification to criticism: a non-justificational concept of criticism

Bartley could have offered an ideal form of non-justificational epistemology for formulation of his philosophy of pancritical rationalism. If he had done so, the question of how a *rational belief* may be evaluated as *true* could have received a correct answer and Bartley could have based his pancritical rationalism on a non-justificational theory of knowledge. However, Bartley did not follow this ideal path.

Instead, Bartley focused on the idea of the separation of justification and criticism, leading him to a non-justificational conception of criticism:

> The classical account of criticism, which pervades almost all philosophical literature, from the Greeks to the present day, is a *justificationist theory of criticism*. According to this account, the way to examine and criticize an idea is to see whether and how it may be justified.
>
> (1984b: 222)

Bartley seeks to replace a justificational concept of criticism with a non-justificational one due to the infinite regress involved with justification, but not with criticism. Hence, the transition from justification to criticism leads Bartley to a tenable non-justificational concept of criticism in which a position or a belief that cannot be justified may be criticized. Thus, Bartley discovers a new epistemological foundation for his theory of pancritical rationalism.

Bartley (1984a: 115) asks what it means to talk of the fusion of justification and criticism and replies that one answer is that to

> criticize a view is to see whether it can be logically derived from – i.e. "justified by" – the rational criterion or authority. On an empiricist view, such as Hume's, for instance, the strongest criticism of any particular theory was that it could not be justified or established properly – in his case by an appeal to sense experience.

48   William Bartley's pancritical rationalism

Bartley's idea of the separation of justification and criticism is used to show that the meaning of 'critical' itself in the philosophy of critical rationalism would suffer infinite regress if defined by the justificationist concept of criticism. Hence, rescuing critical rationalism from justificationism requires a non-justificational conception of criticism.

In the following quotation, Bartley (1984b: 223) proposes the separation of justification and criticism to show how epistemology contributes to a non-justificational concept of criticism necessary in the philosophy of critical rationalism for prevention of infinite regress:

> If one could continue to ask: "How do you know?", that line of questioning would never end: it would engender an infinite regress. Thus it is supposed that one must stop with an authority – or dogma, or presupposition – *which acts as justifier*. Since this justifier cannot itself be justified, and since the only way to criticize something is to attempt to justify it, these justifiers cannot be criticized. Dogmas, it is concluded, are *necessary*. The logical structure of argumentation itself appeared to vouch for, even to require, dogmatism.
>
> What I did in *The Retreat to Commitment* was to show that *no authorities or justifiers in this sense were needed in criticism*. I separated the notions of justification and criticism (for the first time explicitly) and showed that criticism can be carried out successfully and satisfactorily without engendering any infinite regress, and hence without requiring any resort to justification whatever . . . That is, when I declare that all statements are criticizable, I mean that it is not necessary, in criticism, in order to avoid infinite regress, to declare a dogma that cannot be criticized (since it is unjustifiable) . . . I mean that there is not some point in every argument which is exempted from criticism . . .

By means of separating justification and criticism, Bartley discovers an innovational way of replacing the idea of *irrational faith* in reason in Popper's epistemology with a *rational faith*. In the context of such a separation, Bartley's critique of the justified true belief account of knowledge and its outcome for pancritical rationalism are understandable. Like Popper, Bartley criticizes the justificationist account of knowledge, arguing that dogmatic epistemology is untenable because neither sense experience nor intellectual intuition are infallible premises for justification of a conclusion of deductive inference. Like Popper, Bartley knows that sceptic epistemology also originates from justificationism. By accepting the justified true belief account of knowledge and arguing that fallible premises cannot justify a conclusion, the sceptic rejects objective knowledge. However, unlike Popper, Bartley's intention is to show that the sceptic denial of objective knowledge is baseless upon rejection of the idea of knowledge as justified true belief. Hence, the critical rationalist should not establish his own critique of panrationalism (uncritical rationalism) upon the basis of the sceptic's *justificational* critique of dogmatism.

In validation of Popper's critique of the justificationist theory of science, Bartley admits that scientific knowledge is created through conjecture and refutation. However, he employs the conception of *non-justificational criticism* in order to expand the theory of science to the philosophy of critical rationalism. Bartley (1964: 23) argues: "The main originality of Popper's position lies in the fact that it is the first *non justificational philosophy of criticism* in the history of philosophy". As argued earlier, Bartley's concept of the separation of justification and criticism is a major epistemological contribution to the idea of critical rationalism. Let us now investigate how Bartley applies this separation to criticize Popper's critical rationalism in terms of irrational faith in reason.

Epistemology and the separation of justification and criticism

Bartley argues that non-justificational criticism is in Popper's logic of science, although he does not use it to seek its implication for a general theory of knowledge addressing the question of how we know. With his non-justificational critique of Hume's problem of induction, Popper offers the novel theory of science that a scientific theory can be identified as true if and only if no empirical evidence rejects its prediction. Hence, notwithstanding the Humean justificational view of science, Popper's non-justificational solution overcomes the problem of induction in favour of a conjectural theory of science. A scientific claim is a conjecture whose objectivity depends on the absence of counterevidence. Bartley realizes that the non-justificational nature of Popper's logic of science is manifested in conjecture and refutation: a scientific theory is criticized due to its refutation through a false prediction, not because its premises are known to be false.

Bartley (1964: 20) argues that the justificationist conception of rationalism is derived from two dogmas: "(1) The assumption that criticism is necessarily fused with justification; and (2) the assumption that the quality and degree of rationality pass through the relationship of logical deducibility from justifying premises to justified conclusions". Motivated by the separation of justification and criticism, Bartley endeavours to expand the non-justificational logic of Popper's theory of science to his own theory of rationality. To this end, he refers to the idea of the problem-solving ability of a metaphysical theory offered by Popper for defining a standard against which such a theory can be examined.

Bartley argues, therefore, that a theory of rationality can be judged according to its ability to solve the problem of the rationalist's identity, telling us that not only our scientific, but also our philosophical conjectures are refutable. Bartley (1984a: 127) points out:

> We have at least four means of eliminating error by criticizing our conjectures and speculations. These checks are listed . . .

(1) The check of *logic*: Is the theory in question consistent?

(2) The check of *sense observation*: Is the theory *empirically* refutable by some sense observation? And if it is, do we know of any refutation of it?

(3) The check of *scientific theory*: Is the theory, whether or not it is in conflict with sense observation, in conflict with any scientific hypothesis?

(4) The check of the *problem*: What problem is the theory intended to solve? Does it do so successfully?

Among these four means of error detection, the case for checking the theory against whatever problem it is intended to solve has special importance for an understanding of the separation of justification and criticism in regard to pancritical rationalism. From Bartley's perspective, a theory of rationality can be examined against the standard of whether or not it solves the problem it is intended to solve. This type of critical assessment demonstrates the reason why Bartley regards the demarcation between 'critical' beliefs and 'non-critical' ones as more fundamental than the demarcation between science and non-science. As Gerard Radnitzky (1982: 1061) argues: ". . . the question whether or not a position (statement, view-point, standard, etc.) can be justified is misleading. The issue is whether it can *survive* when exposed to systematic criticism". By admitting this legitimate question, a theory of knowledge is to be introduced for showing how a metaphysical theory may be refuted.

Elsewhere, Bartley (1968: 41) argues that

> . . . Popper has written that the problem of demarcating science from non-science is the central problem of the theory of knowledge; and in his *Conjectures and Refutations* he has described the solution to the problem of demarcation as the "*key* to most of the fundamental problems of the philosophy of science".

Bartley then asserts that Popper's criterion for the demarcation between science and non-science corresponds to a problem with little relevance in comparison with the more fundamental problem of demarcating 'critical' from 'non-critical' theories. Bartley continues:

> Theories, including not only the scientific . . . but also philosophical theories such as theories of rationality and theories of demarcation are, in my view as in Popper's *guesses*, hopefully but not necessary "stations on the road to truth".
>
> (Ibid.: 43)

Hence, metaphysical theories can be examined through conjecture and refutation as well as scientific ones. What, however, does refutation of a philosophical conjecture mean?

While not substantially changing Popper's epistemology, Bartley expands the non-justificational concept of criticism from the theory of science to the philosophy of pancritical rationalism. Nevertheless, whereas observable empirical evidence rejects the prediction of a theory in science, the refutability of a metaphysical theory, such as the theory of rationality, is not apparent. Its failure to solve the problem it claims to solve indicates a key ambiguity in Bartley's non-justificational epistemology: what kind of *deductive inference* may be used to refute a theory of rationality due to its failure to solve the problem of 'rational belief' if the falsity of a conclusion in metaphysics cannot be retransmitted to the premises?

From a logical perspective, the problem-solving capacity of a theory does not show how a non-empirical theory may be rejected due to its refuted conclusion. Logic only allows us to transfer either the truth of the premises to the conclusion (modus ponens) or the falsity of conclusion to at least one of the premises (modus tollens). How, then, does the problem-solving capacity of a metaphysical theory apply the formal logic for transferring the falsity of the conclusion to the set of premises when empirical refutation makes no sense? In order to know whether a theory can address the problem it intends to solve, we should first explore whether the theory in question is false or true. The failure of a theory to solve the problem in question does not explain how logical rules are used to transfer the falsity of the conclusion to the premises. Popper applied the principle of falsifiability in order to demarcate science from metaphysics. In the refutation of a metaphysical theory such as the theory of rationality, however, the standard of problem-solving ability of a theory cannot perform a *logical* role similar to the one played by the principle of falsification in science.

Nevertheless, Bartley expands the non-justificational logic of science to his theory of pancritical rationalism by separating justification from criticism and arguing that a claim of rationality need not be justified to be considered true. It is, however, possible to judge a theory of rationality according to its ability to solve the problem in question. It is on the basis of the non-justificational concept of criticism that Bartley uses Popper's epistemology to present pancritical rationalism and that Bartley's theory of rationality is to be understood within the context of Popper's epistemology.

Section II: rationality as a moral attitude: Bartley's critique

Bartley's non-justificationist concept of criticism paves the way for understanding his critique of Popper's irrational faith in reason. By defining the problem of 'rationality theory' as one of the rationalist's identity, Bartley attempts to show that Popper's critical rationalism does not solve the problem in question and argues that, instead of expanding his non-justificationist logic of science to the philosophy of rationality, Popper founds his argument in favour of critical rationalism over uncritical rationalism on justificational logic: if *rational belief in reason* requires justification by argument or experience and if such justification is untenable, one's belief in critical reason is *irrational belief*. In fact, this is Popper's solution to the problem of the identity of a critical rationalist: unable to justify all of his positions or beliefs, the critical rationalist ought to accept criticism and learn from it through an irrational faith in reason or a moral attitude. Bartley's dissatisfaction with this explanation of critical rationalist identity led to his investigation of the epistemological origin of Popper's justificationist concept of rationality.

Popper's critical rationalism and the limits of rationality

Bartley argues that the idea of irrational faith in reason originates in the notion of the limits of rationality. According to Bartley (1984a: 73–74), the limits of rationality mean that

> ... one cannot, without arguing in a circle, justify the rationality of a standard of rationality by appealing to that standard. Yet, if certain beliefs – for example, the standard itself – are held to be immune from the demand for rational justification and from the question "How do you know?", they can be said to be held irrationally or dogmatically. And, so it is claimed, argument about the radically different beliefs held in this way is pointless ... *The limits of rational argument within any particular way of life* seem, then, to be defined by reference to that object or belief in respect to which commitment is made or imposed, in respect to which argument is brought to a close. Thus reason is relativized to one's halting place or standards, and cannot arbitrate among different standards (emphasis added).

In short, the idea of the limits of rationality implies that, with justification of a claim of rationality as the standard for its truth, the problem of infinite regress forces the rationalist to admit the limitations of his rational argument simply because infinite regress must be stopped at some point.

Bartley situates Popper's irrational faith in reason in a wider perspective of the limits of rational argument, declaring that, in contrast to his non-justificationist theory of science, Popper's critical rationalism takes a justificational approach. Popper admits that the limits of rationality originate in the sceptic's rejection of objective knowledge: unable to justify a claim of knowledge by argument or experience, the sceptic has no way to prove his claim. Nevertheless, despite the sceptic's rejection of objective knowledge and rationalism, Popper does not acknowledge the logical consequences of such a justificational critique of uncritical rationalism, i.e. irrationalism. Instead, Popper claims that critical rationalism can be accepted with a concession to a minimum of irrationalism. Bartley criticizes Popper's irrational faith in reason for its justificationist notion of the limits of rational argument.

William Bartley's pancritical rationalism   53

According to Bartley, Popper follows the sceptic's position regarding comprehensive rationalism because both take a justificational approach to the problems of rationality. While recognizing the sceptic's criticism, Popper does not follow the logical result of such criticism and becomes involved in a paradoxical situation by defending critical rationalism in terms of an irrational faith in reason. On the one hand, Popper refuses to accept the sceptic's irrationalism while, on the other, rejecting rationalism in its comprehensive sense because it cannot be justified by argument or experience. Under these conditions, the only option remaining for Popper, who does not want to give up justificationism, is that one can *justify* faith in reason with an *irrational* commitment! This defence of critical rationalism is unacceptable for Bartley; however, due to its origin in the sceptic's justificational critique of rationalism and the dogmatist's justificational call for irrationally stopping infinite regress at some point. In sum, Bartley recognizes that the paradox in Popper's critical rationalism originates in its justificationism.

As observed by Mariano Artigas (2002: 36):

> Popper presents "rationalism" in opposition to the kind of irrationalism which refuses argument, and adds the qualification 'critical' in order to emphasise that, unlike classical or "comprehensive" rationalism, which only admits that which can be justified by positive reasons, critical rationalism acknowledges that we cannot provide such positive justification.

This raises the question of the meaning of the term 'critical' in Popper's critical rationalism and means that, unable to justify our belief in comprehensive rationalism, our very belief in rationalism ought to be shaped by an irrational belief. In this case, the term 'critical' does not benefit from an epistemological meaning, and Popper cannot explain how our moral attitude of openness to criticism allows us to use logic in order to learn from our errors. Artigas (2002: 37) rightly recognizes that: "According to Bartley, behind this problem there exists a meta-context contaminated by a justificationist philosophy about true belief". Bartley argues that Popper's critical rationalism originates in the 'justified true belief' account of knowledge.

Bartley (1984a: 74) reminds us that two consequences seem to follow acceptance of the limits of rational argument:

> The "truth" of one's beliefs is then ultimately rooted not in their self-evidence or in their universality but in one's whim, or in the belief, say, that God has commanded one to accept these standards. A man's standards are *true for him* because of his subjective commitment to them. An irrationalist thus has an *excuse for his subjective irrationalism*, and a secure refuge from any criticism of any subjective commitment: he has a *tu quoque* or boomerang argument. To any critic, the irrationalist can reply: *tu quoque*, reminding him that people whose rationality is similarly limited should not berate others for admitting to and acting on the limitation. If everyone – as a matter of logic – must make

an irrational commitment at some point, if no one can escape subjective commitment, then no one can be criticized simply because he has made such a commitment, no matter how idiosyncratic.

Bartley uses the *tu quoque* (you, too) argument to show that Popper's justificationism leads him to irrational faith in reason. However, Bartley maintains that rejection of justificationism does not involve the need to admit an irrational commitment to any position, since no attempt has been made to justify any position that leads to infinite regress and irrational commitment. All rational beliefs can be held open to criticism.

The epistemological origin of popper's irrational faith in reason

The very logic Popper uses in comparing the difference between critical rationalism and uncritical rationalism is epistemological: the uncritical rationalist cannot justify his belief by argument or experience. Popper (1994 [2013]: 435) expresses uncritical rationalism as an attitude: "I am not prepared to accept anything that cannot be defended by means of argument or experience". Then, he argues that this attitude itself cannot be defended by argument or experience and is thus untenable. By definition, Popper's argument against uncritical rationalism and for critical rationalism is *epistemological*, not *moral*.

Popper concludes that the impossibility of justification of a belief by positive reasoning leads to an open choice of either enduring irrational faith in reason or becoming an irrationalist. He calls the first option critical rationalism. Bartley recognizes that the epistemology of Popper's critical rationalism implies that *a belief is rational if and only if it can be justified*, an epistemology Popper has already rejected by his own philosophy of science. Nevertheless, Popper (1994 [2013]: 431) claims critical rationalism to be a moral attitude: the 'attitude' of readiness to listen to critical arguments and of learning from error. It is an attitude of admitting that 'I may be wrong and you may be right, and by an effort, we may get nearer to the truth'. It now becomes clearer why Bartley situates Popper's irrational faith reason in the wider context of the justificational epistemology of the limits of rationality.

Bartley argues as follows: if Popper admits that non-empirical theories are discussable rationally, why should he not accept the theory of rationality as discussable? Sceski (2007: 70) leads us to see the sense in which Popper regards these theories as discussable:

> In general, the irrefutability of statements can be approached from two perspectives: logically irrefutable and empirically irrefutable. The former according to Popper is equivalent to logically consistent, and the truth of a theory cannot possibly be inferred from its consistency. . . . However, despite

their irrefutability, metaphysical claims can be critically evaluated and even tentatively classified as false in two ways: (1) in light of the problem situation that gave rise to them, and (2) in reference to other theories accepted as well-corroborated background knowledge.

Popper (1962: 199) writes,

> Now if we look upon a theory as a proposed solution to a set of problems, then the theory immediately lends itself to critical discussion – even if it is non-empirical and irrefutable. For we can now ask such questions as: Does it solve the problem? Does it solve it better than other theories? Has it perhaps merely shifted the problem? Is the solution simple? . . . Questions of this kind show a critical discussion even of irrefutable theories may well be possible.

However, Popper does not make use of these remarks to ask himself whether his theory of critical rationalism solves the problem of the rationalist's belief in critical reason.

Bartley (1984a) argues that Popper's irrational faith in reason confronts the rationalist with an identity problem. If a critical rationalist has faith in reason irrationally and if this behaviour is also permitted for an irrationalist, Popper's critical rationalism does not offer the rationalist a consistent identity for distinguishing himself from the irrationalist because both the rationalist and the irrationalist may make an irrational commitment at some point. Bartley uses his own epistemological standard to criticize Popper's critical rationalism, arguing that Popper's irrational faith in reason can be refuted according to the problem-solving ability of a metaphysical theory.

Perhaps a deeper problem with Popper's critical rationalism is that, by definition, a *moral* openness to criticism cannot show the rationalist how he can evaluate his beliefs and gain experience from error. To this end, the rationalist must be able to relate the falsity of his belief to its premises logically, but how can such moral openness without any epistemological basis enable the rationalist to learn from criticism? An irrational faith in reason is unable to show the actor how to apply reason in order to examine the beliefs guiding his behaviour. From the perspective of action theory, the definition of critical rationalism as a moral attitude prevents the actor from seeing how human action may be derived from critical reason. Hence, the role of critical reason in the determination of human action remains unexplained.

Section III: Bartley's pancritical rationalism

Bartley's recognition of critical rationalism as a *theory* of rationality makes an important contribution to the explanatory function of critical reason in human action. Inspired by his non-justificational epistemology, Bartley (1964: 6) argues

56 William Bartley's pancritical rationalism

in "Rationality versus the Theory of Rationality", that, ". . . if to defend a position rationally is to give good reasons in justification of it", it would appear that one cannot offer a stopping point to prevent infinite regress. Hence, an irrational faith in reason would be the natural consequence of the definition of rationality in terms of giving justifying reasons. In order to introduce critical rationalism as a theory of rationality, Bartley replaces justificationist epistemology with the non-justificational philosophy of criticism. Bartley's strategy for turning critical rationalism into a theory of rationality is to use the general separation of justification and criticism for examination of the rationalist's position itself.

The problem of rationalist identity and pancritical rationalism

Pancritical rationalism is the theory of rationality offered by Bartley for answering the question of whether it is possible to remain a rationalist. It was after discovering the non-justificational concept of criticism that Bartley found a solution for the problem of rationalist identity (1984b: 238). The main idea of Bartley's theory of rationality can be summarized as follows: it is a mistake to call upon the rationalist to offer good reasons for justifying his beliefs as true because justification involves the infinite regress. Hence, unlike Popper, Bartley does not argue that the rationalist who cannot justify all of his claims of rationality by argument or experience should then opt to be rationalist with irrational faith. With the separation of justification and criticism, Bartley's pancritical rationalism can, however, recount that it is not mistake for the rationalist to seek falsifying reasons for defending his beliefs as true as long as they are not shown to be false by argument or experience because, unlike justification, *criticism* does not face the logical problem of infinite regress.

Bartley thus argues that uncritical rationalism is to be criticized from a non-justificational perspective: the demand for justification should be rejected. He asks why a rational belief should be justified when the 'justificational account of rationality' is untenable. Bartley argues that the problem of a rationalist's identity should not be dealt with in terms of how the rationalist can justify all of his rationality claims, but in terms of how the rationalist holds open all of his beliefs to criticism, respecting only the beliefs that survive a severe test as rational. To theorize pancritical rationalism, Bartley uses the distinction between justification and criticism to show how the transition from an 'irrational' to a 'rational' faith in reason improves Popper's critical rationalism. Bartley (1984a: 85) writes:

> Let us consider this search for identity and integrity in rationalism, and in so doing examine three possible conceptions of rationalist identity:
> *panrationalism (or comprehensive rationalism)*
> *critical rationalism*
> *pancritical rationalism (or comprehensively critical rationalism)*

William Bartley's pancritical rationalism 57

The story of modern philosophy can be told to a large extent in terms of the history of panrationalism or comprehensive rationalism. It is, for the most part, the story of the failure of panrationalism to defeat sceptical and fideistic contentions about the limits of rationality.

While Popper compares critical rationalism with uncritical rationalism, Bartley attempts to show that both uncritical and critical rationalism propose a justificational concept of rationality. Bartley's new classification allows clarification that the real confrontation is to be sought between the justificational concepts of rationalist identity, i.e. uncritical rationalism and critical rationalism, on the one hand, and pancritical rationalism, on the other.

Bartley (1984a: 118) argues that, whereas the justificationist concept of rationality implies that the rationalist should justify all his beliefs or positions by argument or experience, without which the solution would be an irrational faith in reason, the non-justificational concept of rationality

> . . . permits a rationalist to be characterized as one who is willing to entertain any position and holds *all* his positions, including his most fundamental standards, goals, and decisions, and his basic philosophical position itself, open to criticism; one who protects nothing from criticism by justifying it irrationally; one who never cuts off an argument by resorting to faith or irrational commitment to justify some belief that has been under severe critical fire; one who is committed, attached, addicted, to no position.

Bartley then states the essence of his theory of rationality "I shall call this conception *pancritical rationalism*".

Bartley (1984a: 118) argues that the pancritical rationalism solution to the problem of rationalist identity differs from the uncritical rationalism solution

> in having altogether abandoned the ideal of comprehensive *rational* justification. And it also differs from critical rationalism, wherein a rationalist accepted that his position was rationally unjustifiable but went on to justify it irrationally by his personal and social moral commitment to standards and practices that were not themselves open to assessment or criticism since . . . criticism and rational justification are fused.

As observed by Bartley, we

> cannot go on justifying our beliefs forever since the question of the correctness of the conclusion shifts back to the question of the correctness of the premises; and if the premises are never established or justified, neither is the conclusion. Since we want to justify and cannot do so *rationally*, irrational

58 William Bartley's pancritical rationalism

justification or commitment seems the only resort. So, if rationality lies in justification, it is severely limited by the necessity for commitment.

In this way, Bartley argues that uncritical rationalism and critical rationalism claim that rationality lies in justification and that, therefore, their solutions to the problem of rationalist identity involve infinite regress. Bartley continues, however,

> ... if rationality lies in criticism, and if we can subject everything to criticism and continued test, including the rationalist way of life itself, without leading to infinite regress, circularity, the need to justify, or other such difficulty, then rationality is in this sense unlimited.
>
> (1984a: 118–119)

In fact, Bartley presents his theory of pancritical rationalism through a critical examination of Popper's idea of irrational faith in reason, intending to improve Popper's critical rationalism by removing its justificationist origin.

As pointed out by Noretta Koertge (1974: 76), Bartley's theory of rationality attempts to provide "an interesting new answer to the old question of whether the adaption of a rational approach to life is itself an irrational (or perhaps a rational) decision". Inspired by Popper's use of a shift from justification to criticism in his innovative solution to the problem of induction, Bartley offers his own solution to the problem of rationality by integrating a similar epistemological shift from justification to criticism in the concept of rationality. According to Bartley, pancritical rationalism means that for "a theory to be held rationally it is not only necessary that it be criticisable – it must also be possible that some criticism might *succeed* in discrediting the theory" (Koertge 1974: 77). In brief, pancritical rationalism defines a 'rational belief' as a belief that is open to criticism, but has not yet been falsified.

Pancritical rationalism: critical evaluations

Critical reflections on pancritical rationalism are noteworthy although the details of these reflections are not directly relevant to my concerns in this section. Nevertheless, my intention is to review some of the major reflections.[1] J.W.N. Watkins (1969, 1971) offers one of the major critiques of pancritical rationalism.[2] In brief, Watkins's main argument is that defining pancritical rationalism in terms of the openness of all positions or beliefs to criticism blocks this self-applicable theory from 'real' criticism because refutation makes it criticisable, as does withstanding severe refutation: hence, the theory prevails in both cases.

As Watkins (1969: 59) points out,

> No opponent could show that some standard used by a comprehensively critical rationalist is uncriticisable in the sense that it is not open to adverse

comment of *any* kind. Suppose, however, that he produces a cogent argument purporting to show that it is not open to anything that Bartley counts as genuine criticism. Then that would constitute a *highly demanding criticism* of the standard in question, *in view of CCR [Comprehensively Critical Rationalism] itself*, which requires a rationalist to hold *all* his positions open to criticism. Hence, it is *impossible* for a critic to show that a critical standard necessarily used by a comprehensively critical rationalist is uncriticisable.

Watkins focuses upon the necessary condition of pancritical rationalism, forgetting the sufficient condition. Whereas the openness of all beliefs to criticism is a necessary condition of pancritical rationalism, the sufficient condition implies that such an open belief to criticism is a rational belief if it survives severe test. Bartley (1984b: 241) describes Watkins's critique as follows:

> Watkins claims that pancritical rationalism was a perfect example of a dictatorial strategy in the sense that it permits me to win however the argument may go: a defender of pancritical rationalism, he contends, is *assured* victory over his critics however good their criticisms, for his position is never at risk.

We will see that this allegation is extrinsic to the crux of Bartley's discussion of this matter.

In 'Towards a Theory of Openness to Criticism,' Tom Settle et al. (1974: 85) point out:

> *CCR* requires that all positions, including *CCR*, be held open to criticism. Watkins argued that *CCR* could never be overthrown since even the most devastating criticism reinforced its criticizability. We rebutted this attach by distinguishing between criticizability as a necessary condition for holding *CCR* and criticizability as a sufficient condition: *CCR* would be dogmatic if criticizability were held to be a sufficient condition for holding a view rationally. But in Bartley's work it clearly is intended solely as a necessary condition.

Watkins's critique implies that being able to criticize CCR would permit it to remain a valid theory even if it is refuted by argument of experience. This is, however, an incorrect interpretation of Bartley's pancritical rationalism.

As noted earlier, according to Koertge (1974: 77), Bartley's pancritical rationalism implies that for "a theory to be held rationally it is not only necessary that it be criticizable – it must also be possible that some criticism might *succeed* in discrediting the theory". Hence, Bartley's solution for the problem of rational belief is meant to show that a rational belief ought first to be held open to criticism, then, upon potential refutation of the belief by criticism, the refuted belief is considered irrational. Bartley argues that, since criticism does not involve infinite regress,

60 William Bartley's pancritical rationalism

there is no logical obstacle for holding all positions or beliefs open to criticism in order to see whether or not they survive a severe test and become 'rational' positions or beliefs.

In defence of Bartley's pancritical rationalism, Joseph Agassi et al. (1971: 45) argue that

> Popper has equated the empirical character of scientific theories with their refutability; refutable theories are thus to be entertained with especial seriousness in science. It does not follow that scientists have to embrace those theories whose refutability has been decisively demonstrated by their having been refuted. Analogously, Bartley has equated rationality with openness to criticism or criticisability: criticisable doctrines are thus to be entertained with especial seriousness by rational minded men. Analogously, it does not follow that Bartley or Watkins or any other rationally inclined person has to embrace doctrines which have been successfully criticised.

The preceding statements make the baselessness of Watkins's critique of pancritical rationalism understandable.

In 'On Critical and Pancritical Rationalism', Antoni Diller (2012: 128) poses a similar critique of pancritical rationalism:

> . . . pancritical rationalism is not a better version of rationalism than critical rationalism. Popper does indeed say that the attitude of reasonableness is accepted by means of an irrational decision. This, however, is not fideism, as the attitude accepted is not a theory; at its core are several moral principles. The decision to treat arguments seriously is irrational because it is a moral decision. Rational discourse, for Popper, is guided by the regulative idea of truth. Moral principles, unlike theories, are capable neither of being true nor of being false.

On the basis of the premise that irrational faith in reason is a moral attitude not a theory, Diller claims that Popper's critical rationalism is not a kind of fideism.

Why then should critical rationalism not be a theory? Popper's defence of critical rationalism clearly shows that his argument that critical rationalism is not a theory, but a moral attitude implies that he has already ruled out the possibility of a 'rational' faith in reason due to his justificationism. Popper argues that, since the rationalist cannot justify all his theories by argument or experience, neither can he justify a theory of comprehensive rationalism. As claimed by Diller, Popper's argument does not reflect moral reasoning. Instead, it echoes an epistemological argument. Just as Popper argued that inductive reasoning cannot justify its conclusion by a limited amount of evidence, he also argued that, since the rationalist cannot justify all of his rationality claims, he cannot be a comprehensive rationalist. In both cases, Popper's arguments are epistemological rather than moral.

As argued by Bartley (1984a), it is Popper's justificationist epistemology that enforces him to claim that an irrational faith in reason is to be interpreted as a moral attitude and that critical rationalism does not refer to a 'theory' of rationality. In addition, as argued by Bartley (1984a: 199–202), moral claims, such as empirical or metaphysical theories, can be subjected to non-justificational criticism. Hence, Diller's claim that moral principles are not guided by the regulative idea of truth and, unlike theories, are incapable of being true or of being false is *itself* a false claim.

In contrast to Diller's reading of critical rationalism, Hans Albert (1985: 47) defines critical rationalism as a

> . . . new concept of rationality embodied in the principle of critical examination [that] differs from the classical doctrine principally in that it does not necessitate resource to only dogma whatsoever, and does not allow the dogmatization of answers of any sort – of metaphysical or scientific theories, of ethical systems, historical theses, or practical and thus political proposals. Simultaneously all claims for the *infallibility* of any court of appeal are rejected in favor of a thoroughgoing *fallibilism*.

Albert does not openly criticize Popper's irrational faith in reason; however, his interpretation of critical rationalism clearly reflects the spirit of Bartley's pancritical rationalism.

A logical critique of pancritical rationalism

From an epistemological perspective, the meaning of the term 'critical' plays a crucial role in understanding the extent to which the separation of justification and criticism has been integrated in the philosophy of 'critical' rationalism. From a non-justificational viewpoint, the term 'critical' means that, while the rationalist cannot *justify* all of his rationality claims by argument or experience, he can, nevertheless, *criticize* all of them by argument or experience. Popper uses this non-justificationist concept of criticism to solve the problem of induction in the philosophy of science. In Popper's new logic of science, the scientist places the hypothesis under consideration among the premises of the argument while putting the observation reports brought in criticism of the argument at the conclusion (Bartley 1984a: 194). Here, the logical meaning of 'critical' is to be seen in terms of *retransmission of falsity from conclusion to at least one of premises*. It is exactly this logical rule that allows the scientist to discover whether his conjecture is not refuted and thus remains true.

Unfortunately, Popper did not devote an *epistemological* meaning to the term 'critical' when he defined his 'critical' rationalism because his justificationist concept of rationality did not permit him to formulate a 'theory' of critical rationalism on the non-justificational concept of criticism. This led Popper to define critical

62 William Bartley's pancritical rationalism

rationalism as an attitude of readiness to listen to criticism. The term 'critical' does not benefit from an *epistemological meaning* in Popper's philosophy of critical rationalism; hence, his philosophy cannot provide us with a theory of rationality showing how human action is derived from *critical* reason.

Popper (1992: 75) himself describes the notion of *rational criticism* as follows:

> ... all rational criticism takes the form of an attempt to show that unacceptable conclusions can be derived from the assertion we are trying to criticize. If we are successful in deriving, logically, unacceptable conclusions from an assertion, then the assertion may be taken to be refuted.

However, whereas deriving an unacceptable conclusion from an empirical theory, in terms of a conclusion refuted by fact that can logically be retransmitted to at least one of premises, is clear, it is ambiguous how an unacceptable conclusion for a metaphysical theory can be recognized by non-empirical reason and be retransmitted to at least one of premises.

I offer a new critique of Bartley's pancritical rationalism on the basis of the premise that Bartley, similar to Popper, does not suggest a 'logical form' of criticism when he comes to defining the meaning of the term 'critical' in pancritical rationalism. Hence, I conclude that Bartley has not realized the ideal of the separation of justification and criticism in the philosophy of critical rationalism. While Bartley has made an important contribution to this separation by expanding the non-justificational concept of criticism from the theory of science to the theory of rationality, he does not introduce a logical form for identifying the falsity of a metaphysical theory. What Bartley has actually discovered is that Popper has not used his epistemology to subject metaphysical theories to non-justificational criticism. Nevertheless, Bartley argues that pancritical rationalism has solved the problem of the rationalist identity better than panrationalism and critical rationalism.

From these remarks, it follows that a major logical problem with Bartley's pancritical rationalism is that the theory of rationality does not explain how the rules of logic allow the critical rationalist to discover the falsity of his open claims when he holds all of his claims of rationality open to criticism. The notion of the problem-solving ability of a theory does not help us to see how the *very logical act of criticism* takes place during investigation of the problem-solving capacity of such a theory. From a logical perspective, there are two major options for exploring the falsity of a rationality claim: either the critical rationalist applies *modus ponens* to transmit the truth of premises to conclusion in order to *justify* the claim in question or the critical rationalist uses *modus tollens* to retransmit the falsity of conclusion to at least one of its premises. This latter logical rule refers to non-justificational criticism, which does not *justify* a conclusion by its premises, but by *falsifying* at least one of the premises by means of its refuted conclusion. This non-justificational form of criticism *cannot* be applied for refuting a non-empirical theory such a theory of rationality.

William Bartley's pancritical rationalism 63

If my understanding of the matter is correct, Bartley's theory of rationality does not tell the critical rationalist how to use logic in practice to refute his 'open beliefs'. While Bartley's pancritical rationalism has clarified the *necessity* for opening up all beliefs to criticism and provided for passing a severe test to be a *sufficient* condition for being a rational belief, it does not show the critical rationalist how to refute his rationality claims or how to profit from such refutation. Therefore, Bartley's theory of rationality is unable to explain how critical reason works or how human action is driven by learning from criticism.

The lack of a falsifiability criterion with regard to non-empirical theories creates an important challenge for pancritical rationalism: since Bartley does not clarify how a claim of rationality held open to criticism can be refuted logically, he also cannot address the question of how his own theory of rationality would be refutable. While Bartley's response to Watkins' critique indicates that pancritical rationalism is open to criticism and that it be refuted, it fails to solve the problem of rationality. Nevertheless, although the theory does not provide us with a logical criterion for refuting it, the theory of pancritical rationalism remains irrefutable. My *critique* of pancritical rationalism implies that pancritical rationalism is unable to solve the problem of how a claim of rationality, including the claim that pancritical rationalism is 'rational' itself, can be 'criticized' through deductive logic.

Although it is unclear how logic allows us to judge a rational belief that is held open to criticism by argument or experience, it would also not be possible to identify the truth of our rational beliefs. Hence, it can be said that Bartley's pancritical rationalism has not solved the problem of rationalist identity because it does not tell the rationalist how to defend his rational belief in reason.

I draw this lesson from my logical critique of Bartley's pancritical rationalism: if we want to solve the problem of rationality, an alternative theory of knowledge must be formulated to indicate the logical procedures through which a claim of rational belief can be demarcated from an irrational belief.[3] Bartley uses the unfulfilled capacity of Popper's theory of science in order to propose a theory of critical rationalism; however, Popper's theory of science cannot be used to explore the logic of rationality discovery. Chapter 4 presents a non-justificational epistemology to close this gap and to prepare the epistemological basis for a *non-justificationist concept of critical rationalism*.

Notes

1 For details of Bartley's responses to his critics, see appendix 4 in his book, *The Retreat to Commitment*, entitled "On Alleged Paradoxes in Pancritical Rationalism" (1984b: 217–246).
2 Another critique of Bartley's pancritical rationalism is offered by John Post (1972, 1987). As pointed out by Bartley (1984b: 218–219), "Post contends that my position – that all positions, including my own, are open to criticism – produces a semantical paradox,

64 William Bartley's pancritical rationalism

and generates an *uncriticizable* statement". Nevertheless, "My position refers to itself as criticizable: i.e., it is 'self-referential'. Moreover, my position employs, although not exclusively, an interpretation of criticizability in terms of possible falsity – and thus involves the semantical concepts of truth and falsity". Bartley's response to Post's critique is: "Since, as Tarski has shown, any natural language containing semantic terms and the possibility of self-reference may be expected to be inconsistent, and to produce just such paradoxes . . . such paradoxes can be dealt with as they arise, through means similar to those that Tarski himself had suggested, through distinctions of levels of language, through the use of the notion of object and metalanguages".

3 Bartley (1984b: 234) writes that ". . . pancritical rationalism does not involve, and I have never developed, a theory of rationality as a property of statements". However, if the theory of rationality originates the theory of knowledge, a theory of rationality implies the question of whether a claim of rational belief is true or false. Since Bartley does not concern himself with a general non-justificational theory of knowledge, the connection between an 'unfalsified' claim and a 'rational' belief has not attracted his attention.

Bibliography

Agassi, J., Jarvie, I.C. & Settle, T. (1971) "The Grounds of Reason". In: *Philosophy,* 46 (175), pp. 43–50.

Albert, H. (1985) *Treatise on Critical Reason,* Rorty, M.V. (trans.). Princeton, Princeton University Press.

Artigas, M. (2002) *The Ethical Nature of Karl Popper's Theory of Knowledge.* Berlin, Peter Lang.

Bartley, III, W.W. (1984a) *The Retreat to Commitment,* 2nd ed. Chicago, Open Court.

Bartley, III, W.W. (1984b) "On Alleged Paradoxes in Pancritical Rationalism". In: Bartley (ed.) *The Retreat to Commitment,* 2nd ed. Chicago, Open Court, pp. 217–246.

Bartley, III, W.W. (1968) "Theories of Demarcation between Science and Metaphysics". In: Lakatos, I. & Musgrave, A. (eds.) *Problems in the Philosophy of Science.* Amsterdam, North-Holland, pp. 40–64.

Bartley, III, W.W. (1964) "Rationality versus the Theory of Rationality". In: Bunge, M. (ed.) *The Critical Approaches to Science and Philosophy, In Honor of Karl R. Popper.* London, Free Press of Glencoe, pp. 3–31.

Diller, A. (2012) "On Critical and Pancritical Rationalism". In: *Philosophy of the Social Sciences,* 43 (2), pp. 27–156.

Koertge, N. (1974) "Bartley's Theory of Rationality". In: *Philosophy of the Social Sciences,* 4, pp. 75–81.

Popper, K.R. (1994 [2013]) *The Open Society and Its Enemies.* New One-Volume ed., Ryan A. (intr.), Gombrich, E.H. (essay). Princeton, Princeton University Press.

Popper, K.R. (1992) *In Search of a Better World, Lectures and Essays from Thirty Years.* London, Routledge.

Popper, K.R. (1962) *Conjectures and Refutations: The Growth of Scientific Knowledge.* New York, Basic Books.

Post, J. (1987) "The Possible Liar". In: *Nous,* 4, pp. 405–409.

Post, J. (1972) "Paradox in Critical Rationalism and Related Theories". In: *Philosophical Forum,* 3 (1), pp. 72–61.

Radnitzky, G. (1982) "In Defense of Self-Applicable Critical Rationalism". In: *Partial Volume,* 2, pp. 1025–1069.

Sceski, J.H. (2007) *Popper, Objectivity and the Growth of Knowledge*. London, Continuum International.

Settle, T., Jarvie, I.C. & Agassi, J. (1974) "Towards a Theory of Openness to Criticism". In: *Philosophy of the Social Sciences*, 4, pp. 83–90.

Watkins, J.W.N. (1971) "CCR: A Refutation". In: *Philosophy*, 46 (175), pp. 56–61.

Watkins, J.W.N. (1969) "Comprehensively Critical Rationalism". In: *Philosophy*, 44 (167), pp. 57–62.

Chapter 4

Towards a non-justificationist epistemology

Masoud Mohammadi Alamuti

Introduction

In order to reinvent critical rationalism into a new theory of rationality showing how a claim of rationality held open to criticism may be refuted in practice, a new theory of knowledge is needed to demarcate 'true belief' from 'false belief'. Although Popper and Bartley realize in their epistemology that the justified true belief account of knowledge cannot prepare the ground for a theory of critical rationalism, they fail to present a non-justificationist alternative extending beyond the philosophy of science. Proceeding in four sections, this chapter aims to narrow that gap in the epistemology of critical rationalism, arguing that justificationist epistemologies, whether dogmatic or sceptic, have neglected to address the problem of objective knowledge due to the meaning of justified *true belief* that they give to knowledge. A new solution to the problem of objective knowledge is proposed: the idea of expanding the general differentiation between justification and criticism first introduced by Bartley (1964, 1984) to the concept of objective knowledge leading to the idea of knowledge as *unfalsified conjecture*.

Chapter 4 argues that the idea of knowledge as unfalsified conjecture directs us towards a non-justificational form of deduction, preparing the ground for the introduction of a *new theory of falsification* applicable not only in science but also in metaphysics. Finally, the non-justificationist concept of knowledge, the deductive form of inference and the theory of falsification are used to offer a new theory of knowledge: *a non-justificationist epistemology*.

Section I: objective knowledge: the failure of justificationist solutions

From Chapter 1, we have learned that neither dogmatist nor sceptic epistemology offers an acceptable solution to the problem of objective knowledge mainly because they define knowledge as justified true belief. In addressing the failure, the justificationist concept of knowledge to solve the problem of objective knowledge, I briefly return to the idea of justified true belief *itself*.

The justified true belief account of knowledge and infinite regress in proofs

As correctly observed by Musgrave (1974: 561),

> At the basis of the traditional theory of knowledge is the assumption that knowledge is a special kind of *belief:* Knowledge consists of those beliefs which can be justified. According to this concept of knowledge, to say "I know *X*" means something like "I believe *X*, I can justify my belief in *X*, and *X* is true".

In fact, the concept of knowledge as justified true belief implies that knowledge is not only a special kind of belief, but also a belief that is true and whose truth is justified by positive reasons. Hence, the justified true belief account of knowledge consists of three assumptions: (a) knowledge is a special kind of belief, (b) this knowledge claim (belief) can be known as true and (c) the truth of such a knowledge claim (belief) is to be justified by arguments or experiences.

After these observations, I now explore the role of the premise of knowledge as 'justified true belief' in the argument of justificationist epistemology and its failure to solve the problem of knowledge intended to be solved. Acceptance of such a justificationist reading of objective knowledge as the premise of the theory of knowledge, it would *force* the theory to use this *model* for the process; that is, the conclusion of a rational argument could be realized in practice. Hence, the following two main conditions are to be satisfied in order to model the formation of a claim of knowledge capable of producing 'justified true belief' as the final result:

(a) The premises of such a claim of knowledge are to be infallible.
(b) The forms of inference are to be indisputable in order to transmit the truth of the infallible premises to the justifiable conclusion or to retransmit the falsity from the conclusion to the premises.

According to justificationist epistemology, the knowing subject who aims to prove his claim of knowledge as true (objective) should use infallible premises, whether sense experience or intellectual intuition, and a valid form of inference then unmistakably transmits the truth of the premises to the conclusion. This is the way a justificationist theory of knowledge designs a model for the process of *forming justified true belief.* The concept of knowledge as justified true belief directs the justificationist epistemologist in his search for *infallible premises and undisputable rules for inferences transmitting the truth of premises to conclusion.* In other words, from the *very beginning,* the *demand for justification* – reflected in the concept of objective knowledge – dictates the two conditions a justificationist theory of knowledge ought to meet in order to realize the goal of justified true belief.

68 Towards a non-justificationist epistemology

As Musgrave (1974: 561–562) argues,

> The history of the theory of knowledge is in large measure the history of a great debate about whether man could know anything, in this sense of "know" . . . . Dogmatists were the champions of "objectivity": they insisted that objective truth can be known, that we do have a means of proving it. Now the chief weapon in the sceptic armoury was the infinite regress of proofs.

The problem of infinite regress, the main problem confronting a justificationist theory of knowledge, shows that the demand for justifying a belief as true by its premises is mistaken from the start. Musgrave (1974: 562) writes that the problem of infinite regress implies,

> To prove that a statement X is true we must produce other statement (s) Y from which X logically follows: Y then establishes X in the sense that, given that Y is true, X must be true also. But obviously the truth of Y needs in its turn to be established, as so on ad infinitum. Sceptics concluded that it is impossible really to establish the objective truth of any statement, and therefore that knowledge, in the traditional sense of that term, is impossible.

If this argument is correct, then it could be concluded that it is the demand for *justification* of the assumption of the premises as infallible that leads to the problem of the *infinite regress of proofs*. Infinite regress arises because we want to prove the premise as *true* and, to do so, we must argue either that the premise itself is true because it is self-evident or that it rests on a different true premise. However, since the premise is also not infallible, it must be established on a different infallible premise, but that different premise is fallible, too. In short, infinite regress means that one cannot stop the demand for justification of the premises as true because they always remain fallible.

It is noteworthy that even the demand for presenting infallible premises originates in the definition of knowledge as justified true belief. In other words, this reading of objective knowledge implies that a belief is true if and only if it can be justified; hence, this justified true belief account of knowledge is demonstrated through fulfilment of the following two conditions: (i) conclusion of a rational argument is to be *justified* indisputably by its *premises* and (ii) the *premises* must be assumed *infallible* so the truth of such premises can be transmitted to conclusion by a valid inference. Since dogmatist epistemology, whether intellectualism or empiricism, cannot prove the existence of infallible intellectual intuition or sense experience, the truth of the conclusion would be improvable even under the assumption of an undisputable form of reasoning. Thus, the problem of infinite regress takes shape and creates the main challenge for justificationist theories of knowledge in solving the problem of objective knowledge they intend to solve.

Objective knowledge: dogmatic and sceptic epistemologies

It has been argued in Chapter 1 that dogmatic epistemology consists of intellectualism and empiricism. Viewed from the justified true belief perspective, intellectualist theorists, such as Descartes and Kant, claim the existence of principles in the intellect which do not require establishment by further proofs because they are self-evident or a priori true. Thus, intellectualists attempt to stop infinite regress of proofs at the point of self-evident intellectual intuition. However, since such intuition is not infallible, the intellectualist cannot address the question of how a claim of knowledge can be justified based on premises which are not self-evident, even if the truth of premises may be transmitted to conclusion by a valid inference.

The same argument can be made in regard to empiricist theories, like those of Bacon and Locke, who claim that there are infallible sense experiences that serve as undisputable premises for justifying the conclusion of a rational argument. While the intellectualist can apply deductive logic to justify a conclusion by infallible premises, the empiricist cannot use deductive logic for the same purpose. Hence, the empiricist employs inductive logic to justify a conclusion by a limited number of observations. Thus, the intellectualist suffers from the fact that intellectual intuitions cannot be self-evident, while the empiricist deals with the problem of induction, i.e. that even if all sense experiences were infallible, inductive inference could not logically transfer the truth of such premises to conclusion. In sum, these two dogmatist epistemologies suffer from the infinite regress of proofs. Notably, these epistemologies are called *dogmatic* because they must *stop* infinite regress at some point, whether by an *irrational* decision or by an authority.

However, justificationist epistemology is not limited to dogmatism; scepticism is another justificationist school of epistemology. As argued in Chapter 1, what the dogmatist and the sceptic share is the admission of the justified true belief account of knowledge. While the dogmatists champion objectivity of knowledge because of their claim that intellectual intuitions or sense experience perform as infallible premises of a rational argument in which the truth of the premises *necessitates* the truth of the conclusion, the sceptics argue that the conclusion of such an argument would not be a justified true belief since the premises cannot be justified by experience or argument as true, even if valid deductive logic is used.

In addition, the sceptic, such as Hume, reminds us that inductive reasoning cannot use such experiences for concluding a universal law, even if the epistemologist can assume that the sense experiences are undisputable. Hence, while the dogmatic school attempts to stop the infinite regress of the premises by claiming that there are unquestionable intuitions or experiences, the sceptic school tries to show that infinite regress is unstoppable because neither an infallible premise nor a valid inductive inference exists for transferring the truth of the premises to the conclusion when objective knowledge is defined as justified true belief. Hence, objective knowledge in this sense of the term is untenable.

70 Towards a non-justificationist epistemology

Justificationist epistemology suffers from infinite regress because neither the dogmatists nor the sceptics can offer a right answer to the question of whether or not objective knowledge is possible. In fact, it is the *justified true belief* account of knowledge that forces the dogmatist to assume that that there should be infallible premises for justification of a claim of knowledge as the conclusion of a rational argument and likewise forces the sceptic to argue that disputable premises cannot allow the conclusion of a rational argument to be justified as a true belief. In short, a solution to the crisis of justificationist epistemology is to be sought in the fundamental shift from *justification* to *criticism* in regard to the *concept* of objective knowledge *itself*.

Section II: objective knowledge as 'unfalsified conjecture'

As previously discussed, Popper discovered that the very practice of science challenges the justified true belief account of knowledge and made a plea for conjectural knowledge. He did not, however, offer a systematic answer to the question of what conjectural knowledge itself is. It can be argued that the notion of objective knowledge as 'unfalsified conjecture' is implicitly assumed in Popper's theory of science, but limited to the realm of scientific knowledge rather than to human knowledge as a whole. Hence, a general concept of knowledge in terms of 'unfalsified conjectures' covering science and metaphysics shapes neither Popper's nor subsequently Bartley's epistemology.

Karl Popper's reading of conjectural knowledge

As pointed out by Sceski (2007: 8), "Popper is the first to see things rightly. The goal is not to justify our theories as conclusively or even probably true; rather, the aim is to make 'fallible knowledge claims objective' as part of the quest for truth". Popper (1972) proposed the idea of 'conjectural knowledge' as a solution to the problem of induction, arguing that giving up the demand for justification of the logic of conjecture and refutation would change the inductive logic of science. While observational reports, no matter how many, are unable to justify a universal law of science as their conclusion, only one piece of falsifying evidence, such as 'snow is black', can refute the universal law of 'all snow is white'. Popper's theory of science thus rests on a conjectural conception of knowledge. Making a shift from justification to criticism, Popper introduces his method of scientific discovery as a process in which objective knowledge is created by proposing bold conjectures and subjecting them to severe empirical tests.

Hence, the concept of scientific knowledge as 'unfalsified conjecture' is an inseparable part of Popper's theory of knowledge. The idea of conjectural knowledge guides Popper's formulation of a solution to the problem of induction. Popper realizes that the Humean problem of induction arises from the justificationist account of knowledge and that the sceptic Hume understands that verifying observations, no matter how many, cannot justify a universal law of science. Popper (1962) proposes resolving the Humean problem of induction by applying the notion of conjectural knowledge because there is no need to justify a universal law that the logic of science assumes inductively.

It should be added here that Popper's theory of science puts forth a bold hypothesis among the premises of a deductive argument. If the conclusion of such an argument is refuted by even one observational report, then the logical form *of modus tollens* allows the scientist to retransmit the falsity of the conclusion to at least one of the premises which includes such a bold hypothesis. Therefore, if the empirical test does not refute the hypothesis proposed, then the result may be objective knowledge. This process of conjecture and refutation demonstrates Popper's theory of falsification, according to which a scientific theory must be open to empirical refutation and is to be subjected to logical criticism in terms of retransmission of the falsity from the conclusion to at least one of the premises. In brief, Popper's epistemology of science is 'critical' in the sense that it uses experience to criticize a scientific theory by means of *modus tollens* rather than by justifying it through experience.

However, in Popper's epistemology, the notion of conjectural knowledge finds its expression mainly in the realm of scientific knowledge due to its focus on the openness of the hypotheses to empirical refutation and the logical form applied to test such hypotheses in the form of *modus tollens*, which is applicable only in the realm of science. Hence, Popper's notion of conjectural knowledge becomes a solution to the problem of induction in the logic of science, but not a solution to the problem of objective knowledge in epistemology.

Like Popper, Bartley recognizes that the justified true belief account of knowledge does not serve his non-justificationist philosophy of criticism. While he agreeing with Popper's theory of science, Bartley detects an unfulfilled capacity within it that leads to a difference between Popper's position and his own in regard to the concept of knowledge as unfalsified conjecture. Bartley admits the conjectural logic of science, arguing that non-justificationist criticism is expandable to the realm of metaphorical theories in general and to the theory of rationality in particular. In one sense, Bartley aims to expand the notion of 'unfalsified conjecture' as the definition of objective knowledge from science to metaphysics, while not explicitly arguing for proposing it as an alternative for the justified true belief account of knowledge.

Similar to Popper, Bartley argues that non-empirical theories can be criticized for their problem-solving capacities and uses the notion of problem-solving ability to examine objectivity of pancritical rationalism as a theory of rational belief. While Bartley may be right in saying that pancritical rationalism has addressed the problem in question better than rival theories, pancritical rationalism does not tell us how a rational belief can be refuted logically like the refutation of a scientific theory by *modus tollens*.

72 Towards a non-justificationist epistemology

Objective knowledge: from justification to criticism

The notion of knowledge as justified true belief leads the dogmatist to argue that a claim of knowledge can be *justified* as true by its premises. It also enforces the sceptic's argument that the dogmatist's argument is untenable since the premises are disputable. Hence, the justificationist account of knowledge prevents both the dogmatist and the sceptic from solving the problem of objective knowledge.

Inspired by Bartley's (1964, 1984) notion of the separation between justification and criticism, I argue that the concept of objective knowledge requires this separation to rescue itself from the infinite regress of proofs. My central idea is as follows: *while a claim of knowledge cannot be justified by its premises, it can be falsified by its premises*. This idea aims to internalize the separation between justification and criticism in the concept of objective knowledge. Our claims of knowledge, whether metaphysical or empirical, could be objective; that is true, not because they are justifiable by premises through undisputable inferences, but because they are refutable by premises through valid, but conjectural forms of reasoning.

By this separation between justification and criticism in the very definition of objective knowledge, an alternative to the *justified true belief* account of knowledge is attained. In the following sections, I argue how this new concept of knowledge directs us to a non-justificationist epistemology extending beyond Popper's theory of science.

As argued in Chapter 1, the justified true belief account of knowledge consists of three conditions:

(1) A believes that *P*.
(2) *P* is *true*.
(3) A can *justify* his belief that *P is true*. (*Justified True Belief*)

If the idea of knowledge as justified true belief is substituted by the idea of 'unfalsified conjecture', what would the three conditions for objective knowledge be? I propose the following formulation:

(1) A believes that *P*.
(2) *P* is *not false*.
(3) A can *defend* his belief in that *P is not false*. (*Unfalsified Conjecture*)

In comparison with the justified true belief account of knowledge, the conjectural account implies that *P*, as a knowledge claim of A, need not be a *justified belief* in order to be a *true belief*. While A cannot justify his belief that *P* is true, he can *defend* his belief that *P* is not *false*. We now have a new concept of knowledge that takes into account the separation between justification and criticism and defines objective knowledge as 'unfalsified conjecture'.

On the basis of this new concept of knowledge, a claim of knowledge, whether empirical or metaphysical, could be an objective claim if and only if it has been held open to criticism and has not yet been refuted by argument or experience. The idea of knowledge as unfalsified conjecture calls for a new logic of knowledge. While the non-justificationist model of criticism, as proposed by Popper and Bartley, is applicable merely at the level of empirical theories by means of modus tollens retransmitting the falsity from conclusion to the premises, the new logic of knowledge is to be formulated on the basis of the idea that conclusion of a valid deductive argument can only be *falsified* by the premises rather than *justified* by them. In this way, the ground is prepared for a new theory of falsification for examining metaphysical theories, such as a philosophical theory of rationality, and we would subsequently be able to see how a theory of rational belief that is held open to criticism might be refuted logically.

Section III: deductive logic: a non-justificational theory

This section aims to employ the notion of 'unfalsified conjecture' for introducing a new deductive inference that is central to an alternative theory of knowledge for the epistemology of justified true belief and enables us to expand the separation between *justification* and *criticism* from the concept of objective knowledge to inference for transmitting the truth or falsity from the premises to the conclusion.

My main thesis for the separation between justification and criticism in regard to the deductive form of reasoning is that conclusion of a rational argument in a justificationist form of deduction, whether true or false, is *justifiable* by means of the truth or falsity of its constituent premises. In a non-justificationist form, however, the conclusion of a rational argument, whether true or false, is *refutable* by means of the falsity of its constituent premises. The main question of formal logic is: 'What is the logical relation between the premises and the conclusion?' This question is answered by a justificationist model of deduction saying that conclusion, whether true or false, can be justified by premises, whether true or false.

However, by integrating the separation between justification and criticism into the theory of deductive logic, the untenable demand of justifying the conclusion through the premises that involves infinite regress is substituted by the demand for criticizing the conclusion through the premises. I want to show that the demand for justification is not permitted in the form of inference if it is not allowed in the conception of knowledge. Hence, instead of defining the relation between the premises and the conclusion in a justificational way, we ought to formulate a new logic of deduction to define this relation in a non-justificational manner.

74 Towards a non-justificationist epistemology

In order to see what a non-justificational form of deduction might be like, we should first look at the classical version of a valid deductive argument. As observed by P.F. Strawson (2011: 2), classically,

> ... an argument is valid only if it would be inconsistent (or self-contradictory) to assert the premises while denying the conclusion; or, in other words, only if the truth of the premises is inconsistent with the falsity of the conclusion. A deductive argument is a sort of threat, which takes the form: if you accept these premises as true, then you must accept this conclusion as true as well, on pain of self-contradiction.

The term 'must' in this passage indicates that, in a valid deductive argument, the truth of the premises *necessitates* the truth of the conclusion because the conclusion has been *unquestionably justified* by the premises.

It is worthy of note that the two major forms of deduction in classical logic, *modus ponens* and *modus tollens*, suffer from the same justificationist problem. As argued by William H. Brenner (2009: 31), two particularly common inference patterns or forms of argument:

modus ponens

If the rod is copper, then it conducts electricity.
The rod is copper.
Therefore, it conducts electricity.

modus tollens

If the rod is copper, then it conducts electricity.
It does not conduct electricity.
Therefore, it is not copper.

Given these two common forms of deduction, we can recognize the reason why they are actually *justificationist forms of deduction*: in an argument form of modus ponens, such as the example above, the truth of the premises *necessitates* the truth of the conclusion. The same can be said in regard to the argument form of modus tollens: as shown in the example above, the truth of the first premise and the falsity of the second premise necessitate the falsity of the conclusion. Since both premises are not true, the conclusion cannot be true. Modus tollens is also interpreted in the following way: if the conclusion of a valid deduction is false, then at least one of premises must be false. Yet, the justificationist nature of modus tollens is the same: in this reading, the false conclusion *unquestionably* entails the falsity of at least one premise.

Popper used *modus tollens* to show that a non-justificationist critique of scientific hypothesis is possible through retransmission of the falsity from the conclusion to at least one of premises. If, however, the modus tollens suffers from justificationism in the sense argued above, how could it be the logic for non-justificationist criticism? It is true that this special form of deduction can retransmit the falsity of the conclusion to at least one of the premises, but it *does so* in a justificational manner. While Popper and Bartley claim that *modus tollens* offers the logic of science for a non-justificationist form of criticism, i.e. refutation of a scientific claim by retransmitting the falsity of its prediction to at least one of its premises, the preceding arguments imply that modus tollens also *justifies* refutation of a universal theory by empirical evidence. If the demand for justification is false, then modus tollens, like modus ponens, involves the infinite regress of proofs.

Popper (1992: 75), however, argues,

> Deductive logic is the theory of the validity of logical inferences . . . A necessary and crucial condition for the validity of a logical inference is the following: if the premises of a valid inference are *true* then the conclusion must also be *true* . . . . We can say: if all the premises are true and the inference is valid, then the conclusion *must* also be true; and if, consequently, the conclusion is false in a valid inference, then it is not possible for all the premises to be true. This trivial but decisively important result may also be expressed in the following manner: deductive logic is not only the theory of the *transmission of truth* from the premises to the conclusion, but it is also, at the same time, the theory of the *retransmission of falsity* from the conclusion to at least one of the premises.

The justificational nature of the deductive form of modus tollens enables us to realize that Popper's logic of science rests on a *justificationist* form of criticism.

Like Popper, Bartley (1984: 133) argues:

> The idea of *testing* and *revising* in the light of tests, or – more simply – the idea of critical argument, presupposes the notion of *deducibility*, i.e., the idea of the *retransmission of falsity* from conclusion to premises . . . That is, when the conclusion of a valid argument is discovered to be false, that falsity is retransmitted to the premises whence it must have come: at least one of these premises must be reevaluated.

Actually, Bartley faces a similar problem to Popper's. Bartley's idea of critical argument presupposes a justificationist notion of deducibility in the form of modus tollens because retransmission of falsity from the conclusion to at least one of the premises takes place infallibly. Under Bartley's terms, modus tollens may be called *a justificational form of criticism*.

In addition to the problem that *modus tollens* itself is unable to retransmit the falsity of the conclusion to one of the premises, the form of modus tollens is not suitable for refutation of a non-empirical theory simply because

76 Towards a non-justificationist epistemology

an observation is unable to falsify the conclusion of a metaphysical theory. In contrast, classical logic offers *modus ponens* for transmutation of the truth from the premises to the conclusion. Similar to modus tollens, modus ponens is a justificational inference that cannot be used as a logical rule for a non-justificational criticism.

The idea of unfalsified conjecture and the non-justificational model of deduction

The idea of knowledge as unfalsified conjecture confronts the logician with the following new problem. Classical logic focuses on the question of how deductive inference transmits the truth or falsity of the premises to the conclusion in order to show that it is justified true belief. However, if the idea of knowledge as justified true belief is to be given up in favour of an unfalsified-conjectural account of knowledge, there is no need to *justify* the conclusion of a rational argument as true or false by means of its logical relation to the premises because the concept of justified true belief is ruled out as a regulative idea for formulation of the *theory of deductive logic*.

If this argument is sound, then the idea of knowledge as unfalsified conjecture performs as a regulative idea for the theory of deduction in logic. If a valid form of deduction can transmit the truth of the premises to the conclusion, there is no longer a need for defining the aim of such transmission justification of the conclusion by its constituent premises simply because justification involves infinite regress and is thus untenable. Instead, the idea of knowledge as unfalsified conjectures implies that deductive logic should not define the goal of justified true belief as its regulative idea of logical theory. Knowledge as unfalsified conjecture calls for a non-justificational relation between the premises of a rational argument and its conclusion. As noted earlier, my main idea for reinvention of classical logic, in particular for deductive inference, is that, instead of defining the logical relation between the premises and the conclusion as conclusion being able to be *justified* by the premises, we have to define the relation as conclusion being able to be *falsified* by at least one of the premises.

This may reflect a Copernican Revolution in logical theory because it changes the aim of deductive logic, a change from justificationist deduction, which intends to *justify* the conclusion, whether true or false, by its constituent premises, whether true or false, to a non-justificationist deduction, which intends to *falsify* the conclusion by at least one of its constituent premises. In sum, the idea of knowledge as unfalsified conjecture plays a regulative role for the very logic of knowledge, whether metaphysical or empirical, by calling for non-justificational rules of inference to define *a falsifying role* for the premises of a rational argument rather than a *justifying role* for the premises in examination of the truth or falsity of the conclusion of such a rational argument.

Deduction inference: justificational versus non-justificational

Now the ground is prepared for presenting an outline of the non-justificationist deduction at the core of the logical theory by showing its differences from justificationist deduction that shapes the mainstream reading of deductive inference in classical or even modern logic.[1] This comparison is insightful, in particular for showing how Popper's philosophy of critical rationalism originates in a theory of science that ignores the *justificationist nature* of the modus tollens form of inference used to transfer the falsity of the conclusion to the premises.

In a justificational form of deduction like classical logic, the *content* of the premises is not a *matter of concern* because the aim of the logical theory is to address the question of transmission of truth from the premises to the conclusion. Classical logic implies that, given the premises as *true*, a valid form of deduction can transmit the truth of such premises to the conclusion. Hence, classical logic argues that, given that the premises of a valid deductive argument are proved to be true somewhere, then logic guarantees that the truth (or falsity) of premises *necessitates* the truth (or falsity) of the conclusion. We should remind ourselves here that the notion of justified true belief force not only classical logic to assume that *there should be true premises* upon which a true conclusion is inferred by rational argument, but also forces *the logical form* to claim that the truth (or falsity) of justified true premises is indisputably transmitted to the conclusion in order to *necessitate* the conclusion to be justified beliefs. In this sense, we can also see that the two premises of a justificationist theory of knowledge consist of the following: (a) the premises are given as infallible, (b) the form of inference (modus ponens) can *justify* the truth of the conclusion due to the truth of its constituent premises or, to the contrary, the form of inference (modus tollens) can *justify* the falsity of one of the premises due to the falsity of the conclusion. Inspired by the idea of knowledge as unfalsified conjecture, a non-justificationist theory of knowledge revises these two premises.

Returning to the issue of justificationist deduction, classical logic implies that an invalid inference, such as an inductive one, does not create such a necessary relation between true premises and true conclusion because, even if all the premises are given as true, the conclusion might still be false. In fact, it is the nature of inductive inference that it does not enable logic to provide the necessary relation between premises and conclusions. This is the reason why Popper argues that deductive logic can serve the logic of science, but inductive logic cannot. It is worthy of note, however, that neither deductive nor inductive logic can *justify* conclusion of a rational argument by its premises.

The problem with classical logic directing us to discover the *justificational nature* of deductive inference is that the theory of deduction assumes that the truth or falsity of the premises can *infallibly* be transmitted to the conclusion by making the necessary relation between true premises and true conclusion. However,

78 Towards a non-justificationist epistemology

from a non-justificationist perspective, any logical theory such as the theory of deduction is a postulated *conjecture* that can be true or false; hence, why should the theory be immune to error and provide unquestionable rules of inference for transmitting truth from the premises to the conclusion through modus ponens and retransmission of falsity from the conclusion to the premises through modus tollens?

If all postulated theories as knowledge claims are to be held open to criticism in order to explore whether they are false or true, why should our logical theories not also be treated in the same way and regarded as fallible theories? This argument has led me to discover that, unlike classical or modern logic claims for which deduction guarantees the truth of conclusion due to the truth of the premises, justificationism involves the conception of a necessary relation between the premises and the conclusion in deductive inference, which makes both *modus ponens* and *modus tollens* deeply vulnerable to the problem of infinite regress.

In *Logical Pluralism*, Jeffrey C. Beall and Greg Restall (2006: 14) point out,

> One of the oldest features determining properly *logical* consequence is its *necessity*. The truth of the premises of a valid argument *necessitates* the truth of the conclusion of that argument. . . . If you have an argument in which it could be that the premises were true and the conclusion false, then the argument is not deductively valid. This distinguishes the deductive from the *inductive*.

Then the authors identify the *claim* of a necessary relation between the premises and the conclusion in a valid form of deduction as an *epistemological* claim rather than an unquestionable fact:

> We speak crudely when we talk of the conclusion being necessary on the basis of the premises – such talk is too easily taken the wrong way. The conclusion of a valid argument might, of course, be contingent, and it might even be *false*, if the premises of that argument are not all true. The necessity in a valid argument does not attach to the conclusion. *Necessity is borne by transition from the premises to the conclusion.* What is necessary, in an argument from A to B, is not the conclusion B but the connection between A and B. The *conditional if* A *then* B is true of necessity.
>
> (2006: 15, emphasis added)

In fact, Beall and Restall argue that, talking of the necessary relation between the premises and the conclusion entails offering a logical theory that wrongly assumes such a relation as *infallible*. It is the realization that the logical form of relation between A and B cannot be infallible that leads us to discover the *justificational nature* of classical logic.

Beall and Restall (2006: 16) continue,

> None of our commitment to the universal applicability of logical consequence thereby commits us to any special epistemic status for logical consequence. It is another thing entirely to say that the premises of a valid argument must make the conclusion *epistemically certain*, or that the connection between premises and conclusions must be certain. Those are matters for epistemology, and are not merely the concerns of conditionality, possibility and necessity. Taking logical consequences to be necessary does not entail that we ought to take our access to it to be certain. *Necessity need not entail infallibility in logic*, any more than it need do so in mathematics. *We can make mistakes in our judgments of what follows from what"* (emphasis added)[2].

If a theory of logic, just like any other theory, is only a *conjecture* about the relation between premises and conclusion and if the deduction theory, whether in the form of modus ponens or in the form of modus tollens, claims that the truth of the premises *justifies* the truth of the conclusion or claims that the falsity of the conclusion *justifies* refutation of the premises, then it would be wise to conclude that deductive inferences are justificationist and vulnerable to the infinite regress of proofs. Hence, not only are deductive inferences untrustworthy in their claim of justifying a conclusion by its premises, but they also fail to demonstrate how the premises of a valid argument lead to the conclusion.

W.V. Quine recognizes that the logic itself ought to be held open to criticism. As Bartley (1980: 68) points out,

> According to Quine, when a body of beliefs is brought to the test of criticism, any part of it may be revised and rejected in the light of unfavourable criticism. No segment of it, such as the set of analytically true statements, including logic, is so insulated from such continuous revision that we could say in advance that "the mistake could not be here".

However, Bartley (1980: 68) believes that deducibility itself cannot be subjected to criticism if it appears to presuppose minimal logic.

With this clarification in place, we require a non-justificationist theory of deduction to show how the connection between the premises and the conclusion may be defined as fallible conjecture to prevent the theory of logic from involving infinite regress, For the introduction of a non-justificationist model of deductive inference, I suggest that the same separation between justification and criticism as proposed above in relation to the concept of objective knowledge itself is now to be integrated into the theory of deduction. The deductive form of inference is a justificational form of inference because its goal is to *justify* the conclusion of a

80 Towards a non-justificationist epistemology

rational argument by the premises. In other words, it aims to *guarantee* that if all the premises of a valid deduction are true, then the conclusion must also be true (*modus ponens*) and that if the conclusion of a valid deduction cannot be true, then at least one of the premises must be false (*modus tollens*). In both cases, deductive logic aims to justify the necessity for either a true conclusion by the truth of the premises or of at least one premise being false due to an unacceptable conclusion. From this justificationist perspective, there is no qualitative difference between modus ponens and modus tollens on the basis of which Popper establishes his theory of science[3] and Bartley expands that theory to his philosophy of pancritical rationalism.

With such a separation between justification and criticism, the central function of deductive logic changes profoundly: if the final output of a deductive argument is not a justified true belief in terms of its conclusion, why should formal logic be seen in terms of justifying the truth of a knowledge claim due to the trueness of its premises? Quite to the contrary, the main function of formal logic, in particular of the theory of deduction, is to be understood as showing how an unfalsified conjecture can be inferred as the conclusion of a deductive argument through the truth or falsity of its constituent premises. This fundamental reorientation in the function of deduction from *justification of the conclusion by the premises to refutation of the conclusion by the premises* enables the logical theory to avoid infinite regress and to internalize the separation between justification and criticism in deductive reasoning.

A non-justificationist model of deduction allocates a falsifying role to the premises in their logical relation with the conclusion. Even if justification of the conclusion by the premises is impossible, falsification of a conclusion by the premises is still possible because the only one falsifying premise is enough for refuting a conclusion. While justificationist logic gives the premises the role of *justifying* the conclusion, non-justificationist logic gives the premises the role of falsifying the conclusion.

Hence, it can be concluded that, although justificationist logic cannot fulfil its task because, due to the infinite regress involved in justification, deductive inference cannot *guarantee* the conclusion to be true even if all the premises are true, non-justificationist logic can realize this task because only one falsifying proof, whether logical or experimental, is enough for enabling us to deduce refutation of a universal claim as the conclusion without facing infinite regress. Unlike the justified true belief account of knowledge enforcing classical logic regarding premises and form of inference infallible, the unfalsified-conjectural account of knowledge forces the logical theory to take into account not only that the premises of a deductive argument are fallible and open to criticism, but also that the forms of inference are infallible and open to revision. Hence, instead of claiming that the premises *justify* the conclusion, it is to be admitted that the conclusion of a deductive argument can be falsified when even only one of premises is shown to be false.

The theory of falsification: a non-justificational approach

As argued in Chapters 2 and 3, a major problem with the epistemology of critical rationalism is that the criterion for falsifiability fails to show how a non-empirical theory may be refuted logically. Hence, the main logical gap in such an epistemology is that the theories of 'critical' and 'pancritical' rationalism themselves cannot be identified as 'true' or 'false'. However, with the proposed theory of non-justificational deduction, we are now in a position to introduce a *new criterion for falsifiability* that can be applied to examine the falsity or truth of a claim of knowledge, whether metaphysical or scientific.

According to a non-justificational theory of falsification, a claim of knowledge is falsifiable *if and only if all of its premises are held open to criticism* and *non-justificational form of deduction* is used to transmit the falsity or truth of the premises to conclusion. Hence, the criterion for falsifiability is to be redefined so that a conjecture, whether empirical like a scientific theory or metaphysical like a theory of rationality, is seen as refuted if only one of its premises is shown to be rejected by argument or experience. However, if our investigation shows that none of premises are seen to be false, then our non-justificationist deduction can transfer the truth of the premises to the conclusion as objective knowledge. To sum it up, the conclusion of a rational argument can be refuted if even only one of the premises is refuted by experience or argument.

Contrary to Popper's theory of falsification, the non-justificationist theory would be applicable not only for science, but also for metaphysics because, with the discovery of the non-justificational form of deduction, the transmission of falsity from the premises to the conclusion becomes a possibility and serves the logic of science as well as the logic of metaphysics. We no longer require retransmission of the falsity from the conclusion to the premises, as proposed by Popper, and a scientific theory can be examined due to the truth or falsity of its premises. If only one of the premises of a scientific theory is shown to be false by experience, then logic allows us to refute such a hypothesis in terms of the conclusion of a rational argument.[4] It is not unfair to conclude that the non-justificational theory of falsification deeply changes our understanding of 'critical' argument and the very meaning of *critical thinking* because it shows that an argument is indefensible if only one premise of such an argument is shown to be false by experience or reason.

The non-justificationist theory of falsification leads us to a new solution for the problem of demarcation. Bartley (1993) observes that the question of empirical falsifiability should not be situated at the core of the theory of knowledge, as claimed by Popper. Bartley's own proposal is the identification of a demarcation between 'critical' and 'uncritical' theories without, however, introducing a logical form of criticism necessary for examining non-empirical theories, i.e. addressing the question of how to demarcate a 'critical' theory from an 'uncritical' one logically. The non-justificationist criterion for falsifiability, however, allows us to use

82   Towards a non-justificationist epistemology

logic for refuting a claim of knowledge, whether empirical or metaphysical, if one of its constituent premises is shown to be false. It should be added that the question in non-justificationist falsification is not whether *all* the premises are true, but whether *one* of premises is false. The question in the case of empirical hypotheses becomes whether *experience* rejects one of the premises and, in the case of metaphysical theories, whether *logical argument* rejects one of the premises.

Section IV: towards a non-justificational theory of knowledge

The preceding arguments will now be applied in order to formulate a new theory of knowledge. Three major elements are taken into account in the presentation of this theory:

a) The non-justificational concept of objective knowledge is seen as 'unfalsified conjecture'.
b) Non-justificationist deductive inference: The conclusion of a rational argument can be falsified by its constituent premises.
c) The non-justificational criterion for falsifiability: Only one false premise can refute a universal theory as the conclusion of a rational argument.

The concept of objective knowledge and non-justificationist theory of knowledge

The conjectural conception of knowledge plays a leading role in the formulation of a non-justificationist epistemology. The justified true belief account of knowledge leads to three assumptions: (i) the premises of a rational argument are to be infallible in order for the conclusion of such an argument to be justified as true belief. It is noteworthy that a major source of infinite regress in justificationist theories of knowledge is the assumption that the premises of a rational argument must be infallible in order to provide the basis on which justified true belief can be produced.

The second major assumption is that: (ii) the form of inference in a rational argument, whether deductive or inductive, that transmits the truth or falsity of the premises to the conclusion should be accounted as infallible to *necessitate* the truth or falsity of the conclusion. In the case of the sceptic's induction problem, this means that inductive inference cannot *necessitate* the conclusion of a rational argument on the basis of its premises. In short, not only should the premises be undisputable in order to create justified true belief, but also the form of inference must be infallible in order to transmit the truth or falsity of the premises to the conclusion. It can be said the second major source of infinite regress in justificationist theories of knowledge, which prevents them from solving the problem of objective knowledge, is the assumption that logic shows us how to *justify* conclusions *indisputably* by the premises.

Towards a non-justificationist epistemology 83

The justified true belief account of knowledge leads justificationist epistemology to a third major assumption: (iii) the objectivity of a knowledge claim as the conclusion of a rational argument depends on the trueness of all its constituent premises and deductive inference. Hence, a universal claim is a justified true belief (objective knowledge) if and only if the premises and the rules of inference are shown to be true. This third assumption also contributes to infinite regress in justificationist epistemology.

The idea of knowledge as unfalsified conjecture, however, leads a non-justificationist theory of knowledge to three entirely different assumptions. I argue that the following three assumptions internalize the separation between justification and criticism in non-justificationist epistemology: (i) the premises of a rational argument aimed at concluding with a universal theory are to be assumed as *fallible*, and, contrary to justification, this openness to criticism allows the non-justificationist theory of knowledge to avoid the infinite regress of proofs. A premise held open to criticism can be used as a valid premise as long as it is not refuted by experience or argument; nevertheless, it might be criticized by experience and argument in the future. In this manner, the separation between justification and criticism is integrated into our understanding of *the premises* of a rational argument.

The notion of knowledge as unfalsified conjecture directs non-justificationist epistemology to a second major assumption: (ii) if the final product of the knowing process is unfalsified conjecture reflecting the conclusion of a rational argument and if the premises are fallible, then there is no need to assume that the form of inference is to be infallible in order to be able to transmit the truth or falsity of the premises to the conclusion. The logical theory in general and the theory of deduction in particular are to be regarded as valid, but open to criticism regarding the transmission of the truth or falsity of the premises to the conclusion, but do not *necessitate justification* of the conclusion by the premises. However, valid deduction allows the conclusion of a valid deduction to be refuted by at least one of its premises. The assumption that inference as a fallible form of reasoning enables non-justificationist epistemology to avoid infinite regress in terms of the transmission of the truth or falsity of the premises to the conclusion. Thus, the separation between justification and criticism is internalized in the *form of transmission* of the truth or falsity of the premises to the conclusion.

Finally, the notion of knowledge as unfalsified conjecture leads to a third assumption: (iii) the criterion for the objectivity of a universal theory is a non-justificational model of falsification. If the premises and the form of inference are to be accounted as fallible and have not yet been rejected, then there is no reason for defining justification of the conclusion by the premises as the criterion for objectivity, but we can introduce falsification of the conclusion by at least one of premises as our standard for objectivity. This new criterion for objective knowledge empowers non-justificationist epistemology to prevent infinite regress in terms of the objectivity criterion internalizing the separation between justification and criticism in our theory of falsification.

84 Towards a non-justificationist epistemology

A general formula for non-justificationist epistemology

According to the separation between justification and criticism at the aforementioned three levels, we can now formulate the following non-justificationist theory of knowledge:

> **Premise (i)**: Objective knowledge is unfalsified conjecture
> **Premise (ii)**: Premises of a universal claim of knowledge are fallible
> **Premise (iii)**: Deductive inference is used to refute a universal claim of knowledge as its conclusion if at least one of the premises is shown to be false by argument or experience.
>
> ---
>
> **Conclusion**: A universal claim of knowledge is unfalsified conjecture (objective knowledge) if and only if none of its premises are shown to be false by experience or argument.

As observed earlier, a central epistemological question is how a claim of knowledge, whether scientific or metaphysical, can be evaluated to be true or false. I have argued that the *lack of a logical form for critical evaluation of a non-empirical theory* prevented Popper and Bartley from telling us how a theory of rationality such as critical rationalism is to be judged true or false. Henceforward, my non-justificationist theory of knowledge provides us with a criterion for such judgment. A claim of knowledge is to be accounted as true if and only if none of its premises are shown to be false by experience or argument and it is to be identified as false if and only if one of its premises is shown to be untrue by experience or argument.

It is worthy of note that a critical rationalist is not a dogmatist for assuming that none of premises or inference forms of his argument are justifiable and should not be revised, and he is also not a sceptic for not using the fallibility of the premises or inference forms in his argument to mean their falseness and uselessness for deducing objective knowledge. The critical rationalist regards the premises or forms of inference merely as refutable and revisable, but, as long as they are not shown to be false by argument or experience, they are usable as valid premises or inferences for deducing a rational belief.

In *Objective Knowledge*, Popper (1972) argues that a central issue in epistemology is the growth of knowledge. The non-justificationist theory of knowledge enables exploration of the mechanism of knowledge growth: through discovering mistaken premises, forms of inference or the criterion for objectivity itself, we can learn and profit from our errors in order to advance our objective knowledge. Insofar as the premises and forms of our reasoning in regard to our beliefs are open to criticism, we discover potential errors in our scientific or metaphysical beliefs. It is through learning from such *openness to criticism* that our objective knowledge grows.

Towards a non-justificationist epistemology   85

In conclusion, non-justificationist epistemology overcomes the problem of objective knowledge, firstly, by resting on the concept of knowledge as unfalsified conjecture, secondly, by regarding premises fallible and thus avoiding infinite regress and, thirdly, by arguing that the conclusion can be falsified by even one false premise, whether logical or empirical. In Chapter 5, I apply my non-justificationist epistemology in order to introduce a new theory of rationality called a general theory of critical rationalism, is used in the second part of this book to integrate the philosophy of critical rationalism into a sociological theory of society.

Notes

1 The justificational function of the premises of a rational argument in relation to conclusion has rarely been recognised in the logical theory because the influence of the justified true belief account of knowledge in the theory of deductive logic has not yet been appreciated. It seems that modern logic is similar to classical logic in that premises *justify*, rather than falsify conclusion. See Robert J. Ackermann's (1970) *Modern Deductive Logic*.
2 In "On the Criticisability of Logic", Bartley (1984: 247–248) recognises the question of whether and to what extent logic itself is open to criticism. However, he does not detect the justificational relation between premises and conclusion when he writes: "The question arises whether logic can be revised in the sense of denying that true premises always must lead, in any valid inference, to true conclusions". He does not consider the justificationist relation between premises and conclusion to be problematic.
3 Popper himself worked on the theory of deduction; however, he did not recognize that deductive logic defines the relation between premises and conclusion in a justificationist manner. See: Popper (1947) *New Foundations for Logic* and Popper (1948a, 1948b) "*On the Theory of Deduction, Part I and Part II*".
4 My non-justificational criterion for falsifiability contrasts with Popper's, which may lead to a fundamental result for the philosophy of science. In the case of Popper's logic of science, a falsified prediction is retransmitted from conclusion to at least one of the premises. However, according to my criterion, just one falsifying premise, whether empirical or metaphysical, can refute a universal law of science.

Bibliography

Ackermann, R.J. (1970) *Modern Deductive Logic: An Introduction to its Techniques and to its Significance*. London, Palgrave Macmillan.

Bartley, III, W.W. (1993) "Theories of Demarcation between Science and Metaphysics". In: Lakatos, I. & Musgrave, A. (eds.) *Problems in the Philosophy of Science*. Amsterdam, North-Holland, pp. 40–64.

Bartley, III, W.W. (1984) *The Retreat to Commitment*, 2nd ed. Chicago, Open Court.

Bartley, III, W.W. (1980) "On the Criticisability of Logic – A Reply to A. A. Derksen". In: *Philosophy of the Social Sciences*, 10, pp. 67–77.

Bartley, III, W.W. (1964) "Rationality versus the Theory of Rationality". In: Bunge, M. (ed.) *Critical Approaches to Science and Philosophy*. London, Taylor & Francis, pp. 3–31.

Beall, J.C. & Restall, G. (2006) *Logical Pluralism*. Oxford, Clarendon.

Brenner, W.H. (2009) *Philosophy and Logic: An Integrated Introduction*. Notre Dame, University of Notre Dame Press.

Musgrave, A.E. (1974) "The Objectivism of Popper's Epistemology". In: Schilpp, P.A. (ed.) *The Philosophy of Karl Popper*, Book II. La Salle, Open Court, pp. 560–596.

Popper, K.R. (1992) "The Logic of the Social Sciences". In: Bennett, L.J. (trans.) *In Search of a Better World: Lectures and Essays from Thirty Years*. London, Routledge, pp. 64–81.

Popper, K.R. (1972) *Objective Knowledge: An Evolutionary Approach*. Oxford, Oxford University Press.

Popper, K.R. (1962) *Conjectures and Refutations: The Growth of Scientific Knowledge*. New York, Basic Books.

Popper, K.R. (1948a) "On the Theory of Deduction, Part I. Derivation and its Generalizations". In: *Proceedings of the Section of Sciences*, 51, pp. 173–183.

Popper, K.R. (1948b) "On the Theory of Deduction, Part II. The Definitions of Classical and Intuitionist Negation". In: *Proceedings of the Section of Sciences*, 51, pp. 322–331.

Popper, K.R. (1947) "New Foundations for Logic". In: *Mind*, 56, pp. 193–235.

Sceski, J.H. (2007) *Popper, Objectivity and the Growth of Knowledge*. London, Continuum International.

Strawson, P.F. (2011) *Introduction to Logical Theory*. London, Routledge.

Chapter 5

Unfalsified conjecture and critical rationality

Towards a new theory of rationality

Masoud Mohammadi Alamuti

Introduction

My critiques of Popper's *critical* and Bartley's *pancritical* rationalism in Chapters 2 and 3 imply that the philosophy of critical rationalism faces a fundamental problem that originates in justificationist epistemology. The lack of a non-justificationist epistemology prevents Popper from arguing that there is no need to justify a claim of rationality by argument or experience. Hence, Popper claims that if all beliefs are to be justified in order to be true and that if such justification is untenable, then the following two options remain: either to choose irrationalism due to the impossibility of comprehensive rationalism or to opt for an irrational faith in reason, which Popper calls critical rationalism. I argue that this reading of critical rationalism cannot explain why we should hold all beliefs, including the belief in critical rationalism, open to criticism and that, even if it could explain this, it does not inform us how to evaluate such open beliefs logically as true. Hence, Popper's critical rationalism is unable to show how critical reason performs and drives human action.

In the case of Bartley, the lack of a non-justificationist epistemology does not allow him to explore how to assess a claim of rationality that is open to criticism and must survive severe test for being true as an unfalsified (rational) belief. Therefore, despite Bartley's important contribution of defining pancritical rationalism as a theory of rationality rather than a moral attitude of openness to criticism, he fails to address the main question regarding the philosophy of critical rationalism: the failure to account for how critical reason performs in logically judging a claim of rationality to be true in his theory of rationality. Thus, pancritical rationalism, like Popper's critical rationalism, is unable to provide us with a theory of rationality to address the driving role of reason in the formation of human action.

Since neither Popper's critical nor Bartley's pancritical rationalism can prepare a theory of rationality to explain the role of reason in human action, a reinvention of the philosophy of critical rationalism is necessary for application in the ideal types of rational action as the micro-foundations of the macro-theory of society. In this chapter, I suggest that the non-justificational theory of knowledge introduced in the previous chapter can offer a new epistemological basis in terms of the idea

88 Unfalsified conjecture and critical rationality

of objective knowledge as unfalsified conjecture that paves the way for explaining how a claim of rationality that is held open to criticism can logically be judged as a true claim. To this end, I apply the separation between justification and criticism to formulate a general theory of critical rationalism intended to address the question of how critical reason functions.

Section I: from justification to criticism: the unfinished project of critical rationalism

As argued earlier, the general separation between justification and criticism has played a significant role in various stages during the development of the idea of critical rationalism. Recognizing that the justified true belief account of knowledge is not consistent with the practice of science, Popper applied the notion of 'conjectural knowledge' to present a non-justificationist theory of science. The general separation between justification and criticism thus found its first expression in what Bartley (1964) called Popper's non-justificational philosophy of criticism.

Popper's critical rationalism and the separation between justification and criticism

Realizing that justification is superfluous for the existence of scientific knowledge, Popper (1992a [1959]) argues that the Humean problem of induction means that empirical evidence cannot justify the truth of a universal law. By separating justification and criticism, Popper was able to argue that consideration of objective knowledge merely as unfalsified conjecture and not as justified true belief solves the problem of induction because the logic of science shows how to use experience to refute a deductively formulated scientific claim, not how to justify the conclusion of a scientific deduction by its premises.

Popper (1962) discovered that the reinvention of the logic of science is taken place by replacing the inductive method with the method of *conjecture and refutation* using the modus tollens form of inference. Popper (1992b) claims that modus tollens refers to a non-justificationist form of criticism according to which *the rule of retransmission of falsity from the conclusion to the premises* facilitates refutation of a scientific theory by means of the possibility of a false prediction. Ignoring the fact that modus tollens *justifies* the falsity of one premise for refutation of the prediction, Popper supposes that modus tollens provides the logic of science with a non-justificationist form of criticism whose purpose is not to *justify* a universal conclusion by limited sense experiences. However, Popper is wrong to say that modus tollens falsifies a universal law by even only one piece of counter-evidence because of the justifying role that even this one piece of evidence plays in such refutation.

Nevertheless, Popper's usage of the separation between justification and criticism led to the more convincing deductive theory of empirical science as a replacement for the inductive theory of science. Popper realizes that the logical form of modus tollens is not applicable for a non-justificationist examination of metaphysical theories simply because there is no empirical evidence to refute the conclusion of a metaphysical theory. The form of modus ponens, on the other hand, is useless for metaphysics due the undisputable premises in its justification of the truth of the conclusion. Hence, Popper (1963) offers the notion of the problem-solving ability of a metaphysical theory to show that a non-empirical theory can also be criticized despite that the standard of problem-solving does not offer a 'logical form of criticism' for relating the truth or falsity of the conclusion to the truth or falsity of the premises.

Instead of applying his idea of the problem-solving ability of a philosophical theory to see how a claim of rationality might be true, Popper offers a justificational concept of critical rationalism in terms of irrational faith in reason. Instead of pursuing the separation between justification and criticism to demarcate 'rational' from 'irrational' belief, Popper takes a justificationist turn, arguing that the inability of the rationalist to *justify* all of his positions by argument or experience also leads to his inability to *justify* his own belief in critical rationalism. Hence, a critical rationalist should confess a minimum level of irrationalism.

Bartley's pancritical rationalism and the separation between justification and criticism

Upon discovering that Popper did not identify the separation between justification and criticism in his philosophy of critical rationalism when surmising that his logic of science could offer philosophy a non-justificational form of criticism, Bartley (1964, 1984) attempts to expand non-justificationism from the theory of science to the theory of rationality.

Bartley argues that Popper's innovation of the logic of science has an unfulfilled capacity for the philosophy of critical rationalism. Like Popper, he knows that the form of modus tollens is not applicable for refuting a theory of rationality; however, unlike Popper, Bartley does not discount the usefulness of the problem-solving capacity of such a theory of rationality as a standard for considering critical rationalism as a solution to the problem of the rationalist's identity.

Bartley argues that there is no reason for justification of critical rationalism as a theory of rationality if justification of a scientific theory is untenable, reasoning that, just as the scientist cannot *justify* a universal law of science by inductive observations, nor can the rationalist *justify* a universal theory of rationality by deductive argument. Hence, if justification involves *infinite regress* in science, it also faces infinite regress in metaphysics. Bartley (1984) rejected irrational faith in reason as a philosophy for critical rationalism, arguing that the rationalist does not need to admit even a minimum of irrationalism because his claims of rationality need no justification for being true. Instead, Bartley proposes a *rational* faith in critical reason.

90   Unfalsified conjecture and critical rationality

Using an epistemological study of Popper's critical rationalism, Bartley goes on to apply the idea of the separation between justification and criticism for his presentation of a 'theory' of critical rationalism, i.e. pancritical rationalism. According to Bartley (1964), a philosophical 'theory' is formulated on a set of premises and subjected to rational examination to see whether it meets its own standard. Bartley argues in favour of a new epistemological foundation for the idea of critical rationalism since *no position can be justified, while all positions may be criticized*. Bartley reasons that metaphysical theories are criticizable for their inability to solve the problem they claim to solve, so a theory of critical rationalism can also be assessed critically according to its capacity for solving the problem of the rationalist's identity.

Using separation between justification and criticism, Bartley's pancritical rationalist is a person who holds all of his positions open to criticism and admits only the positions surviving a severe test. Bartley (1984) argues that this theory of pancritical rationalism solves the problem of the rationalist's identity better than other theories, meaning panrationalism and critical rationalism. According to Bartley, panrationalism claims that the rationalist can prove all positions by argument, but the 'panrationalist' faces an identity problem due to his inability to prove that the existence of self-evident intellectual intuitions or sense experiences to justify his rational identity. Hence, Bartley's critique of panrationalism is ultimately a critique of the justified true belief account of knowledge. As per Bartley, the theory of panrationalism does not solve the problem of rationalist's identity, nor does Popper's critical rationalism. If justification is the wrong demand, the rationalist is unable to defend his rationalist's identity by an irrational faith in reason.

Bartley claims that pancritical rationalism solves the problem of identity without a self-contradiction: the rationalist holds all his positions open to criticism, accepting only the positions that withstand stringent screening. Thus, the rationalist remains a rationalist because he respects a position, even his own rational faith in reason, as long as it has not been refuted by argument or experience, on the one hand, and does not need to justify his rationalist identity by an irrational faith, on the other. Bartley concludes that pancritical rationalism realizes the ideal of separation between justification and criticism.

Nevertheless, the theory of pancritical rationalism does not *actually* solve the problem of rationalist identity. Even the rationalist who holds all his beliefs open to criticism and accepts only a position that withstands rigorous examination as a rational position cannot claim that merely holding all his positions open to criticism secures his rationalist identity, for the rationalist does not know how to evaluate his claim of rationality as true logically. The standard of the problem-solving ability of a theory does not provide the rationalist with a logical criterion for examining his belief as true or false. Hence, rationalist identity remains unclear because there is no way to identity whether his claims are true.

One important observation regarding the philosophy of critical rationalism relates to the outcome of this philosophy of openness to criticism for the very meaning of *critical thinking*. The moral attitude of listening to criticism emphasized by Popper and Bartley's theory of openness of fundamental beliefs to self-criticism expresses significant progress from dogmatism towards critical thinking, on the one hand, while rejecting irrationalism, on the other. However, we require reinvention of this open philosophy by introducing logical forms through which we can profit from our errors. As I suggest in this chapter, the rise of Popper and Bartley's theories of critical rationalism are important steps towards a better understanding of critical thinking and demands calls for new advances. The unfinished project of critical rationalism requires *rethinking* the meaning of critical thinking through exploration of how non-justificationist epistemology may deeply change our previous concepts of critical thinking.

Section II: unfalsified conjecture and the unfinished project of critical rationalism

The term 'epistemology' of critical rationalism is to be read in the sense that our claims of rationality are themselves epistemic. Hence, a theory of rationality aiming to address the question of the essence of 'rational' belief is reducible to a theory of knowledge. My intention to overcome the justificational origin of Popper's critical rationalism has directed me to rethink the theory of knowledge itself, resulting in the epistemological investigation in Chapter 4. With the non-justificational epistemology in hand, we are in a good position to investigate the question of how the idea of objective knowledge as unfalsified conjecture contributes to solving the problem of rationalist belief. The notion of knowledge as unfalsified conjecture leads us to defining the 'problem' for which a general theory of critical rationalism presents as a solution.

The problem of 'rational belief': an epistemological reading

From an epistemological perspective, the problem of rationality deals with the definition of rationalist identity. Bartley argues that the theory of rationality intends to solve this problem by supporting his claim of a rational-being as the rationalist dealing with the *epistemological question* of whether he can *defend* his belief in 'rationalism' by argument or experience.

Upon closer inspection, one realizes that the debate between *uncritical* and *critical* rationalism implies that the question of rational belief has an epistemological nature questioning *whether all claims of rationality can be subjected to discussion in order to explore their trueness*. This solution reduces the term 'rational' to 'true' and defines 'irrational' as 'false'. By claiming that 'rational' beliefs are ones 'justifiable' by argument or experience, the panrationalist defines the problem of rationality in the context of justificational epistemology, i.e. the conclusion of a rational argument through the premises, is possible, then the belief in panrationalism is tenable. Hence, the panrationalist recognizes the reduction of the problem

92 Unfalsified conjecture and critical rationality

of rational belief to the justifiability of rational beliefs and provides an epistemological solution: an *epistemology of justified true belief*.

In contrast to uncritical rationalism, Popper applies an epistemological argument when introducing critical rationalism as an irrational faith in reason. Within the context of justificationist epistemology, Popper views the problem of the 'rationality theory' as follows: while the 'panrationalist' (uncritical rationalist) claims that all positions are justifiable by argument or experience, panrationalism itself cannot be *justified* by argument or experience because of infinite regress, rendering the problem of rational belief in reason insoluble, as claimed by uncritical rationalism. In other words, Popper considers the problem of rationality as an epistemological one of whether panrationalism is a 'true' position and then rejects the solution the panrationalist offers for the problem in question. We know, however, that Popper's critique of panrationalism involves an epistemological mistake: by admitting the demand for justification as a *legitimate* demand, Popper offers another justificationist solution for the problem of rationality theory: an *irrational* faith in reason. In short, since we cannot *justify* our faith in reason by argument or experience, we ought to *justify* it with a moral choice or an irrational faith.

Bartley's pancritical rationalism originates from a similar epistemological definition of the rationality problem, arguing that the legitimacy of the separation between justification and criticism in the theory of science also implies the viability of its application to the theory of rationality. If so, the problem of rational belief is whether it is possible to be a rationalist. Thus, Bartley's pancritical rationalism also deals with an epistemological question by arguing that the reason why neither panrationalism nor critical rationalism can solve the problem of a rationalist's identity is that both theories presume the justified true belief account of knowledge. Bartley reasons that the untenability of justification of a knowledge claim presents two options: acceptance of panrationalism or admittance of an irrational faith in reason. Bartley's proposal of pancritical rationalism as an alternative solution to the problem of rationalist identity is an epistemological theory implying that the problem is *not* whether the rationalist can or cannot *justify* all of his positions by argument or experience, but rather whether the rationalist can *criticize* all his positions by argument or experience. Bartley's answer to the latter question is affirmative in his theory of pancritical rationalism.

Concisely, the epistemological problem of the theory of rationality can be defined as the question of what rational belief is, just as the question of what objective knowledge is. What links the question of epistemology with the problem of rationality is the connection between the terms 'rational' and 'true'. Recognition of the theory of rationality *itself* as a *claim of knowledge* leads to the question of how epistemology contributes to solving the problem of rational belief. Bartley (1984: 234) did not explicitly define the problem of the 'rationality theory' as a one of *rational belief*, stating,

> . . . pancritical rationalism does not involve, and I have never developed, a theory of rationality as a property of statements. . . . What I had in mind

Unfalsified conjecture and critical rationality   93

when writing of a pancritical rationalist was one who holds his claims open to review even when – and particularly when – he is unable to imagine, let alone specify, what would count against them.

These remarks show that Bartley does not see rationality of a belief as the property of a statement, whereas an epistemological conception of rationality, on the other hand, refers to a rational belief in terms of a knowledge claim expressed in a statement. This observation enables us to see the reason why Bartley did not create a systemic connection between epistemology and pancritical rationalism. In order to explore a non-justificational theory of rationality, I suggest the integration of the epistemological separation between justification and criticism into the theory of rationality itself.

Objective knowledge: a solution for the problem of rational belief

I have diagnosed the problem with Bartley's pancritical rationalism as the lack of a theory of falsification allowing him to identify how to judge a claim of rationality held open to criticism as a non-false claim. While Bartley, among others, argues that openness to criticism only leads to rational belief when the claim in question withstands rigorous examination, the absence of a theory of falsification that includes the empirical and metaphysical theories makes it impossible to determine how such a severe test takes place. If the pancritical rationalist does not know how to refute his rationality claim logically by argument or experience, he also cannot determine whether his claim is 'true' or 'rational'. If my argument is correct, pancritical rationalism has not solved the problem of the rationalist's identity that it intends to solve, and the epistemological reason for this failure is that the context of the justified true belief account of knowledge cannot offer such a general theory of falsification. The objective of my attempt to develop a non-justificationist epistemology as an alternative to the account of objective knowledge is to narrow this gap and find an epistemological solution for the problem of rational belief.

My introduction of objective knowledge as unfalsified conjecture in non-justificational epistemology allows me to find an answer to the question of what rational belief is. A non-justificationist theory of rationality outlines the answer as 'rational belief' being a belief resting on 'objective knowledge', i.e. unfalsified belief. A claim of rationality as an epistemological claim should be treated similarly to other claims of knowledge. Panrationalism, Popper's critical rationalism and Bartley's pancritical rationalism all do not pay enough attention to the subject of a 'rationality' claim actually being a knowledge claim. Just as the theory of knowledge fails to solve the problem of objective knowledge, for instance, in terms of a justified true belief account of knowledge, the panrationalist theory of rationality fails to solve the problem of rational belief. Popper and Bartley attempt to liberate the philosophy of critical rationalism from the justified true

94   Unfalsified conjecture and critical rationality

belief account of knowledge. However, their attempts do not lead to an alternative theory of knowledge to provide them with a general theory of falsification that covers philosophical theories such as the theory of rationality, without which the critical rationalist is unable to judge the truth of his claim of rationality.

According to the non-justificationist standard of objective knowledge, a knowledge-claim is true if none of its premises is shown to be false, then the same is true about a rational belief. Since all claims of knowledge, in terms of the conclusion of a rational argument, are falsifiable by the premises, all claims of rational belief, in terms of the conclusion of a rational argument, are refutable by the premises. In this sense, the non-justificationist epistemology contributes straightforwardly to the theory of rationality. A non-justificationist theory of rationality may be called a *general* theory of critical rationalism because the problem of rational belief is soluble unless the *general* separation between justification and criticism is expanded from epistemology to the theory of rationality. Justification involves infinite regress, whereas criticism does not. Hence, the definition of rationality is a *critical*, not a justificational one.

Like an empirical theory, a rational belief is regarded as a claim of knowledge. The rationalist applies logic in order to judge his claim of rationality, putting a rational belief at the conclusion of his argument, then checking the truth or falsity of the premises. If even one premise is refuted by argument or experience, then the claim of rationality is falsified because non-justificationist deduction transmits the falsity from the premises to the conclusion. However, if none of the premises is shown to be false by argument or experience, then the rational belief in question withstands the test and counts as a 'true belief'.

Non-justificationist epistemology enables the general theory of critical rationalism to provide a solution for defining rational belief as one that is 'rational' if and only if none of its constituent premises are shown to be false, meaning that the rationality of a belief rests on its unfalsified conjecture. Likewise, a belief is 'irrational' if and only if one of its constituent premises is shown to be false by argument or experience.

Now the following formulations can be applied to the general theory of critical rationalism:

Premise (i): A claim of rational belief is a claim of knowledge.

Premise (ii): A claim of rational belief is objective if it is not refuted by its premises.

Premise (iii): The premises of a claim of rational belief are refutable by argument or experience.

Premise (iv): A claim of rational belief can be refuted if it is shown by argument or experience that at least one of its premises is false.

Conclusion: A claim of rationality is a 'rational' belief if and only if none of its premises is shown to be false by argument or experience and is an 'irrational' belief, if and only if one of its premises is shown to be false by argument or experience.

The rationalist puts the conjecture of rational belief at the conclusion of his argument and then attempts to refute conjecture by the severe test of checking the premises of his rational argument. If none of the premises is refuted by argument or experience, the conjecture in question is an unfalsified belief. However, refutation of just one of the premises by argument or experience makes the conjecture in question a falsified belief. If *objective knowledge* is tenable, then *critical rationalism* is also tenable. The separation between justification and criticism enables the theories of knowledge and rationality to find non-justificationist solutions for the problems of knowledge and rationality.

What is outcome of this new theory of rationality for the meaning of critical thinking? The theory defines the term 'critical' through two major points. The first is that all the premises of a critical argument are to be regarded as fallible and, hence, held open to revision, meaning that a critical thinker profits from wrong premises by trying to replace them with new ones. The second is that the forms of inference transmitting the truth or falsity of the premises to the conclusion are to be considered fallible and, hence, held open to review, implying that a critical thinker always profits from incorrect forms of reasoning and attempts to substitute them with new ones. With these points in mind, a critical thinker views the conclusion of his rational argument as a conjecture that is valid as long as argument or experience does not show the premises and forms of inference in his argument to be false. A critical thinker learns from his errors and improves his imperfect, but objective critical rationality.

It is noteworthy that a critical thinker is not a dogmatist because assumes none of the premises or inference forms of his argument to be justifiable and irrevocable. The critical thinker is also not a sceptic because he does not use fallibility of the premises or inference forms of his argument to mean their falseness and uselessness for deducing a rational belief. The critical thinker regards them as refutable and revisable, but usable as valid premises or forms of inference for deducing a rational belief as long as they are not shown to be false by argument or experience.

Section III: towards a new theory of the growth of critical rationality

The general theory of critical rationalism leads us to an understanding of how *critical reason* grows through learning from the incorrectness of the premises and inference forms of a rational argument. One major advantage of the general theory over Popper's and Bartley's theories of critical rationalism is its introduction of the mechanism of the growth of imperfect critical rationality. The possibility of the growth in critical rationality would not be imaginable if critical rationality

96 Unfalsified conjecture and critical rationality

were viewed as a moral attitude, not as a rational belief. In other words, it would be impossible to argue how this moral attitude grows through cognitive learning from error. However, Bartley's definition of critical rationalism as a 'theory' of rationality makes it possible to show that critical rationality may grow through a learning process. Since Bartley does see the problem of rational belief as an epistemological one in its traditional sense, it is for him to suppose how the pancritical rationalist's rational beliefs grow through learning from error. More importantly, the main problem with the pancritical rationalism is its failure to show how to use logic to profit from errors. Without non-justificationist deduction, however, it would be impossible to show how the rationalist criticizes a claim of rationality because the refutability of a claim such as the conclusion of a rational argument is valid if even one of its constituent premises is shown to be false by experience or argument.

Towards a non-justificational model of the growth of rationality

Popper (1963, 1992a) conceptualizes the growth of knowledge in terms of conjectures and refutations by using the logical form of modus tollens to show transmission of the falsity (mistake) of conclusion to the falsity (mistake) of at least one of the premises. Thus, inasmuch as our logical conjectures in science pass the empirical test, the mechanism of falsification causes a reduction in errors. Hence, the process of learning from mistakes takes place in terms of a logical procedure. Nevertheless, this logical mechanism of learning from error is not applicable for metaphysics because there is no empirical prediction whose refutation can be retransmitted logically from the conclusion to the premises in a philosophical theory such as the theory of rationality. Hence, Popper's theory of science is unable to show us the logical process through which growth of critical rationality occurs. In addition, Popper's theory of the growth of knowledge faces the problem of infinite regress because modus tollens *justifies* retransmission of the falsity from the conclusion to the premises. Hence, infinite regress prevents the practice of learning from empirical errors.

Thus, the non-justificationist theory of knowledge offers a non-justificationist form of criticism, i.e. refutation of the conclusion of a rational argument when at least one of its premises is false. This enables us to introduce a *theory of rationality growth*: using the claims of a rational belief as the conclusion of a valid deduction whose refutation originates in the falsity of the premise. Rational beliefs can grow through learning from mistaken premises or inference forms. Our critical rationality grows insofar as argument or experience shows the premises and inference forms of our rationality claims to be false, and we replace them with unfalsified conjectures about the premises and inference forms. Since there is no logical limit for criticism in terms of premises and inferences, the growth of critical rationality does not face a logical limitation. With this theory of rationality growth in mind, we can investigate major possible stages of the growth in critical rationality.

Three major stages of the growth in critical rationality

Three major stages of the growth in critical rationality can be categorized as follows:

a) a transition from irrationalism to dogmatic rationalism
b) a transition from dogmatic rationalism to justificationist critical rationalism
c) a transition from justificationist to non-justificationist critical rationalism

In order to give a brief explanation of each of these major stages of the growth in critical rationality, we ought to show how learning from mistaken premises and inference forms enables the discovery of a new stage of progress in critical rationality.

From irrationalism to dogmatic rationalism

The main claim of irrationalism, the theory of irrationality, is that rational belief is untenable. In order to use our non-justificationist form of deduction to examine this theory, we can regard the claim of irrationalism as the conclusion of the argument (i.e. if a rational belief is untenable, it is irrational), but then have to check whether the premises or inference forms of this argument are true. Even one false premise or inference activates the mechanism of learning from errors, thus and demonstrating how the transition from irrationalism to dogmatic rationalism takes place.

The theory of irrationality may be presented in the form that 'a rational belief is untenable', meaning that the conclusion of such a theory and the main premise consist of (i) 'premises unjustifiable by argument or experience' and (ii) a form of inference implying that the conclusion is justifiable by the premises. However, from a non-justificationist perspective, irrationalism can be refuted due to a mistaken premise or inference form: irrationalism implies that the premises of a rational belief cannot be *justified* by argument or experience, on the one hand, and that the conclusion of such a rational belief cannot be *justified* by the premises, on the other. The problem with the irrationalist's argument is his wrong demand that the premises and inference forms be justified in order to be true. The irrationalist thus applies untenable assumptions for justification of a conclusion by undisputable premises to argue that rationalism is untenable. In other words, the premises and inference forms of irrationalism refute the conclusion.

The aforementioned critique of the irrationalist theory is seen in the critique of dogmatic rationalism concerning irrationalism. According to the general theory of critical rationalism, the transition from *irrationalism* to *dogmatic rationalism* is a progress in critical rationality that takes place by profiting from incorrect premises or inferences. The critique of dogmatic rationalism rejects irrationalism for being self-contradictory. If *no claim* of rationality in terms of the conclusion of a rational argument can be established upon *unjustified premises* through a valid

98　Unfalsified conjecture and critical rationality

inference, then the very claim of 'irrationalism' itself as a *theory* would be faced with the same criticism refuting it due to its inability to justify itself when its premises cannot be proved as unquestionably true.

Viewed from the general theory of critical rationalism, the transition from irrationalism to dogmatic rationalism is an important progress in critical rationality because the dogmatic at least admits that rational beliefs are possible whereas the irrationalist does not accept rational belief as possible. In this line of thought, J.C. Jarvie and Joseph Agassi (1987: 445, 448) point out:

> ... we discussed different kinds or levels of rationality and examined the question of whether magic is rational, whether uncritical rationalism is rational and whether dogmatism is rational. . . . Even when we call it dogmatic, however, we don't censure irrationalism. . . . On the contrary, we argued . . . that dogmatism has its own rationality, too, both in its preferability to impotent scepticism and in its value within a working setting.

The general theory of critical rationalism shows the logical reasons that explain the progress of critical rationality from the irrationality of magic to the rationality of dogmatism.

From dogmatic rationalism to justificationist critical rationalism

The second major stage in the growth of critical rationality can be found in the transition from the dogmatic theory of rationalism to a non-dogmatic (critical) but justificatory theory of rationalism. At this stage, a critique of the justificationist critical rationalist regarding dogmatic rationalism plays a main role.

The non-justificationist theory of rationality enables the following conclusion of the theory of dogmatic rationalism: 'All claims of rational beliefs can be justified as true belief'. The main premises of dogmatic rationalism are: (i) the premises of our rational beliefs are justifiable by argument or experience and (ii) deductive or inductive inference is used for justification of the conclusion. Now the theory of dogmatic rationalism is correct, i.e. all claims of rational belief are justifiable as true belief, provided that the aforementioned premises are true. A justificationist critical rationalist now goes on to question the position of the dogmatic rationalist, arguing that the assumption of all premises being justifiable by argument or experience is itself a false premise because the premises are fallible. Hence, the dogmatic cannot prove his theory of rationality by implying that 'all claims of rational beliefs are justifiable as true on the basis of such disputed premises. In addition, the justificationist critical rationalist questions the validity of inductive induction for transmitting the truth of the premises to the conclusion.

The justificationist critical rationalist agrees with the sceptical irrationalist that premises of our rational beliefs are not justifiable. "Since one statement could be established as true only by logical derivation from another one already established

Unfalsified conjecture and critical rationality   99

as true, and since this leads to an infinite regress, we must conclude that no statement can be proved . . ." (Musgrave 1974: 582). However, due to infinite regress, the justificationist critical rationalist such as Popper does not conclude that rational beliefs are impossible at all.

The transition from dogmatic rationalism to justificationist critical rationalism originates in opening up premises and inferences to criticism. The justificationist critical rationalist argues that the dogmatist cannot defend rationalism because the premises of a rational argument cannot be justified by experience or argument and inductive inference is invalid. Hence, as observed by Popper, the dogmatist's panrationalism would be untenable. Nevertheless, the justificationist rationalist admits that the premises are disputable, without deducing the conclusion of rationalism as untenable. To the contrary, the justificationist rationalist claims that all rationality-claimers are justified in defending their rationality claims if they admit that none of their claims are conclusively true, but that nobody can justify his claims of rationality based on fallible premises.

Justificationist critical rationalism is *critical* because the rationalist does not admit justifiability of his beliefs although the premises are not infallible, and it is *justificationist* because it does not give up the justificationist origin of dogmatic rationalism, just as Popper does not. In fact, the critical rationalist's critique of dogmatic rationalism is itself a justificationist critique: while the dogmatist cannot *justify* his belief, all rationalists may claim that the rationality of their beliefs depends on the premises they have used to develop their rational beliefs. Since nobody can prove that his premises are undisputable, each critical-rationalist is allowed to have his own rationality claims; the premises are valid for themselves.

I call this justificationist version of critical rationalism the liberal theory of rationality, which can be found in John Locke's or John Rawls' readings of rationality. As Ake Petzall (1937: 11) writes, Locke

> . . . wanted to make clear certain ideas to himself and to his friends, but very soon he discovers that he and most of his contemporaries to a frighteningly large extent uncritically accept unproved maxims, which turn out not only to be completely valueless but also directly obstructive to real knowledge. People must be awakened from this uncritical attitude. Dogmatism in the form of scholasticism and uncritical rationalism is, according to Locke, a real danger to the science of the time, because people in general are not yet aware of the fact that they accept unthinkingly "truths" which undermine both knowledge and action.

Locke was a champion of the justificationist version of critical rationalism and noticed that the premises of an argument should not be accepted unequivocally. As observed by Petzall (1937: 12),

> Locke's detailed criticism of the assumption of innate ideas, the teaching of absolutely true maxims, principles that are evident in themselves, etc. is not

100 Unfalsified conjecture and critical rationality

only intended to open the way for more valuable knowledge. It is also meant to invite to independent examination. It is necessary to get rid of the self-assumed authority which with no vestige of right has ventured to act as the dictator of principles and teacher of unquestionable truths; for this authority cannot appeal to any other principle than "the principle of principles, – *that principles must not be questioned*".

Locke rightly realizes that, "There is nothing more dangerous than to base one's opinions uncritically upon unverified principles, especially if they be such as concern morality, which influence men's lives, and give a bias to all their actions". However, Locke also claims that:

> We are endowed with a natural reason, which has in itself power enough to enable us, firstly to reach absolutely true knowledge about those things of which such knowledge is necessary, and secondary to reach satisfactory, if not absolutely true, knowledge about things for which knowledge of this kind is sufficient.
>
> (Petzall 1937: 16)

Locke is a justificationist critical rationalist because he criticizes the infallibility of premises, on the one hand, and claims that absolute true knowledge is possible, on other hand. However, as observed by Alan Musgrave (1974: 569): "Fallible premises cannot justify or prove the conclusions which follow from them, even if these conclusions do follow validly". Hence, a justificationist theory of critical rationalism contradicts itself.

John Rawls argues similarly that none of the incommensurable doctrines of the good in a pluralistic liberal society can justify the truth of their validity claims because justification is impossible. Hence, the individual members of such a liberal society should recognize this pluralism and regulate their social relations based on the overlapping consensus acknowledging the legitimacy of all the incommensurable doctrines of the good as long as they respect each other as reasonable. Like Locke, Rawls is a justificationist critical rationalist: while criticizing dogmatic acceptance of justificationism, Rawls does not allow himself to notice the prospect of rational dialogue among incommensurable doctrines. Rawls (1999: 124) writes,

> A basic feature of liberal democracy is the fact of reasonable pluralism – the fact that a plurality of conflicting reasonable comprehensive doctrines, both religions and nonreligious (or secular), is the normal result of the culture of its free institutions. Different and irreconcilable comprehensive doctrines will be united in supporting the idea of *equal liberty for all doctrines* and the idea of the separation between church and state (emphasis added).

Rawls' argument implies that the incommensurable number of conflicting doctrines can only be rational in a justificational manner to the extent that there is respect for reasonable equal liberty for all. From an epistemological perspective, Rawls' recognition of pluralism originates in the justificationist premise that the conflicting doctrines are 'incommensurable' and cannot debate rationally because they have proved their doctrines of the good as justified true belief and there is no room for them to make a mistake. If, however, we replace this premise with the assumption that these 'comprehensive' doctrines cannot justify their claims as true beliefs due to the fallibility of their premises, then we can conclude that these comprehensive doctrines can hold open themselves to rational criticism and enter into a rational dialogue to discover which one is proved not to be false. In this way, we may move from Rawls' justificationist critical rationalism to Bartley's non-justificationist critical rationalism

As Jarvie (1995: 54) maintains,

> ... a non-justificationist strategy adjudicates between competing claims (not by asking how well each competing view is justified, what foundations it rests upon, but) by asking how criticizable they are and how well criticized they have been. Bartley set out from the ancient argument that the justificationist project faces an insuperable obstacle: any justifying foundation can be undermined by the simple tactic of asking on what it in turn is founded, by what it in turn is justified. This creates a vicious and unstoppable regress, for any cut-off point is arbitrarily.

However, as Bartley (1984: 265) argues, the view that ". . . the refutation is itself open to criticism by the testing of its own consequences" is at the core of non-justificationist epistemology, and this

> ... *process* of testing is, of course, in principle infinite; but there is no infinite *regress*, because the aim of justifying or establishing has been abandoned. . . . Hence a nonjustificational, nonauthoritarian theory of knowledge and rationality is indeed possible.

In fact, if individual members of a liberal society with competing doctrines of the good admit pancritical rationalism, their doctrines become 'commensurable' because they need not be justified in order to count as reasonable; they ought to be open to mutual criticism and learn from errors how to agree on the one not refuted by inter-subjective criticism.

The transition from dogmatic critical rationalism to justificationist critical rationalism is a notable growth in critical rationality due to its implication of the falsity of the idea of all rational beliefs being *justifiable* by argument or experience. This falsity renders the dogmatic defence of rationalism untenable, but this critique remains 'justificational' since the dogmatist cannot '*justify*' the rationality

102 Unfalsified conjecture and critical rationality

of his doctrine and thus fails to defend his position. In addition, the liberal solution for the problem of rational belief itself suffers from justificationism for implying that, since nobody can *justify* his belief in reason, all people should be given equal liberty to defend their comprehensive doctrines as reasonable insofar as they do not claim their doctrines to be unquestionably justifiable. As a result, I propose that this liberal epistemology of rationalism shapes *moral agreement* in a liberal society.

From 'justificationist' to 'non-justificationist' critical rationalism

A third major stage in the growth of critical rationality can be presented in terms of a non-justificationist critique of justificationist critical rationalism. In this stage, the general separation between justification and criticism is internalized in the philosophy of critical rationalism.

Non-justificational critical rationalism emerges through a critique of justificationist critical rationalism. Bartley (1984: 238), for instance, reminds us:

> My characterization of pancritical rationalism stemmed from a critical examination of the panrationalist . . . account, according to which *comprehensive* justification was a *necessary* condition of rationality. . . . Since such justification was impossible, it followed that a rationalist was impossible, and thus the question with which I began my book: "Is it possible to remain a rationalist?".

Similarly, I should confess that my own general theory of critical rationalism is the result of a critique of Bartley's pancritical rationalism because it does not tell the rationalist how to judge a claim of rationality as true or false. Bartley argues:

> Unlike justificationist views of rationality which are exposed to the *tu quoque* of the irrationalist ("You, too, must start with unjustifiable premises"), a theory of rationality which emphasises criticism *may* itself be held rationally – that is, if the theory itself is open to criticism.
>
> (Koertge 1974: 76)

Nevertheless, Bartley's pancritical rationalism does not clarify how pancritical rationalism itself can be refuted *logically*.

Viewed from the general theory of critical rationalism, justificationist critical rationalism may be presented as follows: *all claims of rational beliefs are justifiable only according to the truth of their premises, which cannot be indisputably recognized universally*. The main premises of this position are: (i) the premises of a rational claim cannot be recognized as true by all rationality-claimers and (ii) the premises are valid only for the claimers proposing them. The conclusion of these premises is that the premises of rationality claims are used reasonably to

Unfalsified conjecture and critical rationality   103

defend the rational claims of individuals personally despite the fact that they are not justifiable for all.

Non-justificationist critical rationalism refutes not only the premises of justificationist critical rationalism, but also its forms of inference. If justification leads to infinite regress, then the very demand for justifying a conclusion by its premises is misguided. Hence, the liberal theory of critical rationalism is untenable. Non-justificationist critical rationalism establishes its theory of rationality on the assumption that neither the premises of a rational belief nor its inference forms need to be justified in order to be unfalsified belief. This highest level of progress in critical rationality shows that fallible, but unfalsified premises can provide the foundations for rational beliefs. In addition, since falsification of the conclusion by the premises is logically possible, critical rationalists are right in saying that they can judge the premises of their claims of rationality as true when none of them are shown to be false.

The general theory of critical rationalism implies that *the level of openness* of the premises and inferences to criticism as well as learning from incorrect premises and inferences determine the stages of growth in critical rationality. For the theory of society, the importance of the proposed theory of the growth of rationality is found in its upshot for understanding how rational dialogue among individuals enables them to reach an agreement on common values and to create a peaceful and just social order by preventing them from assuming egoistic behaviour.

Section IV: critical rationality and moral dialogue for common values

The general theory of critical rationalism presents an *entirely new understanding* of how human reason works by replacing a justificationist concept of rationality with a non-justificational one. This replacement prevents our theory of rationality from falling into infinite regress. Infinite regress does not allow our theory of rationality to explain how reason works. Hence, the justificationist theory of rationality faces a fundamental problem: it fails to find an answer to the questions of what a rational belief is and how a rational claim is known to be true. The origin of this failure is the problem of infinite regress. However, using the non-justificationist theory of knowledge, the critical rationalist bases his claim of rationality on unfalsified premises and uses valid inferences to argue that premises not shown to be false by argument or experience render the claim in question *true* and hence *rational*.

A theory of rationality informing us whether our claims of rational belief are true enables us to judge whether our moral claims regarding the good life are true. Using their (critical) reason to make such a moral judgment would enable people to reach an inter-subjective consensus on the meaning of the good life. It is through the epistemology of critical rationalism that we discover the cognitive mechanism for forming a moral dialogue for the creation of common values for the good life. In the following, I address why a justificationist concept of

104   Unfalsified conjecture and critical rationality

rationality cannot explain how people enter into a dialogue for reaching a moral agreement on the ultimate values of the good life.

The justificationist theory of rationality, i.e. the dogmatic theory, claims that a dialogue among rationalists is possible because people begin with infallible premises and use undisputable inferences to justify their conclusions as true belief. By expanding the *justificationist model of rational argument* from an *individual* level to a *societal* one, we can argue that undeniable premises infallibly lead individuals entering into rational discussion to deduce the same true conclusions. However, if justification involves infinite regress, how can individuals convince each other that their premises and inference are infallible? In addition, without such shared premises, their inter-subjective dialogue, may not lead to common beliefs about the ultimate values. Musgrave (1974: 563) addresses this problem elegantly:

> If rational discussion involves justification, and if the ultimate justification is subjective, then it is impossible to have a rational discussion with someone who disagrees over first principles. All one can do in this case is to reassert and try to establish your authority. It follows that rational discussion never reflects *genuine* disagreement at all: for the discussion to be rational, both partners must agree on fundamental premises ("first principles"), and any "disagreement" must be due to somebody's failure correctly to reach the right conclusions. Dogmatists sought to defend rationality, but end up by narrowly circumscribing the role of rational argument: it consists merely in drawing conclusions from commonly "known" premises, agreement upon which can be reached only by non-rational, authoritarian means. . . . (D)ogmatic authoritarianism soon collapses into relativism. For the dogmatist cannot guarantee this subjective criterion of truth will produce universal agreement on "first principles", nor can he guarantee that he will be able to exert his authority over dissenters.

Hence, due to the infinite regress of 'first principles', the *justificationist model of rational dialogue* cannot explain how individuals use their reason for reaching a consensus on common values. The *non-justificationist model of rational dialogue*, however, does not suffer from such infinite regress. The main reason for people's ability to enter into a rational discourse with the aim of moral consensus is that their access to critical reason enables them to draw a true conclusion from unfalsified premises. The philosophy of critical rationalism allows us to understand how people's access to critical reason leads them into rational discussion, transforming their mutual arguments into the agents for reaching a moral agreement. On the basis of Popper's critical rationalism or Bartley's 'pan-critical' rationalism, I come to the conclusion that it is difficult to show how a rational dialogue among individual members of the society takes place in order to reach a moral agreement on common values.

In the case of Popper's critical rationalism, the idea of irrational faith in reason implies that people's critical reason is merely a *moral choice* rather than a *rational decision*. If this concept of critical rationality were applied for modelling rational dialogue among individuals, there would not be any *epistemic basis* for establishing a rational dialogue. It is the individual's moral choices that determine his entrance into a rational dialogue about the values of the good life. Even the role of 'critical reason' has already been ruled out of the concept of 'rational' dialogue because even faith in reason itself is assumed *irrational*.

In the case of Bartley's pancritical rationalism, the idea of 'rationality' as 'openness of all beliefs to criticism and acceptance of the beliefs surviving severe tests,' makes important progress towards addressing the question of rational dialogue among individuals for enabling them to prevent infinite regress of 'first principles'.[1] Bartley's theory of rationality, however, does not deal with the problem of unjustifiable premises preventing the conclusion of a rational dialogue among individuals from being deduced as true. In fact, the main problem with Bartley's theory of rationality and the issue of rational dialogue is that it does not introduce non-justificationist deduction allowing rationalists to use critical reason to falsify conclusion of their arguments by the premises. Hence, defining *rationality* merely as *openness to criticism* would not be enough to show that rational dialogue among individuals is actually possible. By contrast, the general theory of critical rationalism tells us that people who can establish their own moral beliefs about the good life on unfalsified conjectures would have access to objective knowledge requiring common beliefs in ultimate values. The second part of this book aims to apply the general theory of critical rationalism in order to introduce a new sociological theory of society for addressing the question of how people create and change social order through the common values they give to themselves.

Note

1 Bartley (1984: 235) writes, "I was in no way restricting myself to science when I wrote of criticizability: I was concerned with a broad range of ideas, with religion, ethics, theory of value, and metaphysics, as well as with science. In this broader domain, there is not the slightest reasonable hope of always being able to specify potential criticisms in advance, although one may try even here to specify the *sorts* of things that would be critically effective. Yet there is all the more reason, in such circumstances, to continue to hold such theories as open to criticism". Nevertheless, in order to see how a moral claim might be judged as true, it would not be enough to hold the claim in question open to criticism; one should use logic to explore whether the premises of such claim are true.

Bibliography

Bartley III, W.W. (1984) *The Retreat to Commitment*, 2nd ed. Chicago, Open Court.
Bartley III, W.W. (1964) "Rationality versus the Theory of Rationality". In: Bunge, M. (ed.) *Critical Approaches to Science and Philosophy*. London, Taylor & Francis, pp. 3–31.
Jarvie, I.C. (1995) "The Justificationist Roots of Relativism". In: Lewis, C.M. (ed.) *Relativism and Religion*. New York, Palgrave Macmillan, pp. 52–70.
Jarvie, I.C. & Agassi, J. (1987) "The Rationality of Irrationalism". In: Agassi, J. & Jarvie, I.C. (eds.) *Rationality: The Critical View*. Dordrecht, Martinus Nijhoff, pp. 445–451.

106 Unfalsified conjecture and critical rationality

Koertge, N. (1974) "Bartley's Theory of Rationality". In: *Philosophy of the Social Sciences*, 4, pp. 75–81.

Musgrave, A.E. (1974) "The Objectivism of Popper's Epistemology". In: Schilpp, P.A. (ed.) *The Philosophy of Karl Popper*, Book I. La Salle, Open Court, pp. 560–596.

Petzall, A. (1937) "Ethics and Epistemology in John Locke's Essay Concerning Human Understanding". In: Goteborgs *Hogskola Arsskrift*, XLIII (2), pp. 1–83.

Popper, K.R. (1992a [1959]) *The Logic of Scientific Discovery*. London, Routledge.

Popper, K.R. (1992b) "The Logic of the Social Sciences". In: Bennett, L.J. (trans.) *In Search of a Better World: Lectures and Essays from Thirty Years*. London, Routledge, pp. 64–81.

Popper, K.R. (1963) "Optimist, Pessimist and Pragmatist Views of Scientific Knowledge". In: Shearmur, J. & Turner, P.N. (eds.) *Karl Popper, After the Open Society, Selected Social and Political Writings* (2012). London, Routledge. pp. 3–10.

Popper, K.R. (1962) *Conjectures and Refutations: The Growth of Scientific Knowledge*. New York, Basic Books.

Rawls, J. (1999) *The Law of Peoples, with the Idea of Public Reason Revisited*. Cambridge, MA, Harvard University Press.

Chapter 6

Justificationism and the theory of society

Masoud Mohammadi Alamuti

Introduction

The first part of my book 'Epistemology and Critical Rationalism' has suggested new concepts of knowledge as unfalsified conjecture and rational belief as unfalsified belief. Now it would be interesting for a sociologist to know whether the resultant concepts of knowledge and rationality may help him to envision a new theory of society. Hence, this second part of the book inquires how non-justificationist philosophies of knowledge and rationality affect the theory of society and introduces the new idea of critical rationality to a sociological theory of society. Chapter 6, the beginning of the second part, investigates the contributions of justificationist epistemology to the theory of society in classical and modern sociology through four case studies of the ideal types of human action.

Along this line of inquiry, Jeffery C. Alexander et al. (1987: 13, 17) make a notable observation:

> For sociological theory, epistemology becomes "the problem of action": Is the knowing actor rational or interpretive? Yet however action is postulated, the ultimate source of this knowledge remains to be decided. It may be located inside or outside the knowing individual. . . . [T]he micro level can be forcefully brought into more collective theorizing only if subjective interpretation is considered a major characteristic of action.

In addressing the question of how epistemology contributes to the theory of society, Chapter 6 focuses on Emile Durkheim, Max Weber, Talcott Parsons and Jürgen Habermas.

Section I: Emile Durkheim: social epistemology and social order

After briefly reviewing Durkheim's social epistemology and presenting its definition of the meaning of human action, Section I applies the resultant model of action to explain Durkheim's moral solution to the problem of social order.

108 Justificationism and the theory of society

Finally, this section shows that Durkheim's justificationism prevents his theory of society from giving a proper role to human reason in the creation of social order.

Durkheim's social epistemology

Durkheim introduces his social epistemology through a critique of the two leading theories of knowledge of his day: empiricism and apriorism. In *The Elementary Forms*, Durkheim shows how primitive religions shaped the categories of thought for the first time. Durkheim (1995 [1915]: 8–9) points out:

> Men owe to religion not only the content of their knowledge, in significant part, but also the form in which that knowledge is elaborated. At the root of our judgments, there are certain fundamental notions that dominate our entire intellectual life. It is these ideas that philosophers, beginning with Aristotle, have called the categories of understanding: notions of time, space, number, cause, substance, personality. . . . They are like solid frames that confine thought. Thought does not seem to be able to break out of them without destroying itself, since it seems we cannot think of objects that are not in time or space, that cannot be counted, and so forth. . . . Now, when one analyses primitive religious beliefs methodically, one naturally finds the principal categories among them. They are born in and from religion: they are a product of religious thought.

With this quotation in mind, we observe that Durkheim's social epistemology implies that religious ceremonies have formed the various categories of human thought listed above and that Durkheim uses the justified true belief account of knowledge to offer an alternative to empiricism and apriorism.

Durkheim (1995 [1915]: 12–13) states:

> Up to the present, only two doctrines have opposed one another: For some, the categories cannot be derived from experience. They are logically prior to experience and condition it. They are thought of as so many simple data that are irreducible and immanent in the human intellect by virtue of its natural makeup. They are thus called *a priori*. For others, by contrast, the categories are constructed, made out of bits and pieces, and it is the individual who is the artisan of that construction. Both solutions give rise to grave difficulties. Is the empiricist thesis adopted? Then the categories must be stripped of their characteristic properties. In fact, they are distinguished from all other knowledge by their universality and their necessity. . . . Reason, which is none other than the fundamental categories taken together, is vested with an authority that we cannot escape at will. . . . But the characteristics of empirical data are diametrically opposite. A sensation or an image is always linked to a definite object . . . and it expresses the momentary state of a particular consciousness. It is fundamentally individual and subjective. . . . Under these conditions, to

Justificationism and the theory of society   109

reduce reason to experience is to make reason disappear – because it is to reduce the universality and necessity that characterize reason to mere appearance, illusions that might be practically convenient but that correspond to nothing in things.

Durkheim's critique implies that empiricism and apriorism cannot justify their claims of objective knowledge by intellectual intuition or sense experience. However, Durkheim's critique is justificationist and, insofar as the demand for justification guides his debate of universality and necessity, it is the unfulfilled ideal of justified true belief by empiricism and apriorism that legitimates his criticism.

As noted by Rawls (1996: 437), Durkheim's social epistemology implies that

> . . . the categories of the understanding enter the minds of individual persons during enacted practice in such a way as to be empirically valid. . . . It is the socioempirical origin of the six categories in enacted practice that, according to Durkheim, allows his epistemology to overcome the duality of thought and reality.

In fact, Durkheim replaces logical justification of the categories with social justification (Rawls 2004). Hence, the demand for justification remains unchanged in the social epistemology leading to the new concept of reason: *the categories of thought*.

Human action in Durkheim's theory of society

In 'Durkheim's Individual in Society: A Sacred Marriage?', Mark S. Cladis (1992: 78) points out: "Showing how Durkheim's social epistemology springs from his religious investigations will put us in a good position to appreciate his thought on individuals in society". Social epistemology defines 'reason' as categories of thought; hence, it would not be surprising to find rationality of action in such categories of thought. Whereas religious ceremonies shape the categories of thought, religious codes of moral behaviour are what define the meaning of 'rational' action. In Durkheim's model of human action, reason drives action via moral codes of behaviour defining the categories of thought. The resultant concept of rationality implies that individuals can *communicate* the reason for their actions because their categories of thought have already enabled them to respect moral values voluntarily.

As noted by Robert N. Bellah (1973: 151), Durkheim describes human nature as follows:

> Our sensory appetites are necessarily egoistic; they have our individuality and it alone as their object. When we satisfy our hunger, our thirst, and so on, without bringing any other tendency into play, it is ourselves, and ourselves alone, that we satisfy. [Conceptual thought] and moral activity are, on the

110   Justificationism and the theory of society

contrary, distinguished by the fact that the rules of conduct to which they conform can be universalized. Therefore, by definition, they pursue impersonal ends. Morality begins with disinterest, with attachment to something other than ourselves.

With this description, Durkheim argues that the definition of reason as conceptual thought originating in morality enables understanding of the pursuit of self-interest under the influence of human reason. This observation leads Durkheim to his solution for the problem of social order.

Social epistemology, moral codes of behaviours and social order

Now, we are in a good position to realize how Durkheim's social epistemology with its definition of rationality in terms of categories of thought provides his theory of society with a micro-foundation for addressing the problem of social order. Durkheim presents his solution to this problem based on a model of human action consisting of two driving forces: reason and self-interest. Durkheim's model of rational action implies that categories of thought direct human action and enable the actors to communicate and learn how to manage their self-interests based on moral codes: *sacred as well as profane*. Durkheim's solution for the problem of order originates in his social epistemology because the moral origins of rational action enable him to situate the pursuit of self-interest within the context of values common to all. The formation of individuals' reason by moral order in society has created common values that prevent them from turning the pursuit of profits into a conflict of interest and make social order achievable.

Durkheim argues that a utilitarian solution to the problem of order is not acceptable because the pursuit of self-interest without moral respect for others would have the unavoidable consequence of a conflict of interests or, in Hobbesian terms, 'war of all against all'. The place of reason as the categories of thought in Durkheim's action theory does not allow him to accept the utilitarian solution that assumes reason to be a servant of passion. As observed by Bellah (1973: xxiv),

> The mere maximization of self-interest based on exchange of goods could not, in Durkheim's eyes, explain the moral basis of advanced societies. For Durkheim, under the division of labor there is "an occupational morality for each profession" which has an imperative quality . . .

Having so argued, Durkheim leads us to new understanding of organic solidarity in a modern society.

Durkheim suggests his alternative theory of society by arguing that a system of common values, whether traditional or modern, prevents individuals from turning the pursuit of self-interest into a 'war of all against all'. In this sense, Durkheim sees the division of labour as the result of 'naturalistic' social causes, not of thoughtful rational measures by individual men. As noted by Cladis (1992: 79),

> . . . Durkheim attempts to distinguish religion-as-traditionally-understood from other social phenomena by placing practice – rituals – within the special domain of religion . . . He begins to perceive continuity between modern and traditional societies. A common faith is no longer a unique attribute of traditional societies. Modern societies, too, are in need of, and are developing, their own common faiths.

In fact, Durkheim argues that all societies are religious communities because of the values common to all that make social ordering of people possible. It is in this sense that an epistemological reading of reason as morally informed categories of thought enables Durkheim to argue for social order.

Justificationism and Durkheim's theory of society

As argued earlier, Durkheim's social epistemology deeply affects his theory of society. Now, the question is whether social epistemology involves justificationism. What would be the result of such justificationism for addressing the role of reason in the rise of social order? In the first part of the book, I have argued that, due to infinite regress, a justificationist concept of reason cannot show how reason guides action. Access to reason, therefore, would not be a driving force enabling individuals to agree on common values necessary for a peaceful social order.

I draw this conclusion from the previous arguments asserting that Durkheim's theory of society does not give agency to human reason through which individuals could enter into rational dialogue for the creation of common values. Durkheim's social epistemology wants to prove that the reason why categories of thought are objective is not that they are justified by intellectual intuition or sense experience, but because they are justified by religious practices. However, he faces the following epistemological challenge: if justification involves infinite regress, then religious practices are also unable to justify the categories of thought. Hence, Durkheim's social epistemology fails to address the question of how reason performs for his theory of action and would not show how reason drives action so that individuals can reach a moral consensus on the values necessary for making society a civil sphere, rather than a 'war of all against all'.

Talcott Parsons (1968a [1937]: 447) evaluates Durkheim's epistemology as relativist:

> [Durkheim's] epistemology has brought the basis of human reason itself into the same relativistic circle, so as to make the previous relativism itself relative, since the relativism of social types is itself a product of a system of categories which are valid only for the particular social type. This is a doctrine which may be called "social solipsism".

The relativism originating in Durkheim's justificationism does not allow him to recognize an independent actor whose objective knowledge provides him with rationality for thinking of social order without society totally influencing him in turn. Durkheim's actor is a 'rational being' only to the extent that his morally informed categories of thought allow him to be one. The independent thinker does not have a place in Durkheim's ideal type of rational action. Thus, Durkheim's justificationism leads to a micro-foundation for the macro-theory of society upon which it is not *reason* that enables individuals to give themselves the common values necessary for making human society a civil sphere.

Section II: Max Weber: Kantian epistemology and social order

This section defends the claim that Weber's theory of society was inspired by the concept of rationality originating in Kant's theory of knowledge. To this end, the section reviews Kantian epistemology and explores its outcomes for Weber's ideal types of rational action. It then argues that Weber's theory of society was formed upon the action types of 'value' and 'instrumental' rationality.

Immanuel Kant: epistemology and rational action

The importance of Kantian epistemology for Weber's theory of society cannot be appreciated without understanding how Kant's epistemology refers to a *critique* of *pure reason* that leads him to the notion of *practical reason*. Kant argues that the rationalist uses his pure reason to address a practical question of moral theory, namely that of what he should do. Hence, Kant's epistemology directs him to the notion of practical reason pointing to his model of rational action. In the next section, I shall argue how Weber's ideal type of value rationality is linked to Kant's doctrine of practical reason.

Kant's epistemology and his moral philosophy

Kant's theory of knowledge was a proposal for overcoming the Humean problem of induction; for Hume had argued that inductive inference could not justify a universal law by experience. Kant introduced an innovative solution to the Humean problem: the imposition of *a priori true* categories of thought on the external world deductively instead of *justification of* a universal law inductively by experience. Kant's solution was justificationist because it replaced justifying experience with justifying intellect.

In developing his critique of pure reason, Kant argues that a synthetic metaphysical judgment is to be justified in order to be true, but cannot be justified because its correspondence to the categories of intellect cannot be achieved. In the case of empirical judgment, however, such correspondence is possible. It is worthy of note that Kant's epistemological revolution was his argument that instead of corresponding judgment to objects,

> we must suppose that objects must conform to our knowledge. For, "we can know *a priori* of things only what we ourselves put into them" . . . But Kant's deduction only licenses our use of the principles of the pure understanding for objects *as we experience them*, that is, as "phenomena".
>
> (Korsgaard 2000: 9)

Viewed from a non-justificationist perspective, Kant's critique of pure reason assumes that a judgment is true if and only if it can be justified. However, since justification involves infinite regress, it is not only metaphysical theories that cannot be justified by argument, but also scientific theories that cannot be justified by experience. Therefore, the critique of pure reason itself suffers from justificationism, making Kant's moral philosophy problematic, too.

According to Kant, the basic task of moral philosophy is to address the question 'What should I do?' Kant answers that a human as a 'rational' creature can use 'pure' reason to justify the rightness of his action. Thus, the 'practical' usage of 'pure' reason shapes the concept of rational action in order to address the question of 'What should I do?' Having said that, just as Kant's critique of pure reason suffers from infinite regress, so does its usage for defining 'practical' reason.

Kantian model of rational action

Kant's moral philosophy argues that all persons as *rational beings* must be respected as the end-in-themselves. Kant's golden moral law is that one should act in a way that his/her conduct exemplifies the actions all human beings: the maxim of acting according to a universal moral law. Kant (1956 [1787]) argues that, in world of free will, it is this universal moral law that drives human behaviour. In short, Kant uses pure reason to infer a 'practical' consequence for being a 'rational' creature in accordance with his moral philosophy.

According to Kant (1956 [1787]: 48), pure reason, while not being able to give an answer to the question of what a person should do, nevertheless implies that the essential character of the law is its universality and that the person acting out of a sense of duty strives for universality. "Everything in nature works in accordance with laws. Only a rational being has the capacity to act *in accordance with the representations* of laws, that is, in accordance with principles, has a *will*" (Kant 1997 [1785]: 24). Kant calls the principle that you give yourself and that you act on a 'maxim'. Just as Kant's theory of science, his moral philosophy claims that universal moral law can be justified by categorical imperative.

114 Justificationism and the theory of society

Kant's doctrine of practical reason contributes meaningfully to his theory of rational action.

> Rational beings are the determiners of ends – *the one who set value on things*. So a rational being must value rational nature as an end in itself, and it is with this end in view that we act only on maxims which could be universal laws. Since we are the ones who make rational nature our end, we are the *ones who give ourselves this law*. We are *autonomous*.
>
> (Korsgaard 2000: 22, emphasis added)

Kant's moral man applies pure reason for a 'practical purpose'. He is a rational being who determines his own action ends. Kant's theory of practical reason suggests that it is reason, not passion, that drives action.

Kantian origin of Weber's models of rational action

The ideal types of rational action play an important role in Weberian sociology. The first step in an examination of the micro-foundation of Weber's theory of society is the discovery of the contribution of Kant's epistemology to Weber's analysis of social order.

Weber is primarily interested in the question of the conditions under which rationalization of the conduct of life has come about for the individual in pursuit of his or her ideals. It is no accident that Weber calls for sociology to relate all social processes to the active or passive individual (Mommsen 2006: 39). For Weber,

> Rationalization is simply the overall effect of the extension of either instrumental or value-rationality. The growth of value-rationality within the religious sphere that includes moves to a more ordered, coherent and applicable religious doctrine would have been an example of religious rationalization. The extension of instrumental rationality in the modern world, for instance Weber's account of bureaucratic rationality, would be another example of rationalization.
>
> (Whimster and Lash 2006: 16–17)

The important question remains of how the Kantian actor, as a rational being determining the ends of his action, plays a central role in the Weberian theory of society.

Kant's epistemology and Weber's meaningful action

The unity of the Kantian system with its distinction between pure, practical and aesthetic judgments is what led Weber to the separate development of his Western rationalization in the social, cultural and personal spheres. The action types of instrumental and value rationality are also inspired by Kant's demarcation between pure reason and practical reason on the one hand, and his moral philosophy on the other.

Weber (1968: 4) argues for speaking of action insofar as the acting individual attaches a subjective meaning to his behaviour, meaning that the concept of action postulates a realm of ideas (called meanings or ultimate values) and a realm of nature (as the medium of the realization of ideas in nature).

> It is a humanism in the sense that the mechanism is supposed to operate solely at the level of the individual human subject. Weber insists that social relationships and social collectivises are always in principle reducible to the actions of individuals.
>
> (Hindess 2006: 139)

Weber's concept of meaningful action can be linked to Kant's rational actor, who chooses the ends of his behaviour. In addition, the term 'meaningful' here refers to the notion of ultimate values chosen by a rational actor. Weber defines meaningful action as one that takes the behaviour of others into consideration, for what connects individuals to each other is, in fact, the ultimate meaning they give to the good life. According to Weber, "Human behaviour is rational to the extent that it conforms to meanings and values, and non-rational to the extent that it does not" (Hindess 2006: 139). It is for this reason that Weber emphasizes the construction of *ideal types of rational action*. The term 'meaningful action' understood in the context of Kantian epistemology offers Weber the notion of human autonomy: the individual actor is capable of determining the ends of his action due to his capacity for choosing the ultimate values of his action.

Martin Albrow (2006: 167–168) recognizes the contribution of Kant's epistemology to Weber's concepts of rationality:

> In the notion of human reason he [Kant] brought together both scientific knowledge and moral rules, each governed by the idea of law. . . . Kant's critiques established reason as the unifying factor between nature and humanity, and made the understanding of both dependent on transcendental ideas such as universal causality and perfect freedom. The reason the tag "rational" could be applied by Weber so easily to action where means were chosen to achieve purposes was that for Kant reason was exhibited in two related respects. Knowledge of means involves knowledge of laws, "how nature works", and that knowledge is advanced by science, which is governed by the transcendental ideas. It is a faculty of the human mind that permits the discovery of laws in nature. Secondly, the employment of those laws for an end of whatever kind is an objective principle valid for every rational being.

Hence, Weber uses the Kantian theory of science to develop his action type of instrumental rationality. The means is effective in the realization of

116 Justificationism and the theory of society

a given goal if there is objective knowledge to justify its efficiency. More importantly, the term 'rational' in Weber's ideal type of value rationality is to be viewed within the context of Kant's moral philosophy. For Weber, ultimate values chosen by a rational actor to give a meaning to his life are a voluntarily choice.

As Albrow (2006: 168–169) points out, the fact that

> ... Weber applied the tag 'rational' to action that adhered to values is fully comprehensible only within the framework of Kantian philosophy. . . . Action is being measured against a rule that it is expected to express. . . . For Kant the supreme product of human reason was the idea of the undetermined human subject freely following the rules of duty or moral obligation. The human personality developed through that free choice of adhering to principles. The subject was also the transcendental premise of understanding nature through laws.

To sum it up, Weber's ideal types of action originate in Kantian epistemology. "Reason, borne by the subject, provided the unity of the moral and natural worlds. Weber's two types of action are 'rational' because they are derived directly from this Kantian idea of reason" (Albrow 2006: 169). Nevertheless, Weber criticizes one important aspect of Kant's moral philosophy.

Weber's critique of Kant's moral philosophy

Mark Warren (1988: 39) argues that Weber, while influenced by Kant's moral philosophy, does not accept Kant's view that ultimate values can be rationalized by practical reason.

> In the case of moral values, actions cannot be said to have worth unless they result from free choice . . . Weber's concept of personality follows these broadly Kantian lines of reasoning. Like Kant, Weber finds an ultimate value in freedom construed as rational agency. . . . One might still argue, however, that Weber's position is implausibly relativistic because he believes – unlike Kant – that a commitment to a rational teleology of personhood is, in the end, a matter of faith . . .

Kant claims that universal moral law exists because rational beings can use their practical reason to justify such a moral law. Weber argues, however, that such justification is logically impossible because agreement on the premises of such a universal moral law cannot be achieved.

As Warren (1988: 39) argues, Weber reasons that commitment to an ultimate value is a matter of faith because ". . . what 'faith' means in this context is simply that all arguments involve axiomatic premises that cannot themselves be rationally demonstrated". Like Popper, Weber claims that rational faith in reason is untenable and that our faith in ultimate values would be an issue of belief.

> What separates Kant from Weber is that Kant held that his premises were exhaustive, and that this commits all humans to them insofar as they are potentially rational beings. Weber simply avoids universalizing his claim because he understands that one cannot argue rationally for the axiom that rational capacities define a fully human life. To do so would be to presuppose what one is trying to demonstrate.
>
> (ibid.)

If, however, Weber is right in saying that Kant's moral law cannot be justified as a universal law, he also ought to admit that the same is true in relation to Kant's theory of science because a universal law in science cannot be justified either. Weber's critique of Kantian moral philosophy is justificationist due to its premise that the truth of a belief is to be justified.

Weber's justificationist critique of Kantian practical reason leads to the conclusion that ultimate values cannot be rationalized if the premises themselves are not justifiable and that only the internal consistency of a given system of values may be examined with rationality. As Warren (1988: 40) reminds us,

> ... Weber equates meaningful action with what is potentially rational, in the sense that, in principle, one who is living a meaningful life can provide a consistent account of his or her actions in relation to both values and circumstances ... While Kant holds that freedom implies the universalizability of maxims of conduct, Weber's universal commitment attaches to the inner consistency of values and their integration with empirical conditions of action.

The following remarks by Warren are worthy of note:

> In Weber's usage, *instrumental rationality* refers to rationalities of means, the most effective way of achieving a goal. *Value rationality* refers to the rationality of goals themselves, that is, the internal coherence of the interpretive schemas that deal with the intrinsic worthiness of an end.
>
> (Warren 1988: 34)

If Kant's epistemology entails infinite regress, Weber's ideal types of action face the same problem.

Weber's justificationism and his theory of society

Weber's critique of the Kantian model of rational action has an important consequence for addressing the problem of social order. With a Kantian perspective,

118 Justificationism and the theory of society

one can argue that all rational beings who consider each other as the end per se are capable of agreeing on the maxim of the moral equality of rational beings as a system of ultimate values necessary for a peaceful social order. Weber's critique of Kant's practical reason, however, does not lead him to this solution for social order. Instead, Weber defines value rationality in terms of using reason to determine the consistency of a value system. Thus, while admitting the conflict of ultimate values in society, Weber's notion of value rationality refers to the internal consistency of a system of values.

Weber's critique of the Kantian doctrine of practical reason leads him to an action type of value rationality that directs him to a different approach to social order. Weber argues that the idea of value rationality in terms of using reason to check the internal consistency of a value system enables him to show that ideational forces contribute to a transition from traditional to modern society. As observed by Talcott Parsons (1963: xxxiii), for Weber:

> Rationalization comprises first the intellectual clarification, specification and systematization of ideas. Ideas are generated by what Weber called the teleological *meanings* of man's conceptions of himself and his place in the universe, conceptions which legitimize man's orientations in and to the world and which give *meaning* to man's various goals. Such ideas imply metaphysical and theological conceptions of cosmos and moral orders, as well as man's position in relation to such wider orders.

Given these considerations, Weber's action type of value rationality finds a central role in his theory of society by exploring how value rationality has enabled people to make their views of the universe and man's place in it more consistent.

In *The Sociology of Religion*, Weber (1963) argues that the ideal type of value rationality allows him to explore how traditional worldviews and the place of man in the world were rationalized to make the rise of modern social order possible. However, Weber's justificationism forced him to limit the role of value rationality to making ultimate values *consistent* rather than *rational* due to his assumption that the premises of ultimate values are to be justified and that, without such justification, the only role remaining for reason is to make them internally consistent.

In *The Protestant Ethic and the Spirit of Capitalism*, Weber uses the action type of value rationality to model the behaviours of individuals participating in the religious reformation.[1] He argues that the religious reformation in Europe led to the rise of a capitalist social order. The central problem for Weber was the origin of bourgeois capitalism with its rational organization of free labour.

> For modern rational capitalism has need, not only of the technical means of production, but of a calculable legal system and of administration in terms of formal rules. Without it adventurous and speculative trading capitalism and all sorts of politically determined capitalisms are possible, but no rational

Justificationism and the theory of society 119

enterprise under individual initiative, with fixed capital and certainty of calculations. Such a legal system and such administration have been available for economic activity in a comparative state of legal and formalistic perfection only in the Occident.

(Weber 2005 [1930]: xxxviii)

Weber argues that it was the Protestant Ethics that made the rise of a capitalist social order possible.

In this line of reasoning, Weber (2005 [1930]: 56) emphasizes the role of Calvinism:

... Calvinism was the faith over which the great political and cultural struggles of the sixteenth and seventeenth centuries were fought ... At that time, and in general even today, the doctrine of predestination was considered its most characteristic dogma.

It is worthy of note that this doctrine and its reform paved the way for the rise of capitalism. In modern Western capitalism, working hard and pursuing material interests to maximize consumption were not the main goals per se; the utility of such things originated in looking at them as ends-in-themselves. Weber argues that the Calvinist reform changed traditional values in Europe making the rise of a rational organization of labour possible.

Weber argues that Calvin improved the *internal* consistency of the doctrine of predestination. According to this doctrine, Weber (2005 [1930]: 57) reminds us that:

Those of mankind that are predestinated unto life, God before the foundation of the world was laid, according to His eternal and immutable purpose, and the secret counsel and good pleasure of His will, hath chosen in Christ unto everlasting glory, out of His mere free grace and love, without any foresight of faith or good works, or perseverance in either of them, or any other thing in the creature as conditions or causes moving Him thereunto, and all to the praise of His glorious grace.

This original reading of the doctrine created an intolerable situation for believers. They could not know whether they were among those receiving God's glorious grace. Hence, Calvin's new theological reading of the doctrine offered a more consistent notion and liberated believers from such a difficult situation.

As observed by Reinhard Bendix (1998: 80),

According to Calvin, men exist for the sake of God. To apply earthly standards of justice to His sovereign decrees is evidence of presumption and lack of faith. We can know only that some men are saved and the rest are damned.

120 Justificationism and the theory of society

To assume otherwise is to believe a manifest contradiction, namely that mere human merit or guilt can influence God's absolutely free decrees.

This theological reform with a new understanding of predestination prepared the moral basis for the rise of capitalism.

Under this condition,

... unremitting labor was not merely a negative good; it was the way of life ordinated by God in which every man must prove himself. The usefulness of labor was judged by the fruits that signify its favor in the sight of God. Profit and wealth were ethically bad only insofar as they led to idleness and dissipation; they were commended insofar as they resulted from the performance of duty.

(Bendix 1998: 83)

Weber's value rationality implies that the actors rationalize the ultimate goals of their actions by defining them based on a more consistent reading of the universe and the place of man within it. Weber's theory of society uses the ideal type of value rationality to show how the rationalization of worldviews and values led to the rise of capitalist society.

Weber argues that the religious reformation prepared the ground for the separation between cultural spheres in a modem society in which science can no longer provide an answer for the ultimate meaning of the universe. Weber's critique of Kantian moral philosophy thus led to the notion of conflicting ultimate values and his analysis of modern society moved from the rise of a Protestant society to the post-religious social order with its characteristic plurality of gods and demons. Weber argued that the transition from the moral solidarity in a traditional society to the plurality of 'gods and demons' in modern society eliminated the need for one system of ultimate values in society. From that time on, the instrumental rationality of bureaucracy and capitalist economy has led modern society to struggle for the attainment of power and wealth. Weber's justificationist critique of Kant's moral philosophy resulted in the failure to argue for a possible rational dialogue for the creation of a peaceful social order.

Section III: Talcott Parsons: epistemology and social order

Kantian epistemology also influences Parsons's theory of society; however, unlike Weber, Parsons does not define modern society in terms of a plurality of gods and demons. Parsons's sociology attempts to show the existence of one system of values upon which social order stands. This section argues that Parsons's theory of society is Kantian in the sense that it uses the idea of practical reason to offer a voluntaristic theory of action, a theory that also reflects Parsons's justificationism.

Kantian epistemology and Parsons's theory of voluntaristic action

Richard Munch (1981: 709–739) has offered an insightful reading of the Kantian foundation of Parsons's sociology. Munch argues that, according to Kant, an interpenetration of intellect and experience shapes scientific knowledge, and Parsons similarly defines human action as an interpenetration of a normative orientation towards the ultimate values and the pursuit of self-interest. Munch (1981: 712) argues that ". . . Talcott Parsons's sociology is everywhere permeated with the structure of the philosophy of Kant". In brief, Munch aims to lead us to see the Kantian foundation of Parsons's sociology.

As Munch (1981: 715) reminds us,

> For Kant, modern scientific knowledge is explainable neither as a habitual generalization from empirical experience, as in Hume's empiricism, nor as a series of deductions from the first principles of reason, as in the rationalism of someone like Descartes, but only as the mutual interaction of theory and experience.

Munch reasons that Parsons's action theory uses the interpenetration of moral obligations and self-interest to address the question of social order.

Kant's theory of knowledge inspires him to propose his notion of practical reason: Kant

> rejects all utilitarian moral theories. Just as we cannot account for the objective necessity of causal laws by reference solely to the content of sense perceptions, so we cannot derive the necessity of a moral law valid for all men at all times from the desires – or the calculation of utility – of individuals. Private calculations of utility may yield different results for different individuals . . . We cannot explain the obligatory force of moral law as the sum of all calculation of utility, because these calculations would yield externally variable results, and we would have made no progress towards a concept of true obligation . . .
>
> (Munch 1981: 716)

Parsons's voluntaristic action theory is Kantian because it answers the question of the conditions for a universally biding moral law.

> Any particular rule of action can be adjudged valid to the extent that it enables us to attain a given end, but there is no direct path from this "hypothetical" validity to a universal, unconditional validity, since our first particular rule might be called into question by other particular rules which function as means to other given ends. To bring order to the multitude of particular rules

122   Justificationism and the theory of society

and to answer the question of their universal validity, we cannot begin from below, but must apply a scheme of categories from above. For Kant, order is produced by a "categorical imperative".

(ibid.: 717)

Munch observes that Parsons applies this same logic to offer his solution for the problem of social order by revealing an interaction between moral obligations and the pursuit of self-interest.

Parsons's unit act and voluntaristic action theory

Parsons's major contribution to the sociological theory of action may be seen in terms of a unification of Durkheim's and Weber's value and instrumental rationalities in one 'unit act'. Parsons (1968a [1937]: 44) introduces the *unit act* in the following way:

> . . . an "act" involves logically the following: (1) It implies an agent, an "actor". (2) For purposes of definition the act must have an "end", a future state of affairs toward which the process of action is oriented. (3) It must be initiated in a "situation" of which the trends of development differ in one or more important respects from the state of affairs to which the action is oriented, the end. This situation is in turn analyzable into two elements: those over which the actor has no control . . . and those over which he has such control. The former may be termed the "conditions" of action, the latter the "means". Finally, (4) there is inherent in the conception of this unit, in its analytical uses, a certain mode of relationship between these elements. That is, in the choice of alternative means to the end, in so far as the situation allows alternatives, there is a "normative orientation" of action.

In Weber's ideal types of action, the rationality of the ends separates from the rationality of the means, whereas Parsons's proposes merging these two types of rational action into *one* unit act. According to Parsons (1968b [1937]: 651), the two ideal types involve specific norms: the efficient adaptation of the means to the ends, called the norm of efficiency, and the norm of legitimacy or moral obligation. Parsons argues that there is no reason whatsoever for the actor not to apply these two types of rationality in *one* unit act.

Like Kant, Parsons (1968a [1937]) argues that ultimate ends of human action cannot be subjective utilities, but are rather moral judgments made by individuals in view of the ends. Parsons recognizes that the utilitarian model of action assumes that the ends of an action are subjective utilities and that the rationality of action is reflected only in the norms of efficiency. This subjective nature of the ends also indicates its randomness. Given the subjectivity and the randomness of utilities as the ends of an action, a rational actor seeks only the most efficient

Justificationism and the theory of society   123

means to realize subjective utilities. Such a utilitarian model cannot address the origin of action ends.

Parsons (1968a [1937]: 61) argues that the utilitarian model proposes a negative conception of the randomness of ends due to a lack of concern for the choice of the ends. The subjective nature and randomness of the ends create a major problem for the utilitarian theory of action: with subjective and random ends, the private calculation of utility may yield varied results for diverse rational actors. Hence, there would not be any objective ground upon which the actor could opt for his preferable ends. Parsons (1968a [1937]: 63–64) argues for only one possible way to escape this limitation:

> If ends were not random, it was because it must be possible for the actor to base his choice of ends on scientific knowledge of some empirical reality. But this tenet had the inevitable logical consequence of assimilating ends to the situation of action and destroying their analytical independence, so essential to the utilitarian position . . . Then action becomes determined entirely by its conditions, for without the independence of ends the distinction between conditions and means becomes meaningless.

Parsons concludes that the utilitarian model of action faces the following 'dilemma':

> . . . either the active agency of the actor in the choice of ends is an independent factor in action, and the end element must be random; or the objectionable implication of the randomness of ends is denied, but then their independence disappears and they are assimilated to the conditions of the situation, that is to elements analyzable in terms of nonsubjective categories . . .

Considering none of these options to be tenable, Parsons offers the voluntaristic action theory to show how the ends of an action can be rationalized by a voluntarily orientation to ultimate values, thus denying the actor the use of instrumental reason to make other human beings the means for his own ends.

As pointed out by Munch (1981: 716), Kant argues that private calculations of utility may yield different results for different individuals.

> The criterion of a moral law, however, is that it is binding for all men at all times. We cannot explain the obligatory force of moral law as the sum of all calculation of utility, because these calculations would yield externally variable results, and we would have made no progress towards a concept of true obligation.

The voluntaristic nature of Parsons's action theory can be understood in the context of Kantian moral philosophy.

124 Justificationism and the theory of society

The Hobbesian Problem of Order and the Parsonian Solution

Parsons (1968a [1937]: 89–91) argues that the Hobbesian problem of social order has central importance for sociology. Hobbes defines the state of nature as the 'war of all against all'.

> . . . Man, he says, is guided by a plurality of passions. The good is simply that which any man desires. . . . But reason is essentially a servant of the passions – it is the faculty of devising ways and means to secure what one desires. Desires are random, there is "no common rule of good and evil to be taken from the nature of the objects themselves". Hence since the passions, the ultimate ends of action, are diverse there is nothing to prevent their pursuit resulting in conflict.

Parsons argues that this Hobbesian observation creates a significant challenge for sociological theory.

Parsons credits Hobbes with being the first thinker to recognize

> . . . the need to explain why human society is not a 'war of all against all'; why, if man is simply a gifted animal, men refrain from unlimited resort to fraud and violence in pursuit of their ends and maintain a stable society at all.
>
> (Wrong 1999: 33)

Parsons writes that Hobbes

> . . . went on to deduce the character of the concrete system which would result if its units were in fact as defined. And in so doing he became involved in an empirical problem which has not yet been encountered, as the present discussion so far has been confined to defining units and noting merely their logical relations in utilitarian thought – the problem of *order*.
>
> (Parsons 1968a [1937]: 91)

Hobbes's problem of order arises from acceptance of the utilitarian action model. If the rationality of action is limited to the means, the pursuit of interests results in a 'war of all against all'. As recognized by Dennis Wrong (1999: 34), "Parsons's entire work represents an effort to solve the Hobbesian problem of order". Parsons's solution to the problem of social order is inspired by Kantian doctrine of practical reason.

Parsons argues that people apply reason in order to control the pursuit of individual interests through respect for the moral law, consequently preventing a 'war of all against all'. Thus, Kantian moral philosophy enables Parsons to develop a model of action showing how individuals use reason to orient their action goals towards a system of common values and let them live in a civil sphere.

Justificationism and the theory of society 125

Common values and socialization: the possibility of social order

In 'The Place of Ultimate Values in Sociological Theory', Parsons (1935: 294–295) argues that his Kantian approach solves the problem of social order. If the ends of an action are viewed in terms of a random plurality, the choice between ends implies a relationship between them and that one end could be an alternative for the other. However, "in so far as the action of an individual is guided by rational choice, its ultimate ends are to be thought of as constituting an integrated system". Parsons continues: "Rationality of action for an individual implies just as much the working-out of such a coherent system of ends as it does a relational selection of means" (ibid.: 294–295). With this point in mind, Parsons (1935: 295) shows the importance of his voluntaristic action theory for solving the problem of order:

> In the first place it may be argued in general and abstract terms that this random variation of systems of ends would be incompatible with the most elementary form of social order. For there would be no guaranty that any large proportion of such systems would include a recognition of other people's ends as valuable in themselves, and there would thus be no necessary limitation on the means that some, at least, would employ to gain their own ends at the expense of others. The relations of individuals then would tend to be resolved into a struggle for power – for the means for each to realize his own ends. This would be, in the absence of constraining factors, a war of all against all – Hobbes's state of nature. In so far, however, as individuals share a *common* system of ultimate ends, this system would, among other things, define what they all held their relations ought to be, would lay down norms determining these relations and limits on the use of others as means, on the acquisition and use of power in general. In so far, then, as action is determined by ultimate ends, the existence of a *system* of such ends common to the members of the community seems to be the only alternative to a state of chaos – a necessary factor in social stability.

The Kantian moral solution to the problem of social order is evident in Parsons's argument: the existence of a system of *common* values is necessary for controlling egotistic behaviours and preventing others from being used as a means for selfish ends.

The conceptual scheme of pattern variables and Parsons's theory of society

Parsons (1935: 299) argues that human action in "pursuit of immediate non-ultimate ends" is subjected "to normative rules which regulate that action in conformity with the common ultimate value-system of the community", reasoning that rationality cannot pertain only to means-ends relationships; rational action

126 Justificationism and the theory of society

does not take place only in an environment of 'random ends'. The normative organization of the chain of 'unit acts' itself, i.e. of intermediate means-ends relationships, has to be addressed within the theoretical framework of the general theory of action, typically relying on an integrated system of ends. Parsons argues that no social order can exist without a coherent system of ends. Without a broad range of social institutions to concretize ultimate values and provide a structure for social action, no conformity of ultimate ends for all of society can be ensured.

Parsons's theory of society implies that practical reason enables us to see the possibility of integrating common values in personal identity. This usage of practical reason finds concerted meaning in the 'socialization process' of making the individual a civilized member of society. As Wrong (1999: xi) observes, Parsons

> . . . regarded "personality" as a system co-equal in its interdependence and partial independence with the "cultural" and "social" systems. Socialization understood as the process by which an individual is inducted into a society by learning and internalizing its norms and cultural patterns . . .

Throughout the socialization process, the rational actor learns to use reason for internalizing common values in the constitution of his action ends. Parsons applies Freud's theory of the superego as a model for internalizing social norms, shaping a psychological model to concretize the notion of value rationality in his voluntaristic theory of action and defining the moral man as an actor guided by a built-in superego and backed by an ego-ideal.

The concept of 'role' is crucial in leading us to explore the connection between the theory of voluntaristic action and the scheme of pattern variables. Wrong (1999: 48) points out:

> Structural-functionalism, especially in its Parsonian version, possessed a powerful, well-developed theory of human nature based on the idea that "the internalization of social norms" is the most important feature of the socialization process, thus linking, as Durkheim had not, a consensual view of society with a conforming and 'role playing' view of individual personality.

Noticing that the individuation process that Freud called ego development may be seen as the inclusion of the individual in the system of moral regulation, Parsons argues:

> . . . the most significant unit of social structures is not the person but the role. The role is that organized sector of an actor's orientation which constitutes and defines his participation in an interactive process. It involves a set of complementary expectations concerning his own actions and those of others with whom he interacts. . . . Roles are institutionalized when they are fully congruous with the prevailing culture patterns and are organized around

expectations of conformity with morally sanctioned patterns of value-orientation shared by the members of the collectivity in which the role functions.

(Parsons and Shils 1962: 23)

This quotation implies that the internalization of values in personal identities takes place through the roles they play in the social division of labour.

An actor in any situation is confronted by a series of major dilemmas of orientation and choice. Parsons describes five dichotomies, formulating these choice alternatives as *pattern variables*. Parsons and Shils (1962: 48) point out:

> ... we may define the five dichotomies as follows. The first is that between accepting an opportunity for gratification without regard for its consequences, on the one hand, and evaluating it with regard to its consequences, on the other. The second is that between considering an act solely with respect to its personal significance, on the one hand, and considering it with respect to its significance for a collectivity or a moral code, on the other. The third is that between evaluating the object of an action in terms of its relations to a generalized frame of reference, on the one hand, and evaluating it in terms of its relations to the actor and his own specific relations to objects, on the other. The fourth is that between seeing the social object with respect to which an action is oriented as a composite of performances (actions), on the one hand, and seeing it as a composite of ascribed qualities, on the other. The fifth is that between conceding to the social object with respect to which action is oriented an undefined set of rights (to be delimited only by feasibility in the light of other demands), on the one hand, and conceding to that social object only a clearly specified set of rights on the other.

Parsons uses the scheme of pattern variables to explain how common values are internalized in personal identities via these five dichotomies to create a *social division of roles* allowing people to pursue their interests peacefully.

Francois Bourricaud (1981: 64) asks whether the theory of pattern variables explains how individual choices are coordinated so as to give rise to social order. The problem is that choice in the domain of the unit act is described in strictly dichotomous terms. Parsons's answer to this question rests on two assertions:

> (1) the actor has at hand a stockpile of resources and possible uses for them; (2) given a context and an actor, there always exists a point of reference, which the actor may or may not take as a norm for his action. Looking at the aggregate, which involves a large number of unit acts and individual actors, we discover that a single actor may simultaneously adopt more than one point of reference ... From the macroscopic standpoint, the compatibility principle requires the existence of either an explicit aggregation procedure or a set of unconscious mechanisms for coordinating the either/or choices made by the individual actors in response to the alternative facing them.

128 Justificationism and the theory of society

Parsons's theory of pattern variables argues that the voluntaristic choices of individual actors, i.e. the either/or responses, are integrated in the rise of social order.

Parsons argues that

> ... at the moment of choosing, the choice appears to strike a balance between costs and benefits. .... If I opt for a universalistic solution, I must forgo the particularistic one. But foregoing the latter *today* may promise that *eventually* certain benefit will accrue for my enjoyment. Socialization is based on a logic of this kind, involving tradeoffs and compensations; these take place constantly, not only among the members of the family within which socialization is being carried out, but also within the mind of the individual being socialized, who must make tradeoffs between one phase of his development and another ...
>
> (Bourricaud 1981: 64)

The pattern variables constitute a system that enters into all the dimensions of action – *means*, *goals*, *norms* and *conditions* – and describes the socialization process internalizing common values in personal identities.

Parsons introduces four functions of the social system: "the economic, [adaptation] concerned with maximizing efficiency and '*means*'; the political [goal attainment], focused on organization and '*goals*'; the solidarity [integration], representing emotional bonds and '*norms*'; and the pattern-maintenance, oriented to stable symbolic patterns and 'values'" (Alexander 1988: 31). Parsons uses a *homologous method* to expand the individual's micro-standpoint to a macro-perspective of social order. His theory of the four functions does not address the question of how individual action plays a *causal force* in the formation of social order. The four functions in the social system are proposed through an analogy with the parallel elements in the unit act. From the micro-macro perspective, this analogy does not define human action as a driving force of social ordering.

Parsons's four functions of the social system serve as his solution to the problem of social order:

> To say that we are members of a social system means that: (1) we are bound by certain constraints that the location of the system vis-à-vis its specific environments imposes; (2) we accept the obligations that the task to be accomplished jointly imposes on all the members of the group; (3) transactions and interchanges with our associates and companions affect us both positively and negatively; (4) we have an interest in maintaining, reinterpreting, or replacing the norms that govern our behaviour and make it meaningful. These four propositions set forth the standpoint of the actor. Looking at the same relations from the standpoint of the system, we again find the four

system functions with which we began: adaptation, goal attainment, integration, and latent pattern-maintenance.

(Bourricaud 1981: 89)

It is upon the basis of such an analogy between the actor's perspective and the social standpoint that Parsons (2005 [1991]) builds his structural-functional theory of social order.

Justificationism and Parsons's theory of society

I suggest that Kantian justificationism has prevented Parsons from addressing the question of how social order is shaped through the socialization process and that the reason for this is that neither Kant nor Parsons can show how the actors play a 'causal' role in the rise of social order by using reason for defining action goals according to ultimate values. Due to the socialization process being a *learning* process and the justificationism of Kant's epistemology and moral theory, infinite regress prevents the doctrine of practical reason from addressing the socialization process through which an individual becomes a member of the society.

In order to address the question of how individuals may affect social order through the internalization of common values in action ends, Parsons applies Freud's theory of ego development. In his attempt to explain the role of human action in the rise of social order, Parsons uses the scheme of pattern variables, which merely develops the individual's standpoint regarding his social membership and the societal standpoint of the system to define the 'differentiation' of roles as a mechanism of the formation of the social system and its four functions. Due to its Kantian origin, Parsons's action theory allows a definition of socialization as a learning process in terms of the correspondence of an individual's rational choices with a given moral law in society. Thus, Parsons's theory of social order creates an *analogy* between two standpoints: the individual and the social. However, this type of micro-macro relation cannot address the role of human agency due to the use of practical reason in the creation of social order. From an epistemological perspective, Parsons's justificationism is an obstacle for the exploration of socialization as a cognitive process linking human action and social order. Since Parsons's sociology is inspired by Kant's epistemology, we have to admit that it is Kant's justificationism that prevents Parsons's action theory from giving a causal role to the human actor in the process of the formation of social order.

Bourricaud (1981: 189) recognizes that "Parsonian sociology has been accused both of confusing the idea of social equilibrium with that of cybernetic regulation and of altogether neglecting the phenomenon of social change". I argue that this accusation is not baseless for Parsons argues that the existence of social order depends on a system of common values, and he takes the common values as a given fact. Considering the two sides of this equation together, we can argue that Parsons's theory of society does not concern itself with the question of how

130 Justificationism and the theory of society

individuals may use reason to give themselves the common values they need to prevent egotistic behaviour. Kant recognizes such a role for practical reason, but Parsons's justificational critique of Kant leads him to the assumption that common values are a *given* fact, so the focus of Parsons's theory of society has become the question of how common values are internalized in personal identities and make a peaceful social order possible.

Section IV: Jürgen Habermas: epistemology and the theory of society

This section studies Jürgen Habermas's theory of society from an epistemological view. With five major arguments, it investigates how consensual epistemology contributes to the theory of society.

Habermas's epistemology: consensus and justification

Firstly, I attempt to show that Habermas's epistemology is a justificationist theory of knowledge due to its introduction of an 'intersubjective consensus' as the standard for testing the validity of a knowledge claim. I begin with the shift proposed by Habermas from traditional epistemology centred on the conscious subject to an epistemology focused on language in order to explore the contributions of Habermas's epistemology to his solution for the problem of social order.

The criterion of truth: 'justified consensus'

In accordance with traditional epistemology, a claim of knowledge is valid if it corresponds to its object. However, Habermas (1981a) argues that in an epistemology focused on language, the object cannot be defined independently of the knowledge-claimer, and it refers to *the state of an affair* shaped within an intersubjective discourse. As observed by Paul Healy (1987: 146),

> ... "facts" are not "things or events on the face of the globe, witnessed or heard or seen", rather, "facts are derived from the states of affairs, and the states of affairs are the propositional content of statements". Given this linguistic definition of facts, the truth problem emerges as an inherently discursive affair. Habermas is then in a position to maintain that . . . the truth problem centres on the validation of claims made in language (states of affairs) rather than on the verification of experience. . . . From there, the concern passes to the specification of the conditions for objectively validating such truth claims.

Habermas summarily argues,

> The validation of truth claims is governed by the ideal of attaining consensus in discourse. . . . Such a consensus is one which derives exclusively from the

dynamics of the discourse itself, from the force of the better argument, and specifically excludes any external constraints or biases.

(ibid.)

Is Habermas's epistemology justificationist? Yes, it is, indeed, because Habermas argues that participants of a discourse have to justify a knowledge claim as true before they can admit its validity. It is for this reason that *truth* is defined as *justified consensus*.

Speech acts and three types of validity claims

The shift from subject-oriented to language-based epistemology leads Habermas to the central importance of 'speech acts' for the theory of knowledge. From Austin's theory of speech acts, Habermas learns that to speak a language is to perform an action. He argues that, in uttering a speech act,

> ... the speaker makes an *offer* which the hearer can either accept or reject. Suppose a flight attendant says to a passenger, "You must stop smoking now". The attendant is making an offer – or ... raising a *validity-claim* – which the passenger can accept by extinguishing the cigarette or reject by saying "Why?" In the latter case the attendant must give some reasons or grounds which would support the validity-claim raised with the original speech-act, for example by pointing out that the plane would soon be landing and that the safety regulations stipulated no smoking at such a time.
>
> (Thompson 1983: 280)

Habermas then achieves an important result:

> The validity-claim raised with a speech-act is thus internally connected with reasons and grounds ... there is a "rationally motivating force" at work within the process of communication. "A speaker can *rationally motivate* a hearer to accept his speech-act offer because ... he can assume the guarantee for providing, if need be, convincing grounds which would stand up to the hearer's criticism of the validity-claim".
>
> (ibid.)

This reading of the speech act is justificationist because the speaker should offer verifying reasons to assure the hearer that his claim is true despite the hearer's criticism.

Habermas argues that three major validity claims relating to three types of object are justifiable by consensus between the speaker and the hearer. In this way, the theory of truth transmits a justificationist standard of validity to the three types of speech act. As pointed out by Thompson (1983: 280),

132 Justificationism and the theory of society

There are, Habermas maintains, at least three validity-claims which are raised with the utterance of speech-acts. A speaker may raise the claim (a) that the statement made is *true* (or the existential presuppositions are satisfied); (b) that the speech-act is *correct* in terms of the prevailing normative context (or the normative context itself is legitimate); (c) that the intention of the speaker is as it is expressed, that is, that the speaker is *sincere* in what he or she says.

In order to discover whether these knowledge claims are valid, the speaker has to offer justifying reasons to persuade the hearer.
Habermas argues:

In raising these claims the speaker takes up relations to any of three objects domains or "worlds", with regard to which a claim can be contested by a hearer: (a) the *objective world* as the totality of entities about which true statements are possible; (b) the *social world* as the totality of legitimately regulated interpersonal relations; (c) the *subjective world* as the totality of experience to which the speaker has privileged access.

(ibid.)

According to Habermas, the speaker and the hearer have to arrive at a justified consensus for each of these speech acts if they want to admit their claim as a justified true belief.

Ideal types of rational action: communicative versus instrumental

Habermas connects knowledge and rationality directly and establishes his theory of action upon consensual epistemology: the rationality of an action depends on the validity of the knowledge claim supporting such an action. While admitting Weber's classifications of value rationality and instrumental rationality, Habermas replaces Kant's practical reason with his own communicative rationality. In addition, Habermas rejects the teleological concept of action, offering instead his own model of action with speech acts.

The speech acts: 'communicative' and 'instrumental' action

Habermas uses his consensual epistemology to define the notion of communicative action. "The threefold articulation of validity-claims, world-relations and modes of language use defines the complex concept of 'communicative action', or, more precisely, 'action oriented to reaching understanding" (Thompson 1983: 281). The idea of knowledge as *justified consensus* leads Habermas to the ideal type of communicative action. Communicative action refers to *all* three types of speech acts through which *validity claims* can be *justified* as true with regard to their objects, for instance the social or physical world. The notion of understanding in the ideal type of communicative action denotes attainment of a justified consensus in all three types of speech acts. Hence, the idea of communicative action rests on consensual epistemology and suffers from the infinite regress of proofs.

In what sense is the ideal type of communicative action to be regarded as a 'rational' action? If an action is 'rational' insofar as it rests on a valid claim of knowledge in terms of justified consensus, then the rationality of communicative action is to be seen in a justified agreement between the two dialogue partners, the speaker and the hearer. In this sense, communicative action is characterized as an action *oriented towards reaching understanding*. Due to the justification involved in infinite regress, it is not surprising that communicative rationality does not lead to an understanding of how reason performs.

Instrumental action can be seen in the same way: an action is 'rational' from an instrumental perspective when efficient means for reaching a given end are employed based on justified experiences. Unlike communicative action, instrumental action *is not* a speech act oriented to mutual understanding, but rather uses knowledge in terms of justified consensus to prove the efficiency of the means for realizing a given end. Another reason instrumental action is not like communicative action is its rationality in enabling the actor to explore efficient means instead of aiming at reaching an understanding. Habermas defines instrumental action as 'action oriented toward success'. It uses objective knowledge rationally in terms of justified experiences to identify whether the means can *successfully* attain the desired end. Thus, valid scientific claims should be the base upon which the 'rationality' of an instrumental action rests.

As pointed out by Thompson (1983: 282),

> In calling an action "rational" we may presume that the actor knows, or has good reason to believe, that the means employed will lead to success; in calling an expression "rational" we may presume that it bears some relation to the world and hence is open to objective – that is, intersubjective – assessment. The former case, by linking the term "rational" to the notion of action oriented to success, offers an intuitive basis for what Habermas calls "cognitive-instrumental rationality". The latter case links the term "rational" to the notion of intersubjective assessment and thereby points towards a broader concept of *communicative rationality* "in which various participants overcome their merely subjective views and, by virtue of the mutuality of rationality motivated conviction, assure themselves of both the unity of the objective world and the intersubjectivity of their life-relations".

Habermas argues that we can *rationalize* the three types of speech acts by basing them upon justified true claims since

> ... an expression may be deemed "rational", not only if it can be assessed in terms of its relation to the objective world, but also if it can be appraised with

134 Justificationism and the theory of society

regard to a social world of legitimate norms or a subjective world of personal experiences.

(ibid.)

From the viewpoint of consensual epistemology, one problem with Habermas's classification of action types into communicative and instrumental actions is that the separation between 'communicative' and 'instrumental' actions loses its basis if the idea of 'rational' action in terms of justified consensus can be applied not only for the ends of the action but also for its means. It should not be a matter of concern that a justified consensus is used for rationalizing the 'ends' or the 'means'. In this sense, an instrumental action might also be categorized as a speech act for identifying the efficiency of the means with regard to the end based on a mutual understanding between the dialogue partners concerning the efficiency of the means.

Communicative rationality and discursive ethics

Although the Weberian action type of value rationality is absent in Habermas's models of rational action, Habermas uses the idea of communicative reason to replace Kantian practical reason. This communicative rationality replaces the subject-centred epistemology with a linguistic-oriented epistemology. Among the three types of validity claims, the type (b) speech act, in which a speaker raises the claim that a statement is correct in terms of the prevailing normative context, has special importance for Habermas's theory of society.

When the idea of communicative rationality is used to define the type (b) speech act, the ultimate ends of an action are no longer rationalized on the basis of Kantian practical reason. If the object of a claim is defined discursively, Kant's moral philosophy ought to give a place to discursive ethics. Habermas thus argues that his consensual epistemology has provided a moral theory with a new knowledge base involving the speaker and the hearer in a debate on the correctness of their moral claims with regard to the prevailing normative context (or the legitimacy of the normative context itself). Speaker and hearer apply their communicative reason to see whether they can arrive at a justified consensus on the moral claims in question. Habermas (1990) claims that his discursive ethics give the rational actor autonomy for exploration of whether his moral claim regarding the ultimate values is 'rational'.

Habermas's theory of society: communicative reason and social order

I have argued that Habermas applies his epistemology to show how communicative reason enables the actors to reach a moral consensus on validity claims regarding ultimate values. Instrumental rationality is also used by the actors to find effective means to realize such ultimate values.

Habermas (1981a: xl) reminds us that

> The concept of communicative action . . . provides access to three intertwined topic complexes: first, a concept of communicative rationality that is sufficiently skeptical in its development but is nevertheless resistant to cognitive-instrumental abridgments of reason; second, a two-level concept of society that connects the "lifeworld" and "system" paradigms . . . and finally, a theory of modernity that explains the type of social pathologies that are today becoming increasingly visible . . .

In brief, the models of rational action enable Habermas to develop his theories of social order and social evolution.

As Thompson (1983: 281) recognizes, the distinction made by Habermas between 'action oriented toward reaching understanding' and 'action oriented towards success' guides him to two different mechanisms of action coordination at the societal level.

> When actors are oriented to the realization of their own ends, when their actions are co-ordinated through egocentric calculations and are appraised in terms of their efficacy, Habermas speaks of "action oriented to success", a category which he further divides into "instrumental action" and "strategies action". When, on the other hand, actors are oriented to reaching an understanding with other actors through a co-operative process of discussion, so that their actions are co-ordinated by, and assessed in terms of, a collective agreement which is the condition for pursuing their own plans, Habermas speaks of "action oriented to reaching understanding".

In this sense, these models of action coordination are used to address the question of social order in terms of a social coordination of personal actions seeking to achieve private goals under a normative agreement.

Unlike Parsons, Habermas is not concerned with the Hobbesian problem of social order. If he were, a potential solution for the problem of social order based on his action types of rationality might be imaginable: due to individual communicative rationality and through an intersubjective process of reaching understanding, rational actors might be able to create a system of ultimate values upon which a peaceful social order could be built. However, Habermas's rejection of the teleological model of action causes him to ignore such a solution for the problem of social order. Unlike Parsons, Habermas does not argue that the action types of value and instrumental rationality ought to be merged into *one* unit act. Hence, communicative action does not lead Habermas to replace Kant's moral theory with discursive ethics in order to show the possibility of a rational discussion on the ultimate values.

136 Justificationism and the theory of society

Habermas's models of rational action and the concept of society

Habermas applies the action types of communicative and instrumental rationality as separate units of human action, each following its own internal logic. As argued earlier, the action type of communicative rationality enables rational actors to coordinate their plans in order to reach an agreement, i.e. a justified consensus on legitimate norms of behaviour. The action type of instrumental rationality also allows rational actors to orient their efforts in order to find effective means when actions are coordinated by egocentric calculation based on the efficiency maxim. With the aid of these two separate unit acts, the problem of social order finds a different solution. Instead of arguing that a system of common values internalized in the actor's personality prevents him from egoistic behaviour, Habermas (1981b) suggests a *two-level concept* of society encompassing the two units of rational action, the 'lifeworld' or everyday communication, on the one hand, and the 'system' of society, on the other: *communicative rationality* as well as *instrumental rationality*.

Habermas argues that

> . . . the notion of life-world as a correlate of the concept of communicative action: it refers to collectively shared background convictions, to the diffuse, unproblematic, horizon *within which* actors communicate with one another and seek to reach an understanding. The life-world of a society or social group preserves and transmits the interpretative work of preceding generations. . . . Actions are not only embedded in the symbolic space of the life-world, but they are also organized into functional systems. Hence societies must be conceived *simultaneously* as system and life-world . . .
>
> (Thompson 1983: 285)

However, the individual's communicative rationality is not accounted as a cognitive capacity that lets actors attain a system of common values and prevents a 'war of all against all'. Since the lifeworld of society and the system components of society follow different forms of logic at the individual level, the resultant social order cannot be analysed in terms of a unified model of rational action. Hence, for the lifeworld of society, a justified consensus among individuals coordinates people's actions through moral consciousness, whereas, for the system component, the individual's pursuit of success, in terms of finding effective tools for realizing personal given ends, leads to a struggle for power and wealth.

Since these two levels of social formation follow different rationales, they also integrate society in different ways: the consensual mechanism of action coordination as a normative form of social ordering based on mutual understanding as well as a systemic form of social ordering of people pursuing wealth and power with the aim of successful achievement of their ends. Hence, an unavoidable tension between the normative and the systemic forms of 'action coordination' as the mechanisms of social ordering is to be expected in Habermas's theory of society.

Habermas's theory of social evolution: the logic of social development

The two concepts of system and lifeworld forms determine key aspects of Habermas's theory of social evolution, with communicative and instrumental action providing an explanation of social evolution through the mechanism of social learning. As Habermas (1981b: 118) observes, ". . . we conceive of societies *simultaneously* as systems and lifeworlds. This concept proves itself in . . . a theory of social evolution that separates the rationalization of the lifeworld from the growing complexity of societal systems . . .". The ideal types of rational action help Habermas to suggest that the expansion of a child's cognitive development to include the stages of moral development in society may lead to awareness of the evolution of society in terms of *normative* and *systemic* integration.

Habermas (1981b: 153–154) understands

> social evolution as a second-order process of differentiation: system and lifeworld are differentiated in the sense that the complexity of the one and the rationality of the other grow. But it is not only qua system and qua lifeworld that they are differentiated; they get differentiated from one another at the same time. It has become conventional for sociologists to distinguish the stages of social evolution as tribal societies, traditional societies, or societies organized around a state, and modern societies . . . From the system perspective, these stages are marked by the appearance of new systematic mechanisms and corresponding levels of complexity. On this plane of analysis, the uncoupling of system and lifeworld is depicted in such a way that the lifeworld, which is at first coextensive with a scarcely differentiated social system, gets cut down more and more to one subsystem among others.

However, from a micro-perspective, the question is how Habermas uses his ideal types of rational action to develop his theory of social evolution.

For Habermas,

> The rationalization of social systems can be characterized in terms of their *growth in complexity*. From this perspective one can analyse the formation and expansion of markets organized around the medium of money and the steady growth of political and administrative organizations. The rationalization of life-worlds, on the other hand, can be characterized in terms of both the *separation of spheres of values and the advancement of levels of learning*.
>
> (Thompson 1983: 287)

Given these two levels of social rationalization, the action type of instrumental rationality shows the extent to which the growth of complexity is an unintended outcome of instrumental actions pursuing self-interest, whereas the sense

138 Justificationism and the theory of society

rationality of the lifeworld makes use of communicative actions in order to improve mutual understanding.

> Habermas argues that social evolution can be understood on an analogy with the moral and intellectual development of individuals growing to maturity. . . . It is in this context that Habermas refers to the moral learning process as "the pacemaker of social evolution".
>
> (Kirkpatrick 2003: 93)

However, this raises the question of whether the equivalence between the individual's maturation and social development explains how human action contributes to social evolution.

In *Communication and the Evolution of Society*, Habermas (1979: 99) argues:

> Cognitive developmental psychology has shown that in ontogenesis there are different stages of moral consciousness, stages that can be described in particular as preconventional, and postconventional patterns of problemsolving. The same patterns turn up again in the social evolution of moral and legal representations. The ontogenetic models are certainly better analyzed and better corroborated than their social-evolutionary counterparts. But it should not surprise us that there are *homologous structures* of consciousness in the history of the species, if we consider that linguistically established intersubjectivity of understanding marks that innovation in the history of the species which first made possible the level of sociocultural learning (emphasis added).

It is this *homologous* expansion of the child's stage of cognitive/moral development to the stages of moral consciousness of society that provides Habermas with his logic of social development.

Michael Schmid (1982: 164) argues that the ontogenesis of the individual refers to a specific developmental logic that can be documented in several spheres:

> in a cognitive sphere (the capacity for formal thought), a moral sphere (the capacity for moral judgment), and in a sphere of interaction (referring to an interactive competence based on normatively guided actions which are oriented to the actions of others).

These remarks underline Habermas's conception of the relation between the stages of normative development in society and the ontogenesis of the individual.

In order to address the question of how worldviews have developed in the transition from a traditional to a modern society,

> . . . Habermas draws on Piaget's ontogenetic studies of cognitive development. These studies suggest that the development of world-views can be

Justificationism and the theory of society 139

grasped as a progressive demarcation of the objective and social worlds from the subjective world of experience – that is, as a "decentration" of an ego-centric understanding of the world. Piaget's work also enables one to distinguish several stages of development *within* the dimension of moral-practical insight. Thus, Habermas employs the distinction between pre-conventional, conventional and post-conventional structures of moral consciousness in order to reconstruct the logic of development of law and morality in the transition from clan societies to the modern day.

(Thompson 1983: 286)[2]

However, communicative reason has not been used to indicate how mature actors rationalize their worldviews in the evolution of social order.

Justificationism and Habermas's theory of society

Habermas's theory of society faces a major problem in *the cognitive possibility of action-coordination due to the infinite regress involved in consensual epistemology*. This cognitive problem leads to a second one regarding the theory of social evolution: *the possibility of social evolution through attainment of a higher level of social integration*. These problems arise because Habermas creates a close link between knowledge as justified consensus and the speech act as an action oriented towards reaching understanding. If Habermas's theories of knowledge and rationality are justificationist, then the mechanism of coordination of individual actions and the logic of its evolution also involve infinite regress and hence cannot tell us how social order shapes and evolves.

If the justificatory nature of the action types of communicative and instrumental rationality is recognized due to its concept of knowledge as justified consensus, then the ideal types of action deal with the dilemma of infinite regress, meaning that the 'rationality' of such actions is under-theorization. In these circumstances, the very possibility of intersubjective coordination of individual actions at the societal level faces the major epistemological problem of infinite regress. If the speakers and the hearers cannot reach understanding because of their incapability to offer each other *justifying reasons*, then their conversation cannot result in a societal coordination of their actions. Hence, one could say that Habermas's theory of knowledge is unable to inform us of how the rise of social order is possible at the lifeworld or system level due to its justificationist foundation. Since a 'rational' action, whether communicative or instrumental, cannot be shaped on the basis of justified consensus, Habermas's models of rational action do not suffice to enable his theory of social order to prove that individuals' actions can be coordinated at the societal level by means of reaching understanding and finding effective means.

The same epistemological critique can be levelled at Habermas's theory of social evolution. If the material complexity and normative solidarity in society evolves and rationality is defined as intersubjective consensus, then the same

140 Justificationism and the theory of society

infinite regress arises. From a micro-perspective, one may argue that individuals' communicative and instrumental reason would pave the way for them to rationalize their actions in order to ensure a higher level of complexity and normative solidarity. However, such an argument cannot be defended because consensual epistemology does not permit a process of social learning with evolving levels of rationalization in society. Since the notion of *justified consensus* involves infinite regress, such an argument would also face the same epistemological problem.

Habermas's epistemology of justified consensus prevents his theory of communicative action form giving human action a 'causal' role in social change. This theory of society argues that we should speak of logic rather than the mechanism, of social evolution since, hypothetically, a child's stages of cognitive development can be expanded analogically to the stages of social development. In Chapter 7, I apply the non-justificationist concept of rationality to show how the philosophy of critical rationalism may help us to suggest a new theory of the society addressing not only the question of social order, but also the problem of social change.

Notes

1 In *Weberian Sociological Theory*, Randall Collins (1990: 19) argues: "The argument that the Calvinist doctrine of predestination gave the psychological impetus for rationalized, entrepreneurial capitalism is only a fragment of a Weber's full theory". Collins continues: "Weber's institutional model characterizes capitalism by a complex of traits; rationalized technology; free labor; unrestricted markets for mass-produced products; and the entrepreneurial organization of capital. . . . In general, the interplay of religious and political organizational forms has been responsible for creating these institutional preconditions" (1990: 46–47). Weber's sociology considers all such institutional developments as preconditions for the rise of capitalism.
2 See Richard Kitchener's (1986) *Piaget's Theory of Knowledge*. Kitchener analyzes Piaget's epistemology in relation to traditional theories of knowledge such as rationalism, empiricism and Kantianism. He then turns to Piaget's own epistemology and explores Piaget's claim that epistemology is autonomous and can become an empirical science.

Bibliography

Albrow, M. (2006) "The Application of the Weberian Concept of Rationalization to Contemporary Conditions". In: Whimster, S. & Lash, S. (eds.) *Max Weber, Rationality and Modernity*. London, Routledge, pp. 164–182.

Alexander, J.C. (1988) *Action and Its Environment: Toward a New Synthesis*. New York, Columbia University Press.

Alexander, J.C., Giesen, B., Munch, R. & Smelser, N.J. (eds.) (1987) *The Micro-Macro Link*. Berkeley, University of California Press.

Bellah, R.N. (ed.) (1973) *Emile Durkheim. On Morality and Society, Selected Writings*. Chicago, University of Chicago Press.

Bendix, R. (1998) *Max Weber: An Intellectual Portrait*. London, Routledge.

Bourricaud, F. (1981) *The Sociology of Talcott Parsons*, Goldhammer, A. Chicago, University of Chicago Press.

Cladis, M.S. (1992) "Durkheim's Individual in Society: A Sacred Marriage?". In: *Journal of the History of Ideas*, 53 (1), pp. 71–90.

Collins, R. (1990) *Weberian Sociological Theory*. New York, Cambridge University Press.

Durkheim, E. (1995 [1915]) *The Elementary Forms of Religious Life*, Fields, K.E. (trans.). New York, Free Press.

Habermas, J. (1990) "Discursive Ethics: Notes on a Program of Philosophical Justification". In: Lenhardt, C. & Nicholson, S.W. (eds.) *Moral Consciousness and Communicative Action*. Cambridge, MIT Press, pp. 43–115.

Habermas, J. (1981a) *The Theory of Communicative Action, Vol. 1: Reason and the Rationalization of Society*, McCarthy, T. (trans.). Boston, Beacon Press.

Habermas, J. (1981b) *The Theory of Communicative Action, Vol. 2: Lifeworld and System: A Critique of Functionalist Reason*, McCarthy, T. (trans.). Boston, Beacon Press.

Habermas, J. (1979) *Communication and the Evolution of Society*, McCarthy, T. (trans.). Boston, Beacon Press.

Healy, P. (1987) "Is Habermas's Consensus Theory a Theory of Truth?". In: *Irish Philosophical Journal*, 4, pp. 145–152.

Hindess, B. (2006) "Rationality and the Characterization of Modern Society". In: Whimster, S. & Lash, S. (eds.) *Max Weber, Rationality and Modernity*. London, Routledge, pp. 137–153.

Kant, I. (1997 [1785]) *Groundwork of the Metaphysics of Morals*, Gregor, M.J. (trans., ed.). Cambridge, Cambridge University Press.

Kant, I. (1956 [1787]) *Critique of Practical Reason*, Beck, L.W. (trans.). Indianapolis, Bobbs-Merrill.

Kirkpatrick, G. (2003) "Evolution or Progress? A (Critical) Defense of Habermas's Theory of Social Development". In: *Thesis Eleven*, 72 (91), pp. 91–112.

Kitchener, R.F. (1986) *Piaget's Theory of Knowledge: Genetic Epistemology & Scientific Reason*. New Haven, Yale University Press.

Korsgaard, C.M. (2000) *Creation of the Kingdom of Ends*. Cambridge, Cambridge University Press.

Mommsen, W. (2006) "Personal Conduct and Societal Change". In: Whimster, S. & Lash, S. (eds.) *Max Weber, Rationality and Modernity*. London, Routledge, pp. 35–51.

Munch, R. (1981) "Talcott Parsons and the Theory of Action. I. The Structure of the Kantian Core". In: *American Journal of Sociology*, 86 (4), pp. 709–739.

Parsons, T. (2005 [1991]) *The Social System*. London, Routledge.

Parsons, T. (1968a [1937]) *The Structure of Social Action*, Vol. I: Marshall, Pareto, Durkheim. New York, Free Press.

Parsons, T. (1968b [1937]) *The Structure of Social Action*, Vol. II: Weber. New York, Free Press.

Parsons, T. (1963) "Introduction". In: Weber, M. (ed.) *The Sociology of Religion*, Fischoff, E. (trans.). Boston, Beacon Press, pp. vi–lxviii.

Parsons, T. (1935) "The Place of Ultimate Values in Sociological Theory". In: *International Journal of Ethics*, 45 (3), pp. 282–316.

Parsons, T. & Shils, E.A. (1962) "Valves, Motives, and Systems of Action". In: Parsons, T. & Shils, E.A. (eds.) *Towards a General Theory of Action*. London, Oxford University Press, pp. 47–243.

Rawls, A.W. (2004) *Epistemology and Practice, Durkheim's The Elementary Forms of Religious Life*. New York, Cambridge University Press.

142 Justificationism and the theory of society

Rawls, A.W. (1996) "Durkheim's Epistemology: The Neglected Argument". In: *American Journal of Sociology*, 102 (2), pp. 430–482.

Schmid, M. (1982) "Habermas's Theory of Social Evolution". In: Thompson, J.B. & Held, D. (eds.) *Habermas, Critical Debates*. London, Palgrave Macmillan, pp. 162–180.

Thompson, J.B. (1983) "Rationality and Social Rationalization: An Assessment of Habermas's Theory of Communicative Action". In: *Sociology*, 17 (2), pp. 278–294.

Warren, M. (1988) "Max Weber's Liberalism for a Nietzschean World". In: *The American Political Science Review*, 82 (1), pp. 31–50.

Weber, M. (2005 [1930]) *The Protestant Ethic and the Spirit of Capitalism*. London, Routledge.

Weber, M. (1968) In: Roth, G. & Wittich, C. (eds.) *Economy and Society: An Outline of Interpretative Sociology*. Berkeley, University of California Press.

Weber, M. (1963) *The Sociology of Religion*, Fischoff, E. (trans.). Boston, Beacon Press.

Whimster, S. & Lash, S. (eds.) (2006) *Max Weber, Rationality and Modernity*. London, Routledge.

Wrong, D.H. (1999) *The Oversocialized Conception of Man*. New Brunswick, Transaction Publishers.

Chapter 7

Critical rationalism and the theory of human action

Masoud Mohammadi Alamuti

Introduction

The question of how human action contributes to social order has a central place in sociological theory. This chapter applies the general theory of critical rationalism for reformulation of the ideal types of value and instrumental rationality. Its argument that the separation of justification and criticism enables the theory of action to avoid infinite regress lies in the very concept of reason that the utilitarian and the normative models of action employ to explain how reason may drive human action. The philosophy of critical rationalism offers a non-justificational concept of reason that lets the theory of action to address the role of rational actors in giving themselves a moral law to govern the pursuit of self-interest necessary for the rise of a peaceful social order. To these ends, the chapter proceeds in five sections.

Section I: non-justificationism and the rationality of action

As observed in Chapter 5, the separation of justification and criticism leads to the new conception that *a belief, whether moral or scientific, is rational if the premises and inference forms through which it is drawn are not shown to be false by argument or experience.* This section uses this new concept of rationality for redefining the ideal types of rational action at the core of the theory of action. For doing this, a look at the justificational foundations of the utilitarian and normative models of human action gives us important insights.

Justificationist theories of action: utilitarian and normative

As argued in Chapter 6, justificationist epistemology has contributed to the theory of action in classical and modern sociology. According to our case studies, justificationism is recognized in Durkheim's social epistemology, in Kantian epistemology, which influences Weber's and Parsons's sociologies, and in Habermas's

144   Critical rationalism and the theory of human action

consensual epistemology. In these case studies, the concept of rationality originates in the justified true belief account of knowledge, and the meaning of *rational* action is defined by such justificationist concepts of rationality.

It is worthy of note that, Durkheim and Parsons use the justificationist concepts of reason to develop a normative theory of action criticizing the utilitarian action theory. The utilitarian model of action implies that the means of action can be based on objective knowledge to inform us of the effective tools for realization of a given end although the action goals are subjective and incapable of being rational. From a non-justificationist perspective, utilitarians may argue that the goals of human action are subjective because the actor is unable to *justify* the moral claims regarding them by positive reasons. In other words, the action goal remains unjustified and is regarded as epistemologically irrational if a validity claim regarding the end of the action is to be justified in order to be considered true, but cannot be verified.

This justificational critique allows the utilitarian theory of action to claim that the goals of action are by nature subjective rather than objective. Since action ends are not based on objective knowledge, i.e. on justified true belief, the utilitarian model assumes them to be subjective. Hence, the utilitarian model claims that the goals of action are determined by passion, whereas the means of action are determined by reason due to the objective knowledge upon which the actor can justify the efficiency of the means for realizing the action end. The main upshot of this epistemological reading of the utilitarian concept of rationality for the theory of action is that *passion* drives action and that *reason* is only a servant of passion usable for finding effective means to actualize a given end.

However, Durkheim and Parsons realize that a peaceful social order cannot come into existence if individual actors follow mere passion and self-interest. Durkheim proposes his social epistemology, arguing that the categories of thought, such as space, time and causality, originate from religious practices. Hence, the rationality of the goals lies in the religious practices defining the categories of thought reflecting them. Durkheim argues that a system of values in society integrated into the categories of thought constructs the moral content of action goals. Unlike utilitarianism, Durkheim's theory views the categories of thought as objective social facts rather than subjective or personal preferences and claims that the objectivity of such categories is justifiable by experience. My argument against this, however, is that justification involves infinite regress, so Durkheim cannot prove the categories of thought as objective by his social epistemology. Thus, Durkheim's normative concept of rationality, in terms of categories of thought originating in society, suffers from infinite regress, which renders it unacceptable as solution to the problem of the rationality of action goals.

As argued in Chapter 6, Parsons presents his voluntaristic action theory as a critique of the utilitarian model. Inspired by Kantian epistemology, Parsons argues that the utilitarian claim that the ends of action are subjective means that, statistically, they are subject to random variation. However, as pointed out by Hans Joas

Critical rationalism and the theory of human action   145

(1996: 11), ". . . any possible statement akin to a law on the distribution of wishes would call into question the free will of each individual". Joas continues:

> To Parsons' mind the dilemma utilitarianism faces thus consists of it having either to assume that free will exists and therefore to assert that goals vary at random, or conversely to assume that goals do not vary at random, at the cost of no longer being able to find a place for free choice and individual decisions in its conceptual framework. Parsons considers the first assumption to be untenable, as there is no sense in human choice from among random goals. . . . Parsons insists that choice already presumes intrinsically unique structures in the sphere of alternative choices, as otherwise choice itself would resemble chance.
>
> (ibid.)

However, acceptance of Kant's epistemology and the resultant moral philosophy does not involve the assumption of goals of action guided by passions. Inspired by the Kantian doctrine of practical reason, Parsons offers a normative model of action.

In accordance with Parsons's voluntaristic model of action, the actor's value rationality determines the action goals by taking on a voluntary orientation towards the moral law existing in society. In fact, the actor *rationalizes* the ends by orienting them towards a system of values (the moral law). Given this Kantian foundation of Parsons's action theory, the problem of infinite regress appears. If Kant's theories of pure and practical reason involve infinite regress, then Parsons's voluntaristic theory of action faces the same problem. Hence, the goals of action cannot be assumed to be 'rationalized' by a voluntarily orientation towards a universal moral law. If Parsons's normative alternative for the utilitarian model is inspired by Kantian epistemology, then the rationality of the goals of action has not actually been addressed by his normative alternative due to its justificationism.

Non-justificationism and the theory of action

It has been argued that the utilitarian model cannot justify the subjectivity of the ends of action, nor can the normative models prove the objectivity and rationality of the ends because of their voluntarily orientation towards a system of values. In both cases, justificationism is what prevents the theory of action from showing the reason why the goals of action or their means may be rationalized through objective knowledge. While the utilitarian action model takes a justificationist position for rejecting the rationality of the ends, the normative model takes a justificationist position to show that rational ends are tenable. However, from a non-justificationist viewpoint, none of these models can defend the rationality of action ends. Thus, these models are unable to address how reason drives action through identifying its goals.

146   Critical rationalism and the theory of human action

My thesis is that the separation of justification and criticism enables us to find a non-justificationist solution to the problem of action theory, in terms not only of the rationality of ends, but also of the rationality of means. The philosophy of critical rationalism points out that an action goal or a means is *rational* if it rests on an 'unfalsified belief' whose premises or inferences are not shown to be false by argument or experience. If our definition of rationality is changed from a justified true belief account to an unfalsified-conjectural account, our ideal types of 'rational' action also ought to be reformulated on the basis of such a separation of justification and criticism.

A non-justificational reading of the concept of rationality in the ideal type of human action means that the rationality of the ends cannot be denied for the unacceptable reason that our claims of rationality regarding the ends cannot be *justified*. If the demand for justification is mistaken, why should the goals of action be justifiable in order to be rational? Neither the ends nor the means are to be justified in order to be objective rather than subjective. However, when the ends or the means of an action are *not* shown to be *false*, then both the means and the ends are considered *rational* because, from an epistemological viewpoint, unfalsified conjectures support the moral validity of the goals in question and the scientific efficiency of the means in question.

Therefore, a non-justificationist concept of rationality renders the utilitarian notion of rationality baseless simply because the ends of the action can be established on critical rationality, just as the means may also be. Hence, neither the ends nor the means of an action require justification in order to be rationalized, they only need to be based on unfalsified beliefs in order to be accounted as rational. This non-justificationist definition of rationality allows refutation of the utilitarian notion of rationality in favour of a critical rationalist action model showing that reason rather than passion drives human action.

The non-justificationist account of rational belief helps us to realize why the normative models of action offered by Weber and Parsons are unable to prove that goals are rational. In the case of Kantian epistemology, the argument is that the actor chooses the ends of the action by using 'pure' reason to address the 'practical' question of what the ultimate ends of our life should be. The notion of practical reason implies that the actor uses it to give himself a universal moral law and that his goals of action are considered rational if they are shaped through orientation towards such a universal moral law. However, due to Kant's justificationism, Weber's and Parsons's ideal types of value rationality face the problem of infinite regress. The proposed non-justificationist concept of rational beliefs as those whose premises and inferences are not shown to be false provides the theory of human action with a new explanation of *rational* ends and means.

Section II: the problem situation in action theory

In order to understand the real problem of action theory, I suggest reformulating the Hobbesian problem of social order. This reformulation prepares the ground for offering a 'critical rationalist theory of action'.

The Hobbesian approach to the problem of action

Hobbes argues that man

> . . . is guided by a plurality of passions. The good is simply that which any man desires. . . . But reason is essentially a servant of the passions – it is the faculty of devising ways and means to secure what one desires. Desires are random, there is "no common rule of good and evil to be taken from the nature of the objects themselves". Hence since the passions, the ultimate ends of action, are diverse there is nothing to prevent their pursuit resulting in conflict.
>
> (Parsons 1968 [1937]: 89)

Parsons rightly observes that this Hobbesian problem creates an important challenge for sociological theory.

This Hobbesian picture of human nature leads Parsons to argue that the very existence of social order means that the Hobbesian definition of the actor as a utility maximizing agent ought to be false. Parsons then proposes his voluntaristic action model: since a system of values guides the ends of an action, one may speak of a moral man as a civilized member of society who does not fight with others. This is what makes a peaceful social order possible. A tautological argument can be seen in such an argument: since human beings are socialized actors, their actions are guided by common values preventing them from a 'war of all against all'. In 'The Oversocialized Conception of Man in Modern Sociology', Dennis H. Wrong (1999: 31–46) recognizes this problem and questions the Hobbesian concept of an actor with a plurality of passions driving action if human beings can be civilized by using reason to control their egoistic behaviour. The assumption that the actor is a Kantian moral man, on the one hand, and a Hobbesian utility maximizer, on the other would be a self-contradiction.

Inspired by Kantian practical reason, Parsons argues that reason drives action. Kant himself goes even further by saying that reason enables the actors to give to themselves a moral law governing their action. Parsons, however, does not follow this line of reasoning, realizing that practical reason has not made it possible for all persons to reach a rational consensus upon one system of values. Nevertheless, Parsons admits that moral humans who respect the existing system of values can rationalize the goals of action and thus justify the idea that it is *reason* that drives action.

Critical rationalism and the problem of action theory

Critical rationalism should be used to address the problem posed by action theory of whether it is reason or passion that drives human action. Kant's practical reason and its critique of utilitarianism lead to an understanding that critical rationalism allows us to reformulate the problem of action theory. From Kant's moral

148 Critical rationalism and the theory of human action

philosophy, the critical rationalist understands the distinction between a rational human being and a non-rational creature: it is the human actor's access to reason that specifies the action of a rational being.

For Kant, it is reason that makes man an *active* being and, as pointed out by Christine Korsgaard (2000: xi),

> ... insofar as we are rational, we also regard ourselves as *action* beings, who are the authors of our thoughts and choices. We do not regard our thoughts and choices merely as things that *happen* to us; rather, thinking and choosing are things that we *do*. To this extent, we must view ourselves as *noumena*.

Kant then comes to argue: "And from this standpoint, we recognize laws that govern our mental powers in a different way than the laws of nature do . . .". With these considerations in mind, it is access to reason that shapes the problem of action when viewing humans as rational beings. For Kant, "The project of critical moral philosophy is to determine what resources we can find in reason for solving the problem which reason itself has set for us" (ibid.). Kant develops his model of action by applying the notion of pure reason to solve the problem of 'What should I do?' Practical reason enables the actor to be an 'active' creature in the sense that he can give himself a moral law to govern his behaviour.

Following Kant's argument, I propose the question of what resources we can find in critical reason for identifying the problem of action. From a critical rationalist perspective, the problem of action theory is defined by the question of *how critical reason drives human action*. With this problem in mind, the ground is prepared for offering a new theory of action.

Section III: critical rationalism, moral philosophy and human action

In one sense, the goal of an action is the state of affairs that the actor attempts to reach. Hence, the role of an actor's access to critical reason in achieving such a state of affairs finds central importance in solving the problem of action theory. While Kant realizes that the resource we find in reason can be used to solve the problem of action, his solution, i.e. practical reason, involves infinite regress. Having said that, a new theory of rationality is required to overcome the 'problem of human action'.

Moral philosophy: from 'practical' reason to 'critical' reason

The separation of justification and criticism in moral philosophy leads to a key reform in the doctrine of practical reason based on the idea critical rationalism. If Kant's justificationism does not allow for showing how reason actually determines the goals of action, then his moral philosophy has failed to fulfil its task. That is

Critical rationalism and the theory of human action   149

reason why the normative approaches of Weber and Parsons cannot address the rationality of action ends and does not provide us with a correct answer to the question of how reason drives action. While their critique of the utilitarian model is valuable, their Kantian alternative is not tenable for it involves infinite regress.

Under this condition, the general theory of critical rationalism suggests a new foundation for the theory of action, showing that it is reason, not a plurality of passions, that guides human action. In his *Critique of Practical Reason*, Kant (1956 [1788]: 29) asks, "How would a free will with nothing constraining or guiding it determine its actions?" His answer is by moral law. Kant argues that there must be an 'uncaused cause' in the noumenal world of rational beings for an unconditional explanation of the phenomenon to be given. The resources that Kant looks for in pure reason to enable him to find a 'practical' solution for the 'problem' of rational action may be interpreted in the following manner: due to a human being's access to reason, there must be an 'uncaused cause' of action reflecting this free will. Kant establishes his theory of practical reason on the aforementioned usage of his resource in terms of pure reason.

However, justificationism forces Kant to conclude wrongly that pure reason cannot justify the objectivity of a metaphysical judgment such as a universal moral law. According to Kant's theory of knowledge, a priori true categories of thought are not imposable on a metaphysical object. Since Kant defines knowledge as justified true belief, his *critique of pure reason* leading to his *critique of practical reason* suffers from infinite regress. In other words, with logical rejection of the demand for justification, Kant's *critique of pure reason* to solve the problem of rational action loses its epistemological foundation. However, the separation of justification and criticism requires a shift from the idea of practical reason as the Kantian solution to the problem of action to the idea of critical reason as a new resource bedded in reason to overcome the problem of human action. Hence, a non-justificationist moral philosophy can enable us to indicate the reason why the ends of an action are not subjective, but capable of being objective and rational.

With this clarification in place, moral philosophy may use the general theory of critical rationalism to show how a moral claim regarding the ends of action can be judged rationally, provided that none of its premises and inferences are shown to be false. According to Kant,

> Rational beings are the determiners of ends – the ones who set value on things. So a rational being must value rational nature as an end in itself; and it is with this end in view that we act only on maxims which could be universal laws. Since we are the ones who make rational nature our end, we are the ones who give ourselves this law. We are autonomous.
>
> (Korsgaard 2000: 22)

However, if justificationism does not allow Kant to prove such a theory of rational action, a new theory rational action is to be presented to offer a non-justificational solution. I suggest the general theory of critical rationalism that lets

150 Critical rationalism and the theory of human action

us have a non-justificational theory of action and shows that critical reason drives action not only through action goals but also through action means.

Section IV: the theory of human action: a critical rationalist formulation

This section introduces a theory of human action based on a non-justificationist conception of rationality and leads to a new reformulation of the two action types of value rationality and instrumental rationality that situates these two in one unit act. The use of non-justificational epistemology to define a belief as rational if its premises and inferences are not shown to be false may be applied to rationalize not only the ends of an action but also its means.

Motivated by Kant's theory of action, I argue that defining the concepts of knowledge and rationality as unfalsified conjectures and beliefs would avoid infinite regress and reveal how the goals and means of an action are capable of being rational. In this sense, the Kantian *agency* of the rational being is found in his access *to critical reason*. This non-justificational concept of reason lets us see how critical reason drives human action. Due to the objective knowledge upon which the actor can rationalize the ends and means of his action, we can say that critical reason rather than passion, guides action. With this non-justificational concept of reason in mind, one can no longer say that the *unjustifiability* of the goals of action by argument or experience is a basis for accounting them as subjective and hence that the action is guided by passions. Thus, non-justificationist concept of reason leads to new ideal types of value and instrumental reason.

The non-justificationist action type of value rationality

In Chapter 6, I have described how that the ideal type of value rationality applied by Weber and Parsons in the development of their own sociological theory originated in Kant's moral philosophy. In brief, human action is guided by practical reason because of the existence of a universal moral law that individuals give themselves and the respect of which enables them to control their egotistic behaviour. However, the infinite regress causing the inability of Kant's practical reason to address the free will of rational beings due to their access to reason is also involved in the Weberian and Parsonian ideal types of value rationality.

In contrast to the above-mentioned similarity to the Kantian theory, the non-justificationist concept of knowledge makes a redefinition of value rationality possible. In his critique of Kant's practical reason, Weber claims that a universal moral law cannot be justified due to the existing plurality of value systems in human societies. Weber's critique of Kantian practical reason is, however, justificational. Inspired by Durkheim and in order to solve the Hobbesian problem of social order, Parsons (1968 [1937]) accepts that there should *one* system of value in a given national society and defines the action type of value rationality in terms of the actor's voluntarily orientation to such a system of values. Thus, the ideal type of value rationality enables Parsons's theory of society to base its claim of a peaceful social order on a unification of the action types of value and instrumental rationality into one unit act. According to this unit act, the actor's reason allows him to choose one system of values as the ultimate source of his action goals by means of which he can manage his egocentric and instrumental pursuit of self-interest in a socialization process. Parsons's unified model action is also called the ends-means framework of human action.[1]

However, even the acceptance of one system of ultimate values in society common to all does not let Kantian practical reason argue that the actor applies reason to internalize the value system in his personality. As argued in Chapter 6, justificationism of the doctrine of practical reason involves the process of socialization in infinite regress. Under these conditions, neither Weber's nor Parsons's ideal types of value rationality can serve as the micro-foundation for a macro-theory of society to show that social order exists because individuals apply practical reason to drive their actions.

On the other hand, when the separation of justification and criticism takes place at the level of the theory of human action, infinite regress is avoided, and the non-justificational action type of value rationality can provide the theory of society with a proper micro-foundation. The ideal type of value rationality concerns the goals of action, which are rational insofar as they follow universal moral law. From the perspective of critical rationalism, the goals of action are rational provided their ultimate values are establishes on unfalsified moral beliefs. If our moral claims regarding such values can be subjected to criticism, then the action ends can be accounted for as *rational* although the moral claims are not shown as false. Thus, critical reason is what drives human action by defining rational ends for an action.

A non-justificationist ideal type of instrumental rationality

The notion of instrumental reason is described by the sociological theories of Weber, Parsons and Habermas as an application of reason for finding the effective means to realize a given end. This concept does not refer to a voluntary orientation towards a system of values, but rather to the pursuit of success. To understand this ideal type of action, a brief reference to the Kantian separation of the spheres of science, ethics and art is insightful.

While Kant separates these spheres of knowledge, what unifies them in their diversity in terms of content is the *form of justification* used by each of them to defend its claims of knowledge. Hence, not only is Kant's theory of ethics justificationist, but also is his theory of science. Whereas Weber and Parsons establish their notion of value rationality on Kant's moral theory, they base their concept of instrumental reason upon his theory of science (Albrow 2006). This means that the actor uses scientific knowledge to justify the effectiveness of a means for the

152 Critical rationalism and the theory of human action

realization of an end. Hence, the problem of infinite regress is involved not only in Kant's theory of ethics in the concept of value rationality, but also in his theory of science in the notion of instrumental reason. Thus, one can fairly argue that Kantian epistemology is unable to address the rationalization of the goals of an action and does not allow instrumental reason to understand the role of reason in finding effective means. The reason for this is simply because both of these ideal types of action rest on the justified true belief account of knowledge and consequently face the infinite regress of proofs.

However, the idea of the separation of justification and criticism leads the micro-foundations of the macro-theory of society to a new action type of instrumental rationality. A non-justificationist theory of science that defines objective knowledge in terms of unfalsified conjecture establishes the concept of reason in the action type of instrumental rationality. If the means of action are effective tools for realizing the goals of action, then they have to be based on knowledge claims that are not shown to be false by experience. The method of conjecture and refutation is applied to discover what means are capable of realizing a given end. Basing the action types of value and instrumental rationality on the non-justificational theory of knowledge prepares the way for unification of these two ideal types in *one* unit act.

Critical rationalism and the 'emancipatory' ideal type of human action

With the understanding of the actor as the author of the goals of action that the philosophy of critical rationalism provides, it is also possible to argue for dividing the ideal action type of value rationality into 'emancipatory' and 'ordinary' action. This distinction directs us to a new understanding of the theory of action. Kantian moral philosophy implies that practical reason gives the actor agency for defining a universal moral law towards which the ends of an action are oriented. I now suggest advancing the general theory of critical rationalism from the role of value rationality according to its Parsonian reading to the role played by 'critical reason', which allows the actors to give themselves a system of values for determining the goals of action. This is what I call an ideal type of emancipatory action.

Non-justificationist epistemology facilitates a significant transition from the oversocialized man to an independent actor reflecting the capacity of the individual actor to create a universal moral law, i.e. a system of values, rather than merely respecting a *given* system of values common to all.

The emancipatory type of rational action

Parsons's (1968 [1937]) theory of voluntaristic action portrays human action through four major elements: (a) the ends (the state of affairs) towards which the process of action shapes, (b) the means by which the ends are to be realized,

Critical rationalism and the theory of human action 153

(c) the environmental (social and natural) conditions within which an action takes place and (d) a normative orientation taken by the actor, i.e. an 'effort' combining the elements of a unit act to shape action as a whole. With this definition of a unit act in mind, the normative orientation of an action refers to the actor's usage of practical reason to internalize a given system of values in the ends of his action. Instrumental reason is also used as the cognitive capacity that the actor employs to find the most effective tools to meet the ends. Human access to instrumental reason allows the actor to realize how the environment of an action may contribute to the goals of the action. However, this definition of a unit act by Parsons forgets the emancipatory nature of Kant's model of rational action, which is critical for seeing an independent role for the actors as the authors of moral law given to themselves by *themselves*.

Due to its usage of pure reason for solving the practical problem of what one should do, Kant's theory of rational action is significant for the emancipatory action type. Reason leads the human being to the realization that his capability to reason enables him to be the author of the moral law governing his action. By means of this moral law, the actor determines what ought to be the goals of his action. The general theory of critical rationalism replaces Kant's practical reason with critical reason, which does not involve infinite regress. In order to be the authors of our goals, we do not have to *justify* the validity claims regarding the goals; we only need to *falsify* them by checking the truth of the premises or inferences upon which the validity claims are formulated.

In this sense, the separation of justification and criticism in the theory of knowledge leads us to a new model of emancipatory action as an alternative not only for the Kantian model of action, but also for its imperfect applications by Weber's and Parsons's models of action. This alternative of emancipatory action for the creation of a system of values and social institutions demarcates itself from ordinarily action people perform in their daily life when taking their system of values as a given fact and using instrumental reason to find the most effective tools for the realization of ultimate values. Whereas Durkheim's and Parsons's justificationist epistemology reflects an oversocialized conception of man as merely respecting established values and institutions, the epistemology of critical rationalism introduces the concept of an emancipated actor using objective knowledge to act independently of his conditions and interests in order to express his capacity to give himself a universal moral law necessary for peaceful social order.

The ordinary type of rational action

The system of common values that individual actors create using critical reason is the basis on which social institutions may be established and becomes the given normative point of reference towards which individuals orient their action goals. The internalization of common values in the personal identities of individual actors refers to the *ordinary type of human action*. Within the context of these daily actions, actors use instrumental reason to consider social and natural conditions and find effective means for realizing the goals of action.

It is only in the ordinary action type that Parsons's unit act finds its correct meaning in the assumption of a system of values and a set of social conditions as the given outcome of human action with the actor's ends and means shaped pursuant to the optimal behaviour of the actor. According to Parsons's definition of the unit act, the actor uses practical reason to integrate common values into his goals through the socialization process. Moreover, the actor applies instrumental reason in his daily life in order to explore effective devices for turning ideal goals into reality. Hence, the action type of emancipatory behaviour remains outside of Parsons's concept model of unit act.

For the critical rationalist action type of ordinary behaviour, the Parsonian unit act requires revision to inform us how an ordinary action occurs. The justificationist psychology Parsons borrowed from Freud's theory of ego development is no longer sufficient for explaining the process of socialization. We can understand the actor's socialization by looking at the process of conjecture and refutation that integrates social values in personal identity. In addition, the actor benefits from instrumental reason to surmise effective means for a given end and check the validity of such a conjecture by experience. Hence, I suggest reformulation of the ordinary type of human action to base it on the epistemology of critical rationalism.

The critical rationalist theory of action proposes firstly examining the unit of action from a vertical perspective to divide it into emancipatory and ordinary action. Secondly, a horizontal viewpoint divides the action unit into value and instrumental actions. In the vertical level, the actor's access to critical reason, in line with Kant's moral philosophy of free will, enables him to use the faculty of reason to give himself a system of ultimate values for addressing the question of what one should do. The philosophy of critical rationalism allows the theory of action to rescue itself from infinite regress. At the horizontal level of ordinary action, critical rationalism enables the action theory to provide a new explanation of the socialization process and reproduction of the social order through individuals' voluntarily respect for an already established value system.

In addition, instrumental reason is used for exploring environmental conditions and formulating effective means with non-justificational eyes via the logic of conjecture and refutation. At this ordinary action level, the action types of value and instrumental rationality are united in *one* unit act, as Parsons (1968 [1937]) has proposed. It is by this unification that integration of a system of values in the interests of the actors does not contradict an instrumental pursuit of effective means and thus prevents a 'war of all against all' in favour of a peaceful social order,

Now I propose my formulation of the critical rationalist theory of human action as follows:

> **Premise (i)**: Critical reason is the author of human action because action goals can be rationalized on the basis of objective knowledge, i.e. unfalsified conjectures about ultimate values.

Critical rationalism and the theory of human action   155

Premise (ii): Critical reason is the author of human action because action means can be rationalized on the basis of objective knowledge, i.e. unfalsified conjectures about effective tools.

Conclusion: Critical reason is the author of human action because not only action means, but also action goals can be rationalized on the basis of objective knowledge, i.e. unfalsified conjectures about ultimate values and effective tools.

In brief, the critical rationalist model of action suggests that actors use critical rationality to determine an action in terms of (a) its *goals* by addressing what the ultimate values in human life should be and (b) the *means* by addressing what the best means are for realizing given goals according to the social and natural conditions surrounding the action in question. The critical rationalist model of human action replaces the oversocialized man in modern sociology with an actor who can use his objective knowledge not only for the creation of a system of values as the moral foundation of a peaceful social order but also for revising the system of values with goal of social change.

Section V: from human action to social order: the rationalization of society

As argued in Chapter 6, the sociological theories of Parsons and Habermas do not link human action and social order in a causal manner. In other words, the theory of society they propose does not show how the individual actors apply practical or communicative reason to reach an agreement upon a system of shared values necessary for social order. In addition, Parsons and Habermas do not explain how the actor employs 'practical' or 'communicative' reason for revising the established values in order to move from one social order to another. What these sociologists actually do is claim that there is a *homologous* relation between the standpoint of the individual and the social standpoint or an analogy between the stages of the person's cognitive/moral progress and the logic of social evolution (Habermas 1979).

From a scientific perspective, however, this kind of micro-macro link does not indicate the causal effect of human action on social order and its change. From a non-justificationist standpoint, the reason for this failure in modern sociology is that ideal types of rational action define the concept of rationality based on justificational epistemology. Insofar as sociologists use theories of knowledge with infinite regress to define 'rational' action, human reason *itself* cannot be an explanatory force for the formation of social order. Such an improper model of human action does not address the role of the actor's access to reason in allowing individuals to reach a rational agreement on a system of value. Hence, social order requiring such a value system cannot be linked to human action in a causal manner.

156   Critical rationalism and the theory of human action

From a non-justificational perspective, it would not be possible to use a justificationist concept of reason to argue that individuals give themselves a peaceful social order through a moral consensus on shared values simply because human reason does not perform as the justificational concept of it proposes. The same reproach applies to the theories of social change in Parsons's and Habermas's sociology for the analogical relation between the stages of the cognitive/moral development of child, as Jean Piaget (1948) and Lawrence Kohlberg (1971) suggest, and the logic of social evolution does not refer to a causal linkage between those stages. In fact, neither Habermas nor Parsons explains how communicative or practical reason enables human actors to revise their moral values and social institutions when they realize that the premises or inference of their values or institutions are shown to be false in the course of social change.

From human action to social order: the question of a causal link

The main advantage of the critical rationalist model of action is that it offers the theory of society a new concept of rationality without infinite regress. With a non-justificational conception of rationality, the action theory leads to addressing how individual actors apply the logic of conjectures and refutations for judging a validity claim regarding ultimate values as true if their premises or inference forms are shown to be false. Logically speaking, rationalization of the goals of an action becomes possible in a non-justificational manner, i.e. upon the basis of unfalsified beliefs rather than justified true beliefs. In addition, the actor may use reason to explore effective means for achieving ends based on scientific conjectures not shown to be refuted by experience.

If the non-justificationist theory of knowledge implies that actors base their goals or means on unfalsified conjectures, whether moral or scientific, at the individual level, then it is logically possible to argue that the actors employ critical reason at the intersubjective level to shape a rational dialogue in order to agree on a system of values and institutions. Since the actors can hold their moral beliefs open to criticism and refute them when they are shown to be false, they may reach a rational consensus on ultimate values that withstands the intersubjective test.

When one admits that human actors can use critical reason to become the authors of a system of common values they *themselves* give to *themselves*, one also accepts that the individual actors are, in fact, the authors of a peaceful social order for themselves. Once a system of shared values is established by the emancipatory actions of individuals, the actors who want to become new members of a society use critical reason for another purpose: for translating the ultimate values into their own personal goals through the process of socialization and the exploration of effective means to realize the ends.

The critical rationalist concepts of value and instrumental reason elucidate how human actors are the originators of social order through the moral law that they

Critical rationalism and the theory of human action 157

give to themselves. A critical rationalist reformulation of Kant's moral philosophy regards human beings – as rational beings – as the originators of social order due to their use of critical reason to agree on a universal moral law. However, this universal moral law does not need to be justified a priori as true, as in Kant's claim, but must be subjected to intersubjective criticism in order to be viewed as objective. The separation of justification and criticism enables the micro-foundations of the macro-theory of society to explain the causal link between human action and social order.

In addition, the aforementioned separation leads to a new analysis of how the actor uses reason to explore effective means for an end. It is an application of the logic of conjectures and refutations with regard to the means versus the ends of action that demarcates the action type of value rationality from the action type of instrumental rationality. In short, the causal link between human action and social order, whether in terms of the creation of ultimate values or with regard to the exploration of effective means, is explained through the non-justificationist theories of knowledge and rationality without facing the problem of the infinite regress of proofs.

Critical reason and the rationalization of society

An expansion of critical rationality from the individual level to a societal one indicates a rationalization of social order through learning from mistaken premises or inferences. In one sense, the emergence of common values and social institutions may be seen in terms of social rationalization. The causal mechanism of this expansion is the voluntarily involvement of the actors in a social dialogue whose logic is understandable through non-justificationist epistemology. Another application of such rationalization is the use of critical reason for internalizing common values into the personality of new members who want to become formal citizens of the society. Finally, the rationalization of the society in terms of the application of critical reason is found in the social structures operating as effective means to realize the ultimate values of individuals.

In the case of social change, the application of critical reason for the rationalization of society can also be explored. Since the actors are capable of using critical reason for revising their rational consensus on ultimate values once they are aware of wrong premises or inferences, they become the authors of social change. Inspired by Kant's action theory, rational actors are the authors not only of the ultimate values (moral law) they have given to themselves for the first time, but also of changing the previous reading of the moral law due to mistaken premises or inferences. Hence, access to critical reason enables human actors to behave as the motors of social change when they realize that the premises upon which they have deduced the ultimate values of their good life might be no longer valid. Then they start to explore how to revise the ultimate values, thus preparing the ground for a parallel change in the institutional structure of society in the areas of

158　Critical rationalism and the theory of human action

law, polity and economy. Hence, the critical rationalist model of action leads to replacement of the logic of social evolution in its Habermasian definition with a causal analysis of social change that regards the actors as agents of social evolution upon their decision to give themselves a new social order to better prevent a 'war of all against all'.

Yet the question remains whether individual actors come to see each other in *one* place and *one* time in order to enter into a rational dialogue on the ultimate values. The answer is negative. People cannot practice this pattern of rational dialogue to see whether they will reach an agreement on the ultimate meaning of the good life. In this case, what alternative model of rational dialogue for coming to an agreement on common values would be possible and could turn such a cultural agreement into the social institutions of law, polity and economy?

Three major agents of social dialogue

To address the aforementioned question, a three-level process of social dialogue is suggested. The three major agents of social dialogue, namely (a) thinkers, (b) social movements and (c) masses are linked together in terms of intersubjective learning, working together to achieve a rational agreement upon a system of moral values and social institutions.

The thinkers, who activate critical rationality sooner than the others, introduce the proposals for the ultimate values that they deem defensible in the context of worldviews and the place of man in them. The concept of the good life within which ultimate values find their own meaning also implies a system of social institutions necessary for realizing the proposed ideal of the good life. The thinkers are the *authors* of an ideal type of social order that they offer society for addressing the question of how people can organize themselves to live together in a peaceful and just social order.

Social movements are the second major agent of social dialogue for the creation of values and institutions. These movements translate the ideal social order into tangible blueprints allowing ordinary persons to engage in a societal dialogue for the creation of social order. The social movements are the authors of social order and its change because of the important casual role they play in turning the ideal social order into a concrete form believable to the public at large.[2] This is the only way that the formation of a rational dialogue among individual members of society is imaginable through the process of social learning from mistaken premises or inferences.

Hence, ordinary people themselves are the third major agent in this rational dialogue for the creation of social order. Like the thinkers and the social movements, ordinary people (the masses) are the authors of the moral law they themselves give themselves due to their access to critical reason. They become the agents of a revision in their moral laws upon realizing that argument has shown their moral beliefs regarding the ideal place of man in a good life in the universe to be false.

Critical rationalism and moral dialogue for social order: a summary

Having learned from the previous arguments, one can argue that justification-ism has prevented the theory of society from defining a causal linkage between human action and social order in terms of an open dialogue among individuals for creating social order. Instead, it has proposed an *analogical* relation between the standpoint of the individual and the social standpoint.

The importance of a theory of action formulated through the philosophy of critical rationalism for the theory of society is its replacement of a justificationist concept of rationality with a non-justificationist one. This means that the action theory *models* human behaviour to give an actor, whether a thinker, a social activist or an ordinary person, the autonomy required for becoming the author of his actions. Hence, the critical rationalist theory of action leads to the mechanism of social dialogue that creates the moral foundation and institutional structure of society.

In summary, justificationist epistemology such as Durkheim's social epistemology, Parsons's idealist epistemology and Habermas's consensual epistemology do not lead to exploration of how human actors use reason to create a system of values necessary for social order. It is the non-justificationist theories of knowledge and rationality that enable the theory of action to show how thinkers, social movements and individuals contribute not only to the rise of a social order but also to its change. In the next chapters, a critical rationalist sociological theory of society will be introduced to apply the proposed theory of action for addressing the role of critical reason in the rationalization of society in some detail.

Notes

1 It is notable that the critical rationalist theory of action admits the ends-means framework of human action, with the goal, however, of understanding the rationalities of the ends and means within the context of the non-justificationist concept of rationality. Hans Joas (1996: 71–72), to the contrary, claims that we need to replace the ends-means framework of action with a reading situating the creativity of action at the core of the unit act. Nevertheless, I suggest that using the ends-means approach does not exclude the actors from being the creators of the ends or the means of their action.
2 See Jeffrey C. Alexander's (2006) *The Civil Sphere*. Alexander writes, "I would like to suggest that civil society should be conceived as a solidary sphere, in which a certain kind of universalizing community comes to be culturally defined and to some degree institutionally enforced. To the degree that this solidary community exists, it is exhibited and sustained by public opinion, deep cultural codes, distinctive organizations – legal, journalistic and associational – and such historically specific interactional practices as civility, criticism, and mutual respect" (2006: 31). This reading of the civil sphere leads an understanding of how thinkers contribute to social movements via the ideal of the universalizing community that they offer these movements and that will then be translated into the concrete definition of a good society for ordinary people.

Bibliography

Albrow, M. (2006) "The Application of the Weberian Concept of Rationalization to Contemporary Conditions". In: Whimster, S. & Lash, S. (eds.), *Max Weber, Rationality and Modernity*. London, Routledge, pp. 164–182.

Alexander, J.C. (2006) *The Civil Sphere*. New York, Oxford University Press.

Habermas, J. (1979) *Communication and the Evolution of Society*, McCarthy, T. (trans.). Boston, Beacon Press.

Joas, H. (1996) *The Creativity of Action*. Cambridge, Polity Press.

Kant, I. (1956 [1788]) *Critique of Practical Reason*, Smith, N.K. (trans.). New York, Palgrave Macmillan.

Kohlberg, L. (1971) "From Is to Ought". In: Mischel, T. (ed.), *Cognitive Development and Epistemology*. New York, Academic Press, pp. 151–236.

Korsgaard, C. (2000) *Creation of the Kingdom of Ends*. Cambridge, Cambridge University Press.

Parsons, T. (1968 [1937]) *The Structure of Social Action*, Vol. I: Marshall, Pareto, Durkheim. New York, The Free Press.

Piaget, J. (1948) *The Moral Judgment of the Child*, Gabain, M. (trans.). New York, The Free Press.

Wrong, D.H. (1999) *The Oversocialized Conception of Man*. New Brunswick, Transaction Publishers.

Chapter 8

The theory of social order
A critical rationalist understanding

Masoud Mohammadi Alamuti

Introduction

The question of how human action contributes to social order holds a central place in sociological theory. Chapter 7 has argued that the theory of action is used to address the problem of social order and that the function of 'reason' in the ideal types of human action ought to be defined by the general theory of critical rationalism offered in Chapter 5. Therefore, it is not surprising that reformulation of the theory of social order based on the philosophy of critical rationalism offers an entirely new account of reason and rationality to sociological theory. It is worth noting that replacement of the justificationist concept of rationality with a non-justificationist one is a *necessary* choice, *not* an optional one, due to the infinite regress involved with justification. The separation of justification and criticism enables the use of a tenable concept of reason in the sociology of social order.

After reformulating the problem of social order, Chapter 8 argues that individual actors apply critical rationality for shaping a set of five metaphysical, moral, legal, political and economic mechanisms to allow them to give *themselves* a peaceful social order. In addition, this chapter presents the role played by ordinary actions in the integration of common values into the personal identities of individuals as civilized members of the society and in the stabilization of their self-imposed social order.

Section I: the problem of social order: a reformulation

In this section, I suggest that a reformulation of the problem of social order from the perspective of critical rationalism is necessary for the sociologist to explain the mechanisms of the *formation of social order*. As Parsons (1968 [1937]) argues, the Hobbesian problem of social order is of central importance for a sociological theory of society since the unintended social consequence of the egoistic behaviour of each person pursuing his own self-interests would be nothing less than a 'war of all against all'. Parsons accepts the problem of social order as Hobbes defined it, but does not admit Hobbes's solution. As Wrong (1999) observes,

162   The theory of social order

Parsons's theory of society, as a whole, is a response to the Hobbesian problem of order. I want to show that Parsons defines the problem of social order in an *improper* manner since he uses a justificational account of reason to address the origins of action goals.

Hobbes: the problem of social order and its solution

Using the concept of 'the state of nature' to show that the pursuit of self-interest leads human society to a situation of war, Thomas Hobbes (1928) argues that people should give all of their rights to a Leviathan, the state, in order to protect themselves from antagonistic action towards one another and to avoid such a state of war. Hobbes's theory of social order presents a solution to the problem of order that defines the state of war based on a concept of action that assumes *passion* as the driving force of action. Hence, the critical rationalist who believes that reason rather than passion guides human action requires a new definition of the problem of order.

In Hobbes's (1928) portrait of human nature, a plurality of passions drive man, and the good, i.e. the goal of action, is simply whatever a person desires. Hobbes claims that reason is a servant of the passions, the faculty of devising ways and means to satisfy his desires. The goals of an action are subjective desires related to one another randomly, and there is "no common rule of good and evil to be taken from the nature of the objects themselves" (1928: 24). As observed by Parsons (1968 [1937]: 89), Hobbes argues that: ". . . since the passions, the ultimate ends of action, are diverse there is nothing to prevent their pursuit resulting in conflict". Each person pursuit of his own desires necessarily involves each one seeking command over the means to realize these desires. Hobbes (1928: 43) argues that the power a man has is "his present means to obtain some future apparent good". However, the consequence is that one man's command over the means to his own ends necessarily means shutting another man out. Thus, power as an immediate end is naturally a source of division between men. Hobbes then argues that, there being no common rule of good and evil in the nature of the human being, unrestricted pursuit of power by individuals pursuing their own self-interest leads human beings to adopt the most efficient means available in their struggle for power: force, fraud or both of these (1928: 66).

Parsons (1968 [1937]: 91) continues with these considerations, saying that Hobbes

> went on to deduce the character of the concrete [social] system which would result if its units were in fact as defined. And in so doing he became involved in an empirical problem which has not yet been encountered . . . [that is] the problem of *order*. This problem, in the sense in which Hobbes posed it, constitutes the most fundamental empirical difficulty of utilitarian thought.

Hobbes's definition of the problem of order as a natural outcome of his own utilitarian model of action made finding a utilitarian solution for it difficult for

The theory of social order 163

him. If individuals are rational only in terms of using reason to find the most effective means for realizing their own desires and if they are not restricted by a common rule of good and evil, then they can only agree to give their rights to the Leviathan of the state in order to preventing a 'war of all against all'. The fear of such a state of things calls for action, and the force of self-preservation leads human beings to use reason, at least a degree of reason, to find a solution for this difficulty in the social contract.

However, Hobbes ignores his own argument that reason, as a servant of the passions, is concerned only with the question of means rather than the question of how people can give up their particular interests for the benefit of a peaceful social order. As Parsons (1968 [1937]: 93) observes: Hobbes's

> . . . solution really involves stretching, at a critical point, the conception of rationality beyond its scope in the rest of the theory, to a point where the actors come to realize the situation as a whole instead of pursuing their own ends in terms of their immediate situation, and then take the action necessary to eliminate force and fraud, and, purchasing security at the sacrifice of the advantages to be gained by their future employment.

If the actors are capable of reaching such an understanding of the state of nature and of sacrificing their self-interests in order to avoid the 'war of all against all', why should the role of reason in action be limited to finding effective means?

John Locke's solution to the problem of social order

Parsons (1968 [1937]: 95–102) claims that Locke's action model is not substantially different from the Hobbesian concept and that individuals use reason to find effective means for their ends in both cases. People agree on ". . . a plurality of discrete individuals each pursuing his own ends independently of the others". Nevertheless, unlike Hobbes, Locke does not consider the goals of action to be *random*. Parsons claims that the Lockean model does not recognize a normative orientation in action and that the

> only explicit treatment of ends at all is that of natural rights which men have "by nature", . . . and which it exists to protect. But all these – life, health, liberty and possessions, – are to be regarded as the universal conditions of the attainment of individual ends, not as the ultimate ends in themselves. They are the things which all rational men want as conditions or means regardless of the character of their ultimate ends.
>
> (1968 [1937]: 95)

Parsons attempts to reduce the role of reason in Locke's action model to finding the most effective means for the ends. Although this reading might be true in

164 The theory of social order

one sense, it is of no assistance in recognizing the role Locke actually devotes to human reason in the creation of a peaceful social order.

Unlike Hobbes in his solution for the problem of the state of nature, Locke (1924: 118–119) argues in *Of Civil Government: Two Treatises* that people use reason to protect their natural rights to life, liberty and property. This role of reason cannot be reduced merely to finding effective means. Like Hobbes, Locke offers a social contract as a solution to the problem of order, but applies a different action model: individuals can use reason to control their egoistic behaviours and to agree on a social contract enabling them to create a civil government. Hence, Locke does not define the problem of social order in terms of a state of war. Locke's model of rational action enables him to see the state of nature in a different way: individuals are rational agents and understand that egoistic behaviour destroys their natural liberties and that the pursuit of self-interest leads to a conflict of interests,

In 'In Defense of Modernity: Talcott Parsons and the Utilitarian Tradition', Leon Mayhew (1984: 1280) writes that the Lockean version of utilities

> ... purports to found order in society on reason in the individual. The individual is presumed to have agreed to the social order (or to civil government) by virtue of the protection and opportunities it provides, that is, because of its calculable benefits or utilities. Such doctrine often takes the form of supposing an original social contract whereby humankind emerged from a presocial or prepolitical state ... What terms would a rational person accept as a part of the social contract? Such a person would not, for example, grant the sovereign absolute power over life and liberty, for the benefits of civil government are not an adequate reward for such a quid pro quo. .... The underlying premise of the contract doctrine is that the ultimate terms and foundations of society and civil government can be derived from understanding *how rational individuals make decisions* (emphasis added).

This quotation clearly expresses the central role Locke devotes to reason in his utilitarian theory of society, a theory Parsons largely ignored.

The problem of social order: a critical rationalist formulation

It is now interesting to argue for replacing the Hobbesian problem of social order with *reason*, not *passion*, guiding action. Chapter 7 has prepared the ground for identifying the problem of social order through critical rationalist philosophy. If the actor has the capacity of using reason to base the ends and means of his action upon unfalsified conjecture, then the problem of social order is no longer one of overcoming the struggle for power and wealth. Locke realized that overcoming self-interest was *not* the *real* problem the theory of society intended to solve and changed his model of action. He understands that the problem of social order is

The theory of social order 165

how individuals can apply reason to guide their decision to create a civil government to protect their natural rights to life, liberty and property from a struggle for power and wealth.

I suggest that acceptance of Locke's definition of reason as justificationist, as observed by Chapter 1, leads to using a non-justificational model of action to redefine the problem of social order. From this non-justificationist view, the problem of social order is *how the individual actors's critical reason allows them to manage thier self-interest while creating a peaceful and just social order*. In other words, the issue regarding social order is how the actors use critical reason to give themselves a moral law that *compels* individual members of society to pursue their own goals peacefully.

Section II: emancipatory actions and the five mechanisms of social ordering

With the problem of social order in mind, we can argue that a critical rationalist theory of social order answers the problem it intends to solve. Among the action types introduced in Chapter 7, the emancipatory action model formulates the act of an independent person who uses critical reason to *give himself* a moral law regardless of his own interests and conditions and thus makes the action manageable. While Kantian moral philosophy proposes the emancipatory action type, the critical rationalist model of action replaces the doctrine of practical reason with the idea of critical rationalism in order to avoid the problem of infinite regress. The use of a non-justificational concept of reason to understand how the rationalization of action goals and means based on unfalsified conjectures takes place internalizes critical rationalism in moral theory.

Expansion of the new model of emancipatory action from the individual level to a social one makes intersubjective dialogue imaginable, whereas such a dialogue remains inexplicable in Kant's moral philosophy, which leads us to see how thinkers, social movements and ordinary persons give *themselves* a *moral law* for supervising their own egoistic behaviours. The action type of ordinary behaviour refers to the act of a rational being who applies critical reason to adapt to his social conditions as given facts and find the most effective means for meeting personal goals under the supervision of the moral law. Broadening the ordinary type of action from the individual to the social level socializes individuals and leads them to use available means for satisfying their ends. Thus, ordinary actions stabilize the social order the actors have given themselves through their own emancipatory actions.

Human action for social ordering: a metaphysical mechanism

To address the question of how emancipatory action leads to the rise of the moral consensus on ultimate values that is necessary for a peaceful social order, we need

166   The theory of social order

to know more about the nature of such a moral agreement. I am contributing to this discussion by uncovering the role of metaphysical views of the universe and man's place within it in shaping the moral consensus on a system of ultimate values. Introducing the metaphysical mechanism of social ordering requires exploration of the relation between worldviews and the ultimate values of human life. The critical rationalist ideal type of emancipatory action enables us to identify this tie. To this objective, a brief reference to Kant's moral philosophy and its influence on Parsons's theory of social order gives insights. The importance of moral philosophy for a *critical rationalist theory of society* lies in the Kantian idea that the actors can *give themselves* a universal moral law for making actions rational. Kant argues not only that 'rational beings' give themselves the moral law to respect human beings as ends-in-themselves, but also that the existence of such a moral law implies that 'rational beings' can treat each other as ends-in-themselves in society and give *themselves* the normative social order that Kant calls a *Kingdom of Ends*.

As observed by Korsgaard (2000: 23), Kant states,

> Each of us has a will that makes laws for itself as if for everyone. Since human beings together legislate the moral law, we form a moral community: a Kingdom of Ends. The Kingdom of Ends is an ideal. It is "a systematic union of different rational beings through common law", a republic of all rational beings. . . . The Kingdom of Ends is also "a whole of rational beings as ends in themselves as well as of the particular ends which each may set for himself", a system of all good ends . . . Each citizen takes his own perfection and the happiness of others as an end and *treats* every other as an end in itself.

This passage describes rational beings as capable of *forming* a normative order in society by giving themselves a moral law enabling them to treat each other as *ends* rather *means* by using practical reason. Kant advances Locke's and Rousseau's contract theories of society by clarifying why it is reason that drives action. However, from Chapter 1 we know that Kant's epistemology involves infinite regress and cannot offer an acceptable correct account of reason, whether pure or practical. Thus, Kantian moral philosophy does not actually explain how reason drives human action for the creation of a Kingdom of Ends.

Kant's justificationism does not let him show how a rational dialogue among individuals takes place for enabling them to organize their relations within the framework of regarding each other as morally equal. Thus, let us consider the possibility of a rational consensus on a *universal* moral law based on a non-justificational concept of reason. Before entering into that discussion, however, a brief reference to Parsons's theory of social order due to its foundations in Kantian moral philosophy is necessary.

Parsons (1935: 295) argues that

> . . . random variation of systems of ends would be incompatible with the most elementary form of social order. For there would be no guaranty that any

large proportion of such systems would include a recognition of other people's ends as valuable in themselves, and there would thus be no necessary limitation on the means that some, at least, would employ to gain their own ends at the expense of others. The relations of individuals then would tend to be resolved into a struggle for power – for the means for each to realize his own ends. This would be, in the absence of constraining factors, a war of all against all – Hobbes's state of nature.

In fact, Parsons uses Kantian moral theory to show that only the assumption that individuals apply practical reason to see humans as the ends-in-themselves enables the discovery of a solution for the problem of social order.

According to Parsons (1935: 295),

> In so far, however, as individuals share a *common* system of ultimate ends, this system would, among other things, define what they all held their relations ought to be, would lay down norms determining these relations and limits on the use of others as means, on the acquisition and use of power in general. In so far, then, as action is determined by ultimate ends, the existence of a *system* of such ends common to the members of the community seems to be the only alternative to a state of chaos – a necessary factor in social stability.

However, Parsons does not accept Kant's view that all human beings, as rational members of different societies, may use practical reason to create a *universal* system of values for the creation of a Kingdom of Ends. Instead, Parsons limits his analysis of social order merely to the members of a national society.

Moreover, Parsons admits that even the rise of a peaceful order in a national society is impossible without a system of values common to all. Like Weber, Parsons claims that the inability to justify the premises of a universal moral law means that the question of how practical reason creates a value system remains unanswered. Parsons does not agree with Kant's argument in its original sense that actors give themselves a universal moral law for supervising the pursuit of self-interest. Thus, Parsons uses the Kantian moral theory in the sense of taking one system of values in a society as a given fact in order for the theory of society to address how the respect of the individuals in a society for their common values makes social order possible. Allow me to explain why I suggest that a non-justificational account of a universal moral law does not counter the critique that Weber and Parsons level at Kant's moral philosophy.

In order to replace the Kantian doctrine of practical reason with a non-justificationist one, critical rationalism can demonstrate how actors are capable of defending a universal moral law by checking whether its premises are true. To this objective, the central problem of moral philosophy shifts from 'What should I do?' to 'What is the meaning of the good life?'. I argue that this shift in the problem of moral philosophy leads to an understanding of the metaphysical mechanism of social ordering.

168   The theory of social order

Within his justificationist mindset, Kant (1956 [1788]) separates metaphysics and moral philosophy, arguing that metaphysical theories that cannot meet the standard of objective knowledge corresponding with the categories of thought limit the application of pure reason in moral philosophy to practical usage: the question of 'What should I do?'. However, a metaphysical claim regarding the universe that cannot be justified as true offers no reason for Kant to concern himself with the issue of whether the actor's worldview contributes to his evaluation of the ultimate values. By replacing the question of what to do in Kant's moral philosophy with the question of the meaning of the good life, I suggest that the way is paved for an exploration of how ontology affects moral theory from the perceptive of critical rationalism. Putting the question of the meaning of the good life at the centre of moral philosophy enables us to address the question of how the actors' worldviews and man's place in it contribute to their emancipatory actions for giving to themselves a universal moral law, i.e. a system of common values.

The question of the meaning of the good life leads to setting the place of the individual in the universe in a *central position* in moral philosophy. From a non-justificational viewpoint, metaphysical theories of the universe can be a subject of rational discussion. Hence, the actor's critical reason guides him to understand whether argument proves a metaphysical theory. Thus, an unfalsified worldview can be used to address the meaning of the good life due to the place that it gives the individual in the universe.

Weber (1963: xxxv) argues that metaphysical ideas give teleological meaning to man's conceptions of himself and his place in the universe that "legitimate man's orientations in and to the world and which give *meaning* to man's various goals. Such ideas imply metaphysical and theological conceptions of cosmic and moral orders, as well as man's position in relation to such wider orders". Weber connects the worldview with man's concept of the good life due to the position the worldview gives man within the universe and speaks of how such a worldview influences the goals of actions through the ultimate values (Parsons 1967). However, Weber's justificationism leads him to claim that reason can only judge the consistency of a worldview rather than its objectivity. As noted earlier, rational inquiry, however, does reveal whether metaphysical claims are objective. Weber does not take into account the significant role critical reason can perform in terms of rationalizing worldviews and giving ultimate meaning to human life. In contrast, a non-justificationist epistemology enables us to see that individuals use reason to evaluate the metaphysical theories that they propose for exploration of the truth of the universe and man's position in it.

This rational capacity for understanding the universe through conjectures and refutations enables actors to initiate emancipatory action for reaching an *ontological* consensus on the meaning of the universe. Recognition of man's position in the context of such ontological agreement is the worldview that contributes to the rise of a system of ultimate values in society, i.e. the rise of a universal moral law

The theory of social order   169

in the Kantian sense. Therefore, worldviews that shape the meaning of the good life through the place in the universe they define for the 'human being' make it possible to explore a metaphysical mechanism for the social ordering of people in society. When individuals use critical reason to initiate a social dialogue for reaching an agreement on the meaning of the universe, they also pave the way for the rise of a moral consensus in society regarding the meaning of the good life. Such a shared concept of the good life at the core of the society's value system enables people to define their action goals with ultimate aim of attaining the good life. This system of goals shared due to man's position in the universe leads us to understand the contribution of metaphysical beliefs to the creation of a peaceful social order.

Since Kant overlooks the origin of moral philosophy in metaphysics, the role of worldviews in shaping the meaning of the good life remains unclear in his theory of society. However, a non-justificationist concept of rationality in which actors can rationalize their worldviews allows us to understand the formation of a moral consensus on the place of man in the universe upon which actors may base their shared meaning of the good life.

Human action for social ordering: a moral mechanism

The proposed causal link between man's position in the universe and the rise of moral consensus on the concept of the good life guides us to a second means for the creation of social order: a *moral mechanism*. A shared system of worldviews would not be sufficient for managing an unlimited pursuit of self-interest by individuals. Additional emancipatory actions by individuals are necessary for deducing logical results from the worldviews concerning the meaning of the good life. Critical reason empowers the actors to explore such logical results and propose a system of moral beliefs about the good life.

The position that the worldviews give the human being in such a metaphysical understanding of the universe addresses the question of how the actor's ontological view of the universe contributes to the meaning of the good life. Martin A. Larson (1970: 57) observes the connection between metaphysics and moral philosophy:

Ethics deal with social relationships or with a man's theory in regard to himself, and attempt to explain how he should act and why. A theory of ethics may depend largely upon metaphysics or theology, but in itself is very different from these . . .

Defined by the logic of critical rationalism, the linkage between a philosophical theory of the universe and a moral theory of the good life explains how the meaning of the good life originates in the position in the universe that a worldview gives man. Emancipatory actions for exploring the logical consequences of

170 The theory of social order

metaphysical beliefs in order to find the meaning of the good life are at the core of the moral mechanism of social ordering.

If non-justificationist epistemology allows actors to rationalize their metaphysical beliefs when the premises or inferences of such beliefs are not shown to be false, actors can also draw the logical conclusions of such unfalsified metaphysical beliefs for man's position in the universe and the resultant outcome for the meaning of the good life. A shared meaning of the good life enables the actors to apply critical reason in order to situate this concept of the good life at the core of the system of values they give themselves for control of their unlimited pursuit of self-interest as a moral solution to the problem of social order.

Taken together, the metaphysical and moral mechanisms of the formation of social order prepare a cultural foundation for the rise of a peaceful social order. This cultural foundation is nothing less than the socially accepted views of the universe and the good life operating as normative peacekeepers of social order in Habermas's (1979) sense. Unlike Parsons's theory of social order, the *critical rationalist theory of society* features actors who create such a cultural base for social order by giving themselves shared views of the universe and the good life. It is noteworthy that critical rationalism gives the Kantian idea of human autonomy an entirely new content. With critical reason driving action, rational beings can agree on a worldview for defining the ultimate virtue of the meaning of the good life.

Like the *epistemic* significance of the universe, the meaning of the good life has a *cognitive* content that benefits from critical rationality. Hence, the ultimate meaning the actors embrace for their lives is the result of the emancipatory actions that make a rational dialogue on moral claims possible. When the actors reach a moral consensus on the meaning of the good life, they form a system of values common to all the members in their society. This shared meaning of the good life is what defines the content of self-interest, hence preventing the actors from conflicting antagonistic interests. This is why I speak of a moral mechanism in the formation of social order. The ultimate ground for a social order existing in peace instead of reflecting a Hobbesian state of war is that the actors' emancipatory usage of critical reason enables them to agree upon common views about the universe and man's position in it. This consensus lets them give themselves a system of ultimate values for shaping the pursuit of self-interest in a morally acceptable manner.

Human action for social ordering: a legal mechanism

A critical rationalist theory of social order answers the question of whether the cultural foundations of social order are sufficient for managing egoistic behaviours by arguing in favour of the creation of a legal system protecting the individual's rights to the good life in order to realize a moral consensus on the ultimate values. Realization of the good life requires this system of rights legalizing the pursuit of the good life and a system of human rights in society that reflects the legal mechanism of social ordering.

Critical reason guides the actors in the exploration of a logical relation between the concepts of the good life and the meaning of human rights. As for our critical rationalist moral philosophy, we need a new legal philosophy based on critical rationalism that searches for the answer to the questions of what the human rights of a rational being are and whether we can use the idea of *equal* access to critical reason in defining the human rights a rational being should have. If the answer to the last question is affirmative, the next question is whether the content of human rights originates in the very concept of the good life.

A critical rationalist philosophy of law answers these questions affirmatively. In non-justificationist legal philosophy, one cannot address the question of a rational being's human rights without recognizing the close ties between human rights and the meaning of the good life, for man's place in the universe is closely related to the human rights of a rational being. Critical rationalist moral philosophy argues that the actors give themselves a shared concept of the good life because they are rational and capable of defending their moral claims by argument. The possibility of having an objective concept of the good life originates in equal access to critical reason. Hence, the critical rationalist philosophy of law can grant each individual an *equal right* to the opportunities for making the good life possible.

The principle of justice appears in moral philosophy first and then becomes a legal concept of equality. The connection between Kant's *principle of justice* and the *notion of rationality* is insightful for the present discussion. As observed by Ross Poole (1996: 71):

> The project of liberalism is to construct an account of justice which resists the subjectivity which it allows to the good. It has been Kant who has provided the main inspiration for the recent liberal theorists who have taken up this challenge. The *principle of justice* is sought, not in the fabric of the external world, nor in the content of individual desire or choice, but in a *structure of human thought and action*. This is, in a sense, a structure of subjectivity; but if it is widely shared, or universal, it will have the requisite impersonal and objective status. A key role in determining the content and the force of the principle is played by the concept of reason. We understand and are subject to the *demands of justice insofar as we are rational beings*. In which case, these demands will not be external constraints, but will in principle be accepted – and perhaps even worked out for themselves – by the very people who are subject to them. The *principles of right* are in this sense self-imposed and their restrictions, *self-restrictions*; they are, therefore, the products of freedom (emphasis added).

This passage shows that Kant builds a logical connection between practical reason and the equal rights of rational beings for self-determination in terms of

172 The theory of social order

the principle of justice. However, the replacement of justificationist reason with non-justificationist reason reveals a new legal philosophy that provides for *equal rights to the good life for rational beings* through their equal access to critical reason.

The principle of justice that stems from the rational nature of human beings links the moral theory with a legal theory to address the question of the human rights of a rational being in relation to the meaning of the good life. The origin of the principle of justice in the rational nature of human being implies a definition of human rights based on the same philosophy of rationality that applies to moral philosophy. Lon Fuller (1963) argues that the inner morality of law lies in the concept of the good life.

With the connection between moral and legal philosophies in mind, actors can initiate emancipatory efforts to turn their moral consensus on the meaning of the good life into a legal system for enforcing moral law. From a critical rationalist perspective, the individual actor cannot justify his theories of human rights, but may subject them to rational discussion to see whether they are false. Once the theories of equal rights to the good life are accounted for as unfalsified conjectures, emancipatory efforts take shape in the legal domain to establish resultant human rights as the law of society people impose on themselves to demarcate lawful from unlawful behaviour.

Upon initiation of the legal mechanism of social ordering, institutions for equal rights to the good life equip society with encouraging and restricting codes of behaviour enabling actors to shape a peaceful social order by obedience to the legal codes of the sacred and profane. Egoistic behaviours cannot be avoided merely by a shared system of values and goals; legal codes of behaviour are necessary for managing the actors' pursuit of self-interest. The role played by the concept of the 'good life' in shaping the moral mechanism of social ordering is the same as the one that the concept of 'human rights' performs in creating the legal mechanism of social ordering.

The *equal access* of individuals to critical reason gives them equal human rights to the good life. According to this philosophy of law, the conception of human rights regulates the legal system in close connection with the meaning of the good life in society. Hence, one could argue that the moral mechanism nourishes the legal mechanism of social ordering. Individuals use critical reason for shaping the institutions of law in order to turn the moral agreement on the good life into enforceable law and equal rights to the good life. The degree of critical rationality that actors use to define their concepts of the good life also determines various meanings for human rights.

Human action for social ordering: a political mechanism

The rise of institutions for human rights marks significant progress towards the goal of the good life. Nevertheless, these institutions require an *enforcement* mechanism, which means that the actors have to initiate emancipatory efforts for

The theory of social order 173

building a political system using the monopoly of power to enforce the law of society. Can the answer to the legal philosopher's concern for defining the human rights of a rational being help the political philosopher find a solution to the question of the political power of a rational being?

With this question in mind, I propose extending the critical rationalist approach in moral and legal philosophies to political philosophy. In order to do so, we have to understand the shaping of a system of governance using a monopoly of force *to impose* the law of society. The concepts of the good life and human rights enable us to address this question in political philosophy.

Kantian philosophy helps us to address the question of a rational being's political power. As rational beings, the actors can actualize their equal rights to the good life by possessing 'equal' power for establishing a government through a monopoly for exercising power. The actors' equal political power originates in their equal access to critical reason. Hence, a rational being's political power can be connected with the moral values and the human rights that they have already given themselves. A critical rationalist theory of politics argues that individuals apply their critical reason to varying extents in the effort to achieve equal power for self-governance.

Using critical reason, the actors can arrive at an agreement on legitimate usage of power for establishing a model of governance to execute the law of society. In fact, the political mechanism of social ordering refers to the actions of rational beings who use their power to give themselves a political law that aims to realize the ideal of equal rights to the good life. The principle of justice originating in the actors' critical reason is extended from the concepts of the good life and human rights to the meaning of legitimate governance. Habermas (2001: 116–117) makes the following relevant observation:

> What basic rights must free and equal citizens mutually accord one another if they want to regulate their common life legitimately by means of positive law? This idea of a constitution-making practice links the expression of popular sovereignty with the creation of a system of rights. Here I assume a principle . . . that a law may claim legitimacy only if all those possibly affected could consent to it after participating in rational discourses. As participants in "discourses", we want to arrive at shared opinions by mutually convincing one another about some issue through arguments . . . Now, if discourses (and bargaining processes) are the place where a reasonable political will can develop, then the presumption of legitimate outcomes, which the democratic procedure is supposed to justify, ultimately rests on an elaborate communicative arrangement: the forms of communication necessary for a reasonable will-formation of the political lawgiver, the conditions that ensure legitimacy, must be legally institutionalized.

This quotation shows how communicative rationality confirms the legitimacy of popular sovereignty through the individual's capacity to participate in rational

174 The theory of social order

discourse to justify not only the law of society, but also its political governance. However, due to the infinite regress that 'communicative reason' involves, I have replaced this concept with the idea of 'critical rationality' to show that it would be possible for 'rational beings' to use their political power for self-determination in the context of what they have already defined as the good life and human rights. Legitimate governance that rational beings give themselves assists them in managing egoistic behaviours in order to support a legitimate social order.

Human action for social ordering: an economic mechanism

In order to realize equal rights to the good life, an additional emancipatory action is necessary: the creation of an economic mechanism aimed at the mobilization of scarce resources for meeting the diverse needs of the good life. Using a critical rationalist economic philosophy, we ask about a 'rational being's economic resources. In answering, it is important to consider the following points: 1) the system of human rights defining the property rights of the means of production on the supply side of the economy and 2) the moral consensus on the meaning of the good life that shapes the individual's preference for goods and services on the demand side of the economy. These two points show that the economic problem in society is the effective mobilization of rational beings' economic resources in order to produce the goods and services necessary for realizing the good life for individuals in the existing institutional setting.

The search for the answer to what economic resources rational beings possess enables the actors to seek how they can create an economic mechanism of social ordering for mobilizing their scarce resources for the good life through institutions of human rights and governance. From the perspective of critical rationalism, it is imperative for realizing the good life that the actors create a mechanism of resource allocation for meeting the needs of the good life in addition to a system of human rights and a political system for enforcing such rights. In brief, emancipatory efforts allow the actors to *give themselves* an economic law of supply and demand for solving the societal economic problem under the conditions that rational beings, whether producers or consumers, employ their resources effectively, i.e. use their means of production or their budgets to realize their goals. As observed by Hans Albert (1999: 82), "The formation of wants is, after all, a social process, shaped to a large extent by the whole cultural environment". The same holds for the production of goods and services as a social process shaped mainly by legal and political surroundings.

As for the rational being's economic resources, we can argue that actors who apply their critical reason to agree on a mechanism of mobilizing scarce resources to satisfy the needs of the good life create an economic mechanism for social ordering. The mechanism of supply and demand as a *spontaneous* system of resource allocation is an undertaking among rational producers to form production plans within the context of the established systems of human rights and governance that

The theory of social order   175

enable them to *give themselves* the economic law of supply and demand. It is also an agreement between rational consumers on shaping their preferences according to their concepts of the good life.

As pointed out by Albert (1999: 79),

> Society appears in the economic perspective as a cooperative unity, endeavoring to overcome the natural scarcity and to bring about the maximal satisfaction of all its members. Leaving out all consideration of conflicts of interests, the ideal of rational behavior, of acting according to the economic principle, is projected to society as a whole, so that the imprecation arises of a functional harmony of interests.

Albert's criticism of the neo-classical economic reading of the market process with its premise of the agents' perfect information about the market conditions[1] encourages replacement of that premise with the agents' imperfect knowledge of market conditions. Critical rationality inspires a regard of the economic agents in the theory of the market process, whether producers or consumers, as rational beings who apply the method of conjecture and refutation to use their imperfect knowledge to *give themselves* the law of supply and demand. These economic agents spontaneously shape a decentralized market economy with the purpose of mobilizing scarce resources to meet the needs of the good life. From this critical rationalist perspective, the market process is a spontaneous trade-off between producers and consumers who use emancipatory actions to give themselves the law of supply and demand.

According to a *critical rationalist theory of the market process*, which space does not allow me to introduce properly here,[2] producers and consumers give themselves the *law of supply and demand* to create a spontaneous coordination between supply and demand by a mechanism of *relative prices*. Producers define their property rights to the means of production according to their human rights and determine the prices of labour (wages) and capital (rent). Consumers, on the other hand, define their preferences based on their shared concept of the good life, thus determining the prices of the goods and services on the demand side of market. In this sense, the actors' social environments shape the supply and demand and determine competitive prices in a spontaneous market process. As Alfred Bosch et al. (1990: 58) point out, "The function of prices is to coordinate producers' and consumers' choices in such a way that these choices become simultaneously realized". A critical rationalist theory of the market process describes the economic mechanism of social ordering by the law of supply and demand that actors give *themselves* based on their shared accounts of the good life and human rights.

The effectiveness of this economic mechanism that economic actors give themselves can be explained from two perspectives, that of the producer and that of the consumer. Firstly, rational producers' supplies develop based on *common* systems of human rights and governance, property rights governing usage of the means of

176   The theory of social order

production, i.e. the workforce, capital and property. Equal access to the rights of the good life prevents producers from misusing the means of production to benefit their own interests. The supply side performs a unification function in coordinating diverse 'production plans' in the economic order of society.

Secondly, similar to the supply side of the market, the demands of rational consumers take shape according to their shared meaning of the good life, so the rationality of common values in society prevents individual demands from being subjective utilities that lead to egotistic behaviours on the demand side of the market. Hence, consumers use critical reason to explore the consistency of their subjective preferences with the ultimate values of the good life in society, making their demands *rational* and controlling unreasonable consumption. From the perspective of the demand side of the economy, the rational consumer's choice is the main coordinator of individual demands for the benefit of the economic order.

From the critical rationalist perspective, the effectiveness of the supplies and demands of rational producers and consumers prepares the ground for understanding the economic mechanism of social ordering. This allocates scarce resources to meet the needs of individuals and prevents the actors from egoistic production or consumption, but also coordinates economic activities in order to provide for equal rights to the good life. The concept of economic efficiency as a proper vehicle for the mobilization of scarce resources to satisfy the needs of the people has a close connection with the *notions* of the good life, human rights and political legitimacy. I suggest that producers' and consumers' objective but imperfect knowledge of market conditions confers an *epistemic* nature onto the concept of economic efficiency.

In summary, access to critical reason enables rational economic actors, the suppliers and consumers, to find a solution for the economic problem in society of how a rational being can employ his resources to realize the good life through institutions of law and governance. The key is voluntary respect for a system of values, law and politics that purposively creates a spontaneous trade-off between supply and demand. Hence, like the meaning of the good life that human beings have given themselves, the concept of human rights and the notion of political legitimacy as well as the law of supply and demand develop through individuals' emancipatory actions and reflect the economic mechanism of social ordering.

Human action for social ordering: a sociological analysis

Now we can integrate the five mechanisms of social ordering, namely metaphysical, moral, legal, political and economic ones, to offer a sociological analysis of social order. The problem of social order is redefined in order to explain how individual actors use their critical reason to agree on a system of common values for avoiding egoistic behaviours for the benefit of a peaceful social order as well as for promoting cooperative actions for the social good. The metaphysical mechanism implies that the actors agree on the meaning of the universe and man's

The theory of social order   177

place in it by rational dialogue. Once rational beings realize that the premises of their worldviews are not shown to be false, their conjectures about the universe will transform into shared worldviews. These unfalsified beliefs about the truth of the universe will then provide the actors with a shared concept of the good life at the core of their value system through the moral mechanism of social order. The critical rationalist theory of social order introduces the shared views of the universe and the good life as normative peacekeepers of social order. Through the creation of common cultural bases, the harmonized goals of human actors prevent conflicts of interest.

The critical rationalist theory of social order then argues that the actors use normative consensus in order to create the system of human rights necessary for turning such an agreement into an enforceable law. The meaning of the good life shapes the contents of human rights by leading to the notion of equal rights for each person to enjoy the opportunity of the good life. Informed by the concept of the good life, the legal mechanism of social ordering enables the actors to establish the institutions of law in society to assure equal rights to the good life for all. However, enforceable law requires executive power for executing the legal standards of equal access to the good life in practice. According to the critical rationalist theory of social order, the political mechanism of social ordering implies that rational actors create a system of governance with legitimacy for using the monopoly of power to enforce the law of society.

Given the moral consensus on legal and political institutions, the critical rationalist theory of social order proceeds to explain the economic mechanism, arguing that the actors use critical reason to solve the economic problem of society by asking how rational agents in the economy can mobilize their resources to meet the needs of their good life. To fulfil this function, the actors on the supply side realize the necessity for shaping their production plans to take into account the workforce, capital and land according to their acceptance of human rights to the good life. This not only avoids conflicts of interests, but also coordinates production plans through the system of enforceable law that defines persons' legal rights in the means of production. On the demand side, the actors realize that the meaning of the good life they have given themselves is what shapes their individual demands for goods and services. This leads the demand side of the market to a coordinated set of subjective preferences according to the existing system of common values upon which the consumers' preferences are shaped to prevent conflicting demands. The spontaneous trade-off between producers and consumers under the consciousness agreement on common values and human rights enables society as a whole to solve its economic problem of allocating scarce resources to peoples' diverse needs.

In this way, the critical rationalist theory of social order explains the rise of a peaceful social order through the set of five emancipatory actions whose meaning are different in each area although individuals use critical reason in all of them to *give themselves* a social order. Moreover, critical reason enables individuals to

178   The theory of social order

give themselves a legal order in order to make moral consensus an enforceable law. Thus, a political order with a monopoly of power to execute that enforceable law emerges along with an economic order providing society with resources required for the realization of equal human rights to the good life. Critical rationality reveals the *rationalization* for a system of *moral, just, legitimate* and *effective* social order based on shared views of the universe, the good life, human rights, political legitimacy and economic efficiency. Inspired by Kant, I offer a critical rationalist theory of social order that applies the general theory of critical rationalism to explain how human actors give themselves a peaceful and just social order.

Section III: ordinary actions and stabilization of social order

The portrait of social order through the sociology of critical rationalism raises the question of the role of ordinary actions in social ordering. In response, I argue that the actors use critical reason to become members of society through a socialization process for stabilizing the existing social order.

From a critical rationalist perspective, the role of ordinary action in the socialization process is not the *creation* of social order. Ordinary actions do not aim to create a moral consensus or a social institution for building social order. Instead, ordinary people's actions take moral values and social institutions as given facts for being civilized members of the society in question, not only through respect for societal values and institutions but also through considering them as the conditions for their pursuit of self-interest.

According to critical rationalist sociology, the actor uses the method of trial and error to discover how to become a member of society by exploring the ultimate values and the social institutions of law, governance and market that condition his actions. Ordinary actions for being a member of society do not question the validity of an established consensus concerning the universe, the good life, human rights, legitimacy and efficiency. Shared values and institutions regarded as *given facts* of *social life* lead to voluntary respect for the established order and to finding effective means for attaining their own goals.

To become a member of society, a critical rationalist theory of socialization explains that the individual actor, with his own social conditions and respect for the existing value consensus and institutions of law, governance and market, uses critical reason to conjecture ways of internalizing the ultimate values in the goals of his actions. The individual's realization that his conjectures are not falsified beliefs leads to his moral socialization in society. From a legal perspective, an individual becomes a member of the society by using critical reason to explore the system of human rights in the society and follows the legal codes of behaviours for justifying his daily behaviours. From a political point of view, an individual becomes a member of society by using critical reason to understand how the political system applies power in society and obeys the decisions of the political governance. Finally, from an economic perspective, an individual becomes a

The theory of social order 179

member of society by using critical reason to understand the supply and demand sides of the market in terms of relative prices for goods and services, on the one hand, and the relative wages for the workforce and the interest rates for capital and land, on the other. In short, the process of the socialization of individuals in society is much more complex than a mere voluntary respect for moral values and includes legal, political and economic dimensions.

In response to the question of the consequences of the individual's membership for the social order, critical rationalist sociology states that individuals who become civilized members of society in its metaphysical, moral, legal, political and economic senses contribute to stabilization of the existing social order. From a metaphysical/moral perspective, the individual actor who applies critical reason to learn and accept the ultimate values of the society is capable of assimilating such ultimate values as a constituent part of his cultural identity and sacrificing his egoistic desires for the benefit of his moral duties. This cultural membership in society prevents the individual from being a destabilizing agent in society. The same holds true for an individual's legal, political and economic membership in society.

From a legal viewpoint, the individual who uses critical reason to learn about the legal codes of behaviour understands that any violation of the standards may lead serious penalties. Hence, his legal obedience contributes to stabilizing the existing social order by preventing unlawful behaviour and encouraging lawful conduct. In a political perspective, the individual who uses critical reason to discover the political obligations governing his social life realizes the consequence of political disobedience for his own well-being. Hence, the individual respects the political obligations in order to achieve his goals. From an economic perspective, the individual who wants to become a member of the society follows the market obligations: he discovers the competitive prices for the means of production and goods and adapts his subjective preferences and production plans accordingly. The adaption of producers and consumers to market prices stabilizes the economic order in society and regulates the equilibrium tendencies between supply and demand.

Unlike emancipatory action, ordinary action cannot explain how an existing social order may transform itself into a new one; ordinary actions mainly stabilize the existing social order without aiming to change it. Chapter 9 is devoted to the question of how emancipatory action that has already operated as an agent of forming social order can lead to understanding how one social order is remoulded into a different one through the actors' use of critical reason to establish new system of moral values and social institutions.

Notes

1 It is remarkable that the neo-classical theory of market economy assumes perfect information through its premise that the ends of economic actions are purely subjective and cannot be coordinated by a rationalized and objective concept of the good. As Alfred Bosch et al (1990: 2) point out, "Both, Neoclassical and Austrian economics,

180 The theory of social order

see economics as the science of means only and not as a theory of action that includes as well reasoning about ends. For both approaches, economics is concerned with the optimal allocation of means for given ends, not with the judgment of ends". However, a critical rationalist theory of the market process assumes that judgment of the ends takes place through the actors' moral consensus on the concept of good life and that it is imperfect critical rationality, not perfect information drives actions.

2 Reformulation of *the rational choice theory* on the basis of critical rationalism can lead us to a new theory of the market process.

Bibliography

Albert, H. (1999) *Between Social Science, Religion and Politics*. Amsterdam, Rodopi.

Bosch, A., Koslowski, P. & Veit, R. (eds.) (1990) *General Equilibrium or Market Process: Neoclassical and Austrian Theories of Economics*. Tubingen, J.C.B. Mohr.

Fuller, L.L. (1963) *The Morality of Law,* Revised ed. New Haven, Yale University Press.

Habermas, J. (2001) *The Postnational Constellation: Political Essays*, Pensky, M. (trans.). Cambridge, MA, MIT Press.

Habermas, J. (1979) *Communication and the Evolution of Society*, McCarthy, T. (trans.). Boston, Beacon Press.

Hobbes, T. (1928) *Leviathan*. London, J.M. Dent & Sons.

Kant, I. (1956 [1788]) *Critique of Practical Reason*, Smith, N.K. (trans.). New York, Palgrave Macmillan.

Korsgaard, C. (2000) *The Creation of the Kingdom of Ends*. Cambridge, Cambridge University Press.

Larson, M.A. (1970) *The Modernity of Milton: A Theological and Philosophical Interpretation*. New York, AMS Press.

Locke, J. (1924) *Of Civil Government: Two Treatises*. London, J.M. Dent & Sons.

Mayhew, L. (1984) "In Defense of Modernity: Talcott Parsons and the Utilitarian Tradition". In: *American Journal of Sociology*, 89 (6), pp. 1273–1305.

Parsons, T. (1968 [1937]) *The Structure of Social Action*, Vol. I: Marshall, Pareto, Durkheim. New York, Free Press.

Parsons, T. (1967) *Sociological Theory and Modern Society*. New York, Free Press.

Parsons, T. (1935) "The Place of Ultimate Values in Sociological Theory". In: *International Journal of Ethics*, 45 (3), pp. 282–316.

Poole, R. (1996) *Morality and Modernity*. London, Routledge.

Weber, M. (1963) *The Sociology of Religion,* Fischoff, E. (trans.). Boston, Beacon Press.

Wrong, D.H. (1999) *The Oversocialized Conception of Man*. New Brunswick, Transaction Publishers.

Chapter 9

Towards a critical rationalist theory of social change

Masoud Mohammadi Alamuti

Introduction

Using the non-justificational concept of knowledge, the philosophy of critical rationalism introduces the concept of rationality as unfalsified beliefs to demonstrate how the actors' cognitive capability to reach an agreement on the meaning of the universe and the good life and lead them to create a peaceful social order. My intention in Chapter 9 is to show that critical reason can alter the social order that individuals have given themselves by revising their common beliefs regarding the universe and man's place within it and encourage them to build new social institutions of law, governance and market.

This chapter presents a theory of social change using a non-justificationist concept of reason. For social change, the importance of critical reason is that it allows the actors to revise the premises or inferences of their common values and social institutions to see whether they are shown to be false by argument or experience. In Chapter 9, Section I uses the emancipatory action type to define the problem of social change. Section II follows with an argument for the cultural mechanism of social change to be explored first of all due to the actors' common views of the universe and the good life that shape their accounts of human rights and political legitimacy. After that, Section III introduces the legal and political mechanisms of social change affecting the governance of society. Subsequently, Section IV reasons that social change needs to transform the resource mobilization system of society to realize the goals of good life. Finally, Section V describes social evolution from the perspective of critical rationalism.

Section I: emancipatory action and the problem of social change

The reformulation of the Hobbesian problem of order in the previous chapter enables better understanding of the problem of social change. The Hobbesian problem of order rests on a mistaken concept of human nature according to which passion guides action. A diagnosis of the justificational origin of that concept

182 Towards a critical rationalist theory of social change

suggests using a non-justificational account of rationality to show that critical reason drives action by the moral law that actors give themselves for avoiding egoistic behaviours and allowing cooperation for social good.

Chapter 8 defined the problem of social order as determining how actors apply critical reason to reach a moral consensus on a shared account of the good life and then establish the institutions of law, governance and market necessary for realizing it. The emancipatory action type formulates the following solution for the problem of social order: from a non-justificationist perspective, a rational agreement on *common beliefs* about the universe and the place of the individual's good life in it becomes possible since the actors' critical rationality does not involve infinite regress. In addition, this normative consensus leads to implementation of rational institutions for a just system of human rights, legitimate political governance to enforce equal rights and an efficient mechanism for resource mobilization to meet the needs of the good life.

This analysis of social order reveals the close tie between the problem of social change and the concept of social order. Critical rationalism enables us to understand the *logical potentiality* for a social order in which the actors *can* use the faculty of reason to reach an agreement on the common values and social institutions necessary for living together in a society. In *The Site of the Social*, Theodore R. Schatzki uses the concept of social 'ordering',[1] to show the problem of social order as problem-shaping in which the actors do not remain passive towards the formation of their social order, but are, instead, the originators of their social order. Schatzki (2002: 6) points out that ". . . 'Ordering', by contrast, designates the dynamic processes that organize-order social existence". With this same vision, I suggest that the problem of social change, i.e. the transition from one form of social organization to another, is affiliated with this kind of dynamic account of social ordering. Hence, the notion of social change ultimately originates in the concept of social ordering.

With this clarified, I apply the emancipatory ideal type of action to formulate the problem of social change by asking how critical reason allows human actors to learn from the incorrect premises of their shared understanding of the universe and the good life in order to revise their common values and social institutions. To formulate a theory of social change to address this problem, I use the insights of the critical rationalist theory of social order presented in Chapter 8.

Section II: critical rationalism and the cultural mechanism of social change

The following pages introduce a theory of social change through a discussion of the three major mechanisms of social change: cultural, governmental and economic ones. This first section devotes itself to the first of them, cultural establishments. However, before describing the cultural mechanism of social change, a brief glance at the Parsonian view of social change may be insightful.

Talcott Parsons's view of social change: an epistemological critique

Parsons's view of social change reasons that the existence of social order depends on a system of values internalized in the actor's definition of self-interest. Voluntarily respect for one another's values prevents the actors from turning the pursuit of self-interest into a war of all against all. Hence, the role of reason in the Parsonian reading of social order is defined in terms of a practical reason for voluntarily respect of a given system of values, rather than critical reasoning for the creation of a system of values they give themselves in a Kantian sense. In this reading of social order, two major points stand out. First, culture as a system of values is what makes social order possible given the problem of egoistic behaviours. Second, the role of reason in shaping human action for social order is limited to a voluntarily respect for a given system of values. This portrait of social order leads to exploration of the reason why Parsons's view of social change is problematic from a non-justificational viewpoint.

Admission of Kantian moral theory to Parsons's social theory would allow the actors to *give* themselves a new system of common values. In Parsons's theory of social change, however, rational actors simply *revise* the moral law they have given themselves. Parsons argues that using their practical reason in this way makes them agents of social change. However, Parsons's view of social change does not comply with this argument, for his justificationist critique of Kantian practical reason prevents him from accepting social change through the actors' restructuration of their values. In his critique of Parsons's theory of society, Alan Touraine (1965: 10–12) argues that Parsons does not accept the existence of values over and above social relationships and regards action as merely implementing pre-existing values rather than as creating new values. However, action is not a mere reaction to a situation related to existing values. *Action creates* these values. Like Touraine (1965), I plan to demonstrate that a critical rationalist theory of society is not a sociology of values, but one of the creation of values.

From a different viewpoint, Stephen P. Savage (1981: 197) states: "What is perhaps most remarkable about many sociological commentaries on Parsons' work is the claim that social change is a non-problem for his social theory". In accordance with his concept of society based on a consensus of values, Parsons does not see the conflict of interest as the main source of social change. Savage explains that

> "Conflict" theorists argue that social relations involve inherent sources of strain. Differential interests and scarce resources are seen to induce conflict relationships; these become a normal part of social functioning and lead in turn to social change. Parsons' work is held to ignore such sources of strain, and to rule out inherent sources of conflict and deviance.

Savage's reply to these allegations is that Parsons does not ignore the role of interests in social order, nor does he forget the role of human action in the creation

184 Towards a critical rationalist theory of social change

of common values. My observation, however, is that even acceptance of Savage's response leaves the main problem with Parsons's view of social change in his ignorance of the role of *reason* in revising a system of values created by the actors *themselves*. Parsons's omission originates in his justificationist critique of the Kantian doctrine of practical reason that rational beings give themselves their ultimate values.

While Parsons (2005 [1991]) recognizes important role of culture in shaping personal identity through the process of socialization that makes a peaceful social order possible, his justificationist concept of rationality does not allow him to define a Kantian role for reason to let the actors become the authors of a universal moral law for themselves. Like Weber, Parsons claims that Kant's moral philosophy cannot *justify* its universal law of respect for all rational beings as ends-in-themselves by argumentation. Like Weber, Parsons argues that human societies reflect a plurality of value systems, so it would be imprudent to say that rational beings reach a moral agreement on a universal system of values.

Like Weber, Parsons realizes that the problem with Kant's moral philosophy is that it speaks of a universal moral law that rational beings give themselves based on the Kantian epistemology that views the categories of thought as *a priori* true. However, not all philosophers, let alone all people, agree on the premise that the categories of thought are justifiable because they are *a priori* true. While Parsons, like Weber, is correct in saying that a moral law cannot be *justified* as a universal truth, he was wrong in saying that a moral conjecture ought to be *justified* in order to be regarded an unfalsified conjecture. Hence, justificationist epistemology is what prevents Weber and Parsons from realizing that actors are capable of reaching a rational consensus on a universal moral law not yet refuted by argument. I argue that a non-justificationist perspective facilitates the argument that a universal moral law that people give themselves for controlling egotistic behaviours can be defended rationally as an unfalsified conjecture when its premises or inference forms are not shown to be false by argument.

With these considerations in mind, we are in a good position to understand why Parsons faces criticism for paying insufficient attention to social change. Without an explanation of how a new system of values replaces an established one in the course of transition from an existing social order to a new one, Parsons (1970) cannot defend his theory of social change. Parsons does not introduce any mechanism to explain the cultural forces of social change as a result of the actors creating new value system because he already regards them as oversocialized human beings who merely implement pre-existing values rather than create new ones, as observed by Dennis Wrong (1999) and Alan Touraine (1965). By defining rational action according to the Kantian doctrine of practical reason, which cannot explain how rational beings reach *universal* moral law, Parsons assesses the actor mainly as an *establisher* of social order rather than as an *originator* of social change.

Critical rationality and cultural change

In order to regard rational actors as agents of social change, we need the concept of an independent actor capable of using critical reason to question his value system. The critical rationalist type of emancipatory action provides us with just such an independent actor whose objective knowledge allows him to question the rightness or wrongness of his value system. Hence, the actors are capable of using *reason* not only for giving themselves a system of values, but also for revising their values. They accomplish this through a non-justificationist concept of rationality that does not involve infinite regress.

Hence, the emancipatory action type of social change whose independent actor uses his critical rationality to revise ultimate values can be applied for modelling a cultural mechanism of social change. From a Kantian perspective, however, a moral law that is justified as true is infallible and cannot be revised. Hence, justificationism prevents a Kantian from arguing that a universal moral law is not implicitly valid forever and can be an unfalsified conjecture open to revision. Now, however, the separation of justification and criticism in the general theory of critical rationalism presents a new concept of reason that allows exploration of possibly incorrect premises or inferences of our rational beliefs regarding the universe and the meaning of the good life. It is *this* concept of reason that enables us to understand the cultural problem of social change. *Emancipatory* action applies reason to make the actor a free agent who imposes moral law on himself. Through this ideal type of action, the rational actor can explore metaphysical and moral elements of the cultural mechanism of social change.

From the non-justificationist perspective, not only metaphysical beliefs about the universe, but also moral theories about the good life may be subjected to rational discussion to determine their truth or falsity. Hence, the cultural mechanisms of social change engender emancipatory actions that criticize established beliefs regarding the role of the universe and the good life as normative peacekeepers of social order. Let me first discuss the metaphysical mechanism of social change.

Reforming metaphysical beliefs for social change

Man's place in the universe is defined in the context of metaphysical beliefs. If cultural change in society means that incorrect premises in the existing value system require reform of the system, then the place of man in the universe is also subject to revision. The non-justificationist theory of knowledge enables us to model emancipatory actions in an effort to discover whether the metaphysical beliefs and the place that they give to man in the universe need to be reformed, and if so, the actors initiate the cultural change necessary for transition from one social order to another.

Thinkers subject metaphysical beliefs to revision upon the realization that their beliefs regarding the universe and the place of man in it are problematic due to incorrect premises or inferences. Then, social movements attempt to translate the metaphysical reforms so that ordinary people can admit the need for such reforms. However, usage of the justified true belief account of knowledge to model metaphysical change involves infinite regress, and, due to the assumed infallibility of the justified metaphysical beliefs, the resultant model cannot explain how the actors may revise their views of the universe to provide a new meaning for man's good life. Such a justificational concept of knowledge does not allow us to explore how the actors use reason to revise their worldviews, even if the premises or inferences are shown to be false. Hence, it is fair to contend that justificationism prevents the theory of social change from identifying the central role the actors play in shaping a cultural change through revising their worldviews to open them to criticism.

In this line of reasoning, Martin Larson (1970: 103–104) offers the following insightful comparison for understanding how traditional worldviews and concepts of the good life have been revised by giving reason its proper role.

> This was the message of Christianity to the world: negate yourself, hate this world and the life thereof, surrender to the unseen, believe in Christ, put yourself in the right relationship with the supernatural, and you will go to Heaven after death . . . The message of Stoicism was this: Depend upon your reason and knowledge to gain virtue; develop your own resources; as there is no life after this, don't worry about the future; gain happiness from the consciousness of right-doing; make yourself absolute, independent of all things external to yourself; derive all good from within.

This comparison emphasizes that changes in modern man's understanding of the universe and the place of man within it would be able to replace the traditional reading of the good life with the pursuit of happiness as an ultimate value. In the same line of reasoning, Stephen L. Collins (1989: 6–7) points out:

> The Tudor idea of order with its manifest concepts of correspondence is part of an eschatologically Christian view of the world. Puritanism, while denying the traditional idea of order and correspondence, still defines a worldview that is eschatologically oriented, that is, based upon a final transcendental truth. Hobbes's political order, however, posits a radical celebration of non-eschatological existence. There is no purpose, beyond natural man who exists as a mobile, motive creature, which predetermines social, personal, or political order.
>
> The move from the Tudor idea of order to Hobbes's is all all-encompassing one. It is possible to identity the establishment of secular values in early modern England by analyzing the structural modifications that characterized the larger metamorphosis in cosmic vision as represented by this changed idea of order. . . . This transition in the idea of order marks a move from the idea

of society to the idea of the state . . . The locus of order shifts from the divine cosmos to the secular sovereign state. The idea of a state, in this context, suggests that social order is separate from divine, natural, or cosmic order. Social order, now, begins to incorporate rational utilitarian authority. And authority is no longer a matter of acquisition or definition; it is only a matter of exercise. Secular order then, redefines the social good.

This passage implies that a fundamental change in worldviews before the rise of a modern social order not only replaced the traditional value system with a secular one, but also created a new account of men's sovereignty in terms of a state that represents the people.

The concept of the good life and social change

The metaphysical reforms for social change lead to the role played by moral beliefs in the cultural mechanism of social change. The logical relation between man's place in the universe and the meaning of the good life previously discussed in the metaphysical reform regarding the meaning of universe prepares the ground for a corresponding change in the concepts of the good life. Emancipatory efforts taken by the actors through the mechanism of thinkers-movements-masses lead to the replacement of old worldviews regarding the concept of decent life with new ones. Revised ontological theories of the universe give the place of man in the universe new substance and encourage the actors to use critical reason for reforming their philosophy of the good life to make it consistent with the rewritten understanding of the universe. Hence, a cultural dialogue among individuals that started with a reform in worldviews may expand to discovering the false premises or inferences used to define the good life.

In the case of metaphysical beliefs, justificationist epistemology prevents us from understanding how the actors become involved in rational discussion concerning the moral philosophy of the good life. From a justificationist perspective, moral theory such as Kant's addresses the question of what man should do. However, admission of this moral theory defines our philosophy of the good life once and forever and allows no revision. Justification of a moral theory entails a consistent, unchanged philosophy of the good life.

The separation of justification and criticism in the philosophy of critical rationalism leads to the insight that an actor can consider his moral theory of the good life as a conjectural solution to the problem of ultimate values. Hence, one's theory of the good life is logically revisable. When none of the premises or inferences are shown to be false by argument, the actor can defend his moral theory as an unfalsified conjecture. This variability of moral theory allows the actor to use critical reason for revising his former understanding of the decent life when even just one premise of the theory is discovered to be false; the actor replaces the falsified concept of the good life with an unfalsified one.

188 Towards a critical rationalist theory of social change

Inspired by critical rationalist moral philosophy, the theory of social change is capable of explaining the moral mechanism of transition from one social order to another. Like Kant, one can argue that the actors use reason to give themselves a moral law for governing their self-interest; hence, all rational beings who can give themselves a universal moral law can consider themselves as the authors of the value system they have given themselves. However, Kant cannot show how the actors use practical reason to initiate a moral dialogue leading to a universal moral law because of the infinite regress involved. A critical rationalist theory of the good life, on the other hand, can lead us to the discovery of how such a moral dialogue takes place and results in a universal moral law. More importantly, Kant's ethics are unable to explain why the actors may hold their moral theories of the good life open to criticism, whereas critical rationalist moral philosophy reasons that the actors can be the agents of social change by replacing their value system with a new one based on revising the premises or inferences that are shown to be untrue.

Therefore, the moral mechanism of social change refers to the emancipatory efforts of actors who discover false premises or inferences in their understanding of the good life. As actors capable of being the authors of their value system, they have the capacity of revising common values by opening up them to criticism. If the existing social order depends on ultimate values, its alteration also takes shape when the actors use critical reason to discover the values that best manage the pursuit of self-interest for the benefit of peaceful social order.

The cultural aspect of social change can be summarized as follows. Since the goals of human actions are shaped by their orientation to their shared beliefs about the universe and the good life, the existence of a system of common values not only prevents the actors from becoming involved in a conflict of goals, but also may enable them to mobilize their actions for the promotion of social good. Moreover, our theory of social change can explain how the actors' capacity for opening up shared beliefs regarding the universe and the good life to criticism, thus allowing them to initiate a cultural dialogue for creating alternative views of the universe and the good life. Critical rationalist sociology views human actors, not only thinkers, but also social movements and ordinary people, as the agents of social change who apply critical reason for participation in social dialogue, thus opening up the assumptions of their fundamental beliefs on the universe and the good life to rational criticism. The cultural mechanism of social change reflects metaphysical and moral learning from error through opening the premises of the beliefs in question to criticism.

From the critical rationalist view, the cultural mechanism of social change represents an evolutionary change by means of which the actors *rationalize* their theories of the universe and the good life. Thus, the cultural aspect of social change reflects metaphysical and moral insights gained by opening up cultural values to rational criticism. The common values towards which action goals are oriented provide a greater cognitive capacity for preventing an irrational pursuit of self-interest through learning from mistakes. Hence, the cultural mechanism of social change contributes to the rise of a more peaceful and just social order due to *rationalization* of fundamental beliefs regarding the meaning of the universe and the good life.

Section III: governance and social change: a critical rationalist approach

From Chapter 8, we know that the concepts of human rights and legitimate governance are deeply rooted in the definition of the good life. As rational creatures, all individuals are eligible for equal rights to decent life. Since the concept of the good life depends on the definition of our worldviews and the place of man within the universe and since equal access to the good life originates in the rational nature of individuals, equal access to critical reason is to be expanded from moral philosophy to legal and political philosophies. According to the non-justificationist concept of rationality, the *definition* of critical reason implies that actors improve their reasoning by learning from mistakes, which leads them to a new understanding of *human equality*. Actors' access to critical reason enables them to achieve more rational accounts of human equality that direct them to a more rational understanding of the decent life, human rights and political legitimacy.

Opening up the law of society to rational criticism

The critical rationalist theory of social change explains the governmental mechanisms of social change, using the ideal type of emancipatory action to show that human agents, i.e. the mechanism of thinkers-social movements-masses, initiate a new level of social dialogue, following their metaphysical-moral dialogue, in order to turn the new moral consensus into improved institutions of law and politics. Hence, the theory of social change models this new level of social cooperation by learning from error. In practice, these two levels of social dialogue for the transition from one social order to another, the metaphysical-moral and the legal-political, are deeply related.

Human agents activate their critical reason to discover why their understanding of human rights and political legitimacy originated in erroneous views of the universe and the good life. From the viewpoint of critical rationalism, critical reason initiates a legal dialogue on the need for reforming flawed visions of human rights in accordance with the ameliorated concepts of the universe and the decent life. From a theoretical perspective, a *critical rationalist legal philosophy* enables us to model the behaviour of actors who realize that their conjectures of human rights are revisable. Through the separation of justification and criticism in the realm of legal philosophy, actors using critical reason can revise their previous beliefs concerning the equal rights of individuals to the good life by discovering the false premises or inferences supporting those beliefs.

190 Towards a critical rationalist theory of social change

Reformulation of the actors' theories of equal rights to the good life paves the way for the rise of a legal dialogue aimed at reforming the content of law in society. Using critical rationality, the actors agree to replace the prior legal order of society with its mistaken premises or inferences regarding the equality of right-holders before the law. The legal mechanism of social change reflects learning from social criticism and shows how the actors explore their new concepts of the universe and the decent life to revise the system of human rights. Reformation of the actors' account of *equal* rights to the good life alone is insufficient; the creation of new legal institutions in society should legalize the enhanced account of human rights.

In the history of the development of law in the modern age, the transition from pre-modern 'natural rights' to modern 'natural rights' presents a good example of the legal mechanism of social change. In *Natural Rights and History*, Leo Strauss (1965: 182–183) writes,

> The premodern natural law doctrines taught the *duties* of man; if they paid any attention at all to his rights, they conceived of them as essentially derivative from his *duties*. As has frequently been observed, in the course of the seventeenth and eighteenth centuries a much greater emphasis was put on *rights* than ever had been done before. . . . The fundamental change from an orientation by natural *duties* to an orientation by natural *rights* finds its clearest and most telling expression in the teaching of Hobbes, who squarely made an unconditional natural right the basis of all natural duties . . . The profound change under consideration can be traced directly to Hobbes's concern with a human guaranty for the actualization of the right social order . . . The actualization of a social order that is defined in terms of man's *duties* is necessarily uncertain and even improbable . . . Quite different is the case of a social order that is defined in terms of the *rights* of man. For the rights in question express, and are meant to express, something that everyone actually desires anyway; they hallow everyone's self-interest as everyone sees it or can easily be brought to see it (emphasis added).

This quotation implies that the rise of the modern concept of natural rights contributed significantly to the transition from a social order based on duty to one based on rights.

Political legitimacy and openness to criticism

The political mechanism of social change makes us aware that the actors are capable of using critical reason to revise the governmental system in society through building new institutions to protect human rights. The political mechanism lets us see individual agents, in terms of thinkers-social movements-masses, apply their critical reason to discover the flawed premises of their theories of good governance in terms of legitimate usage of political power for enforcing the law of society. From the perspective of a *critical rationalist political philosophy*, the individual agents can remodel their political actions as they revise their political theories of legitimate governance upon discovering that the theories of governance are no longer valid due to their incorrect premises or inferences. Hence, the actors, whether the elite or those in social movements, are capable of beginning a political dialogue to persuade each other of political change for establishing a new form of good governance to better enforce the legal ideal of people's equal access to the good life. While an upgrade in the legal order of society assures individuals' equal rights to a decent life, the governmental mechanism of social change cannot fully perform its task without parallel progress in the political order of the society to guarantee individuals the equal right to self-determination.

Thus, the governmental mechanism of social change consists of the legal and political aspects of a social dialogue through which the actors convince each other that the wrong premises or inferences of the previous legal and political systems delegitimize the present form of governance. By using critical reason to investigate the false premises or inferences that make their legal and political institutions unfair and illegitimate, people learn from their prior unsound premises and from *rationalize* the governance of society. Hence, governance benefits from an evolutionary process that allows individual actors to give themselves better systems for enforcing equal rights to the good life, not only for controlling unlimited pursuit of self-interest, but also for advancing joint cooperation for the good of society. In brief, the governmental and the cultural mechanisms act as processes of social change by means of which individuals give themselves a new social order. These *evolving theories of critical reason* enable individuals to discover new theories of the good life, human rights and political legitimacy. However, the justificationist concept of rationality does not explain how the actors revise their own concepts of reason and discover implications for the transition from a flawed social order to a new and better one.

I should emphasize that actors who cannot justify their theories of human rights and governance are not capable of creating infallible mechanisms of social change. Such actors can only hold their theories open to criticism in order to find improved models for human rights and legitimate governance to manage egoistic behaviour. In the transition from old to new governance, a learning process takes place in which individuals adapt to using their equal rights to the good life in a better way.

In modern times, good governance is defined in the following manner:

> Good political governance emphasizes the rule of law, accountability, and transparency. It seeks to achieve these goals through a constitutional framework that is not easily amendable, free and fair multi-party elections, and a clear separation of powers among the executive, judiciary, and the legislative branches of the government.
>
> (Haq 1999: 31)

192 Towards a critical rationalist theory of social change

However, the transition from a monarchy to a liberal democracy during the past few centuries marks a political change that has used not only the modern notion of 'natural rights', but also of good governance in terms of institutions for the rule of law, multi-party elections and a clear separation of powers among the branches of government.

Section IV: critical rationalism and the economic mechanism of social change

In Chapter 8, I have argued that economic agents give themselves the law of supply and demand to create an efficient mechanism of resource allocation in society. The economic actors come to an agreement on defining their production plans according to the property rights the legal order gives them concerning the means of production, on the one hand, and formulating their consumption preferences according to their shared understanding of the good life, on the other. With these agreements in hand, producers and consumers jointly create the law of supply and demand as a *spontaneous* mechanism of resource allocation through which producers supply goods and services to meet the consumers' needs. This mechanism of market economy *automatically* regulates prices to produce an abundant supply of goods at low prices. It is important to remember that such an economic law of supply and demand stems from an agreement between producers and consumers to define production plans and consumer preferences according to their human rights and shared concepts of the good life.

Openness of the economic order to rational criticism

From the non-justificational perspective, a critical rationalist philosophy of economics has the task of exploring the economic mechanism of social change. Since neither producers nor consumers can epistemologically *justify* their production plans and preference patterns according to the accounts of human rights and the good life, the law of supply and demand they give themselves is not an absolute and infallible law, but may be revised to allocate the resources to the needs of people more efficiently. A non-justificational economic philosophy reveals how economic agents, producers as well as consumers, use critical reason to revise the law of supply and demand according to new views of the decent life, human rights and legitimate governance. This new economic order is not a *justified* mechanism of resource allocation, so it is open to revision by producers and consumers, the ultimate originators of the market process.

The critical rationalist philosophy of economics enables us to see that producers and consumers capable of creating an economic order by giving themselves the law of supply and demand can use critical reason to understand the disparities in the market mechanism and revise it in compliance with the new theories of the good life and human rights. This revision of the economic order in view of its shortcomings reveals an explanation of the economic force driving social change. It is economic agents' critical reason that lets them initiate this economic mechanism by allowing producers and consumers to explore the logical consequences of the new systems of equal rights and self-governance as well as their new ultimate values of the good life for *rationalizing* their production plans and preference patterns.

Taking the supply and demand sides of the economy into account, one can argue that critical reason enables producers to integrate a new system of the human rights into their production plans and consumers to incorporate new values of the good life into their preference patterns for goods and services.[2] Hence, a cultural change in terms of the emergence of a new value system and legal-political changes in terms of the formation of a better framework for human rights and institutions of governance enable economic agents to shape emancipatory efforts for the creation of more efficient mechanisms of resource allocation in the process of social change.

In summary, the economic mechanism of social change enables understanding of how producers and consumers can learn from their own mistaken production plans or preference patterns. The transition from one mechanism of resource allocation to another makes the economic order of society more rational by replacing false patterns of production or consumption with new ones that are not shown to be false due to new visions of the good life, human rights and good governance. This will rationalize the economic order of society by achieving a greater capacity for effective mobilization of scarce resources to satisfy people's diverse needs.

Section V: critical rationalism and the evolution of society

It is understandable that the critical rationalist theory of social change leads to a new analysis of social evolution offering a different theoretical perspective. Parsons, for example, defines social evolution as an expansion of society's long-term capacity for adapting to its environment. According to Parsons (1967: 494–495),

A set of 'normative expectations' pertaining to man's relation to his environment delineates the ways in which adaptation should be developed and extended. Within the relevant range, cultural innovations, especially definitions of what man's life *ought* to be, thus replace Darwinian variations in genetic constitution.

As Savage (1981: 212) reminds us, Parsons contends,

History is not simply a process of differentiation and increasing complexity, but of advancing stages of humanity. Human action is distinguished by the

194 Towards a critical rationalist theory of social change

intervention of values in behavior – the more those values dominate and the more explicitly and consistently they operate, the more "human" that action is.

In Parsons' social evolutionary theory, history is the system of humanity's further development. Nevertheless, the role of human reason in a cultural change for social evolution is not the subject of attention in Parsons's theory of social evolution.

Habermas (1979) provides a different theory of social evolution using his theory of communicative action to address the question of social evolution. In brief, Habermas (1979: xxii) argues,

> . . . it is only socialized individuals who learn; but the learning ability of individuals provides a "resource" that can be drawn upon in the formation of new social structures. The results of learning processes find their way into the cultural tradition; they comprise a kind of cognitive potential that can be drawn upon in social movements when unsolvable system problems require a transformation of the basis forms of social integration.

Habermas's theory of communicative rationality suggests an analogy between the stages of the individual's moral consciousness and the stages of social evolution:

> Cognitive developmental psychology has shown that in ontogenesis there are different stages of moral consciousness, stages that can be described in particular as preconventional, and postconventional patterns of problemsolving. The same patterns turn up again in the social evolution of moral and legal representations.
>
> (1979: 99)

As Habermas argues,

> . . . the initial state of archaic societies – characterized by a conventional kinship organization, a preconventional stage of law, and an egocentric interpretation system – could itself be changed only by constructive learning on the part of socialized individuals. It is only in a derivative sense that societies "learn".
>
> (1979: 121)

Nevertheless, Habermas does not speak of an independent actor who applies communicative reason to become an agent of social evolution via the creation of a value system.

Critical rationalism and social evolution as a learning process

Using my general theory of critical rationalism, I suggest that we observe what occurs during social change in order to address social evolution. The actors apply reason to criticize the premises or inference forms of their worldviews regarding the universe and the good life shown to be false. Critical reason guides actors in correcting these worldviews that form the normative foundations of society. Thus, social change through metaphysical and moral learning is the basis for the actors' correction of their conjectures regarding the good life and the development of a more reliable concept of the universe and man's place in it. As Habermas argues, the need for reforming worldviews originates in evolutionary challenges that society masters in the effort to improve its performance in realizing the good life.

Moreover, the transition from an established social order to a more progressive one through critical thinking also leads the actors to correct the systems of human rights, political governance and recourse allocation. Put differently, actors who apply new theories of the universe and the good life also benefit from a more substantial system of human rights to a decent life. From a legal perspective, the new system of the equal rights does not suffer from the mistakes of the former legal system and can thus better realize the moral ideal of equal rights to the good life.

Now the actors are capable of enhancing their model of the legitimate usage of power based on their new reading of human rights. Since the previous model of political governance may have rested on an unsound concept of human rights, the new form of governance uses altered institutions of law to give all the citizens a new role in self-determination of their governance. As people's participation in self-governance improves through learning from mistaken premises or inferences, the capacity of the political order for enforcing just law in society also evolves.

As for the economy, the evolution in society takes place due to the actors' realization that they should change the mistaken assumptions in their accounts of the good life and define their preference patterns according to more reliable moral premises. In addition, realizing that their prior readings of human rights and political legitimacy are no longer tenable due to their false premises or inferences, the actors have to revise their production plans. Hence, economic actors can *reform* the law of supply and demand governing the economic order of society in order to develop a more effective mobilization of scarce resource for the production of diverse goods and services to meet the needs of the good life in a better way.

In sum, critical rationalist sociology leads to realization of how human actors use critical reason to *correct* the mistaken premises or inferences upon which common values and social institutions are shaped. Critical reason leads to the discovery of alternative views of the universe and of a decent life for giving themselves new systems of human rights, political governance and economic order. The societal transition from one social order to an alternative one indicates a *rationalization* of social order towards a higher level of justice and efficiency that

196 Towards a critical rationalist theory of social change

only non-justificationist theories of knowledge and rationality can elucidate. In brief, the concept of rationality as 'unfalsified belief' enables the philosophy of critical rationalism to provide a theory of society for modelling the evolution of human society.

Notes

1 In *The Site of the Social*, Schatzki (2002: 6–17) distinguishes three concepts of social order from each other: regularity/pattern, stability and interdependence suggesting: "An order is an arrangement in which entities also possess meaning and identity" (ibid: 19). Schatzki poses this concept of social order to argue that the subject matter of the theory of social order is a dynamic rather than static social ordering. I suggest the same in the critical rationalist theory of social order.

2 In 'Natural Law and the Rise of Economic Individualism in England,' Alfred Chalk (1951: 337–338) argues that the rise of the modern concept of natural law has played an important role in the formation of market economy. According to Chalk, "... the essential attribute of all natural-law theory is contained in the statement that 'nature will have her course'. ... The medieval interpretation [of the natural law, however], as typified in the writings of Aquinas, was that natural law should be subsumed under the divine law. For Aquinas, the exercise of economic controls was in most instances in strict accord with the principles of both natural and divine law. The medieval doctrine of natural law did not give free play to the self-interest of a group of 'economic men' bargaining in a free market. In most respects, the new sixteenth-century doctrine of the merchant class was the antithesis of the Thomistic view that the church and/or the state should regulate prices whenever they caused undue hardships". Chalk aims to show us that the rise of the modern doctrine of natural law prepared the ground for the emergence of a free market allowing individuals to pursue their self-interests with help of the mechanism of relative prices.

Bibliography

Chalk, A.F. (1951) "Natural Law and the Rise of Economic Individualism in England". In: *Journal of Political Economy*, 59 (4), pp. 332–347.

Collins, S.L. (1989) *From Divine Cosmos to Sovereign State: An Intellectual History of Consciousness and the Idea of Order in Renaissance England*. New York, Oxford University Press.

Habermas, J. (1979) *Communication and the Evolution of Society*, McCarthy, T. (trans.). Boston, Beacon Press.

Haq, Mahbub ul. (1999) *Human Development in South Asia: The Crisis of Governance*. Bangalore, Oxford University.

Larson, M.A. (1970) *The Modernity of Milton: A Theological and Philosophical Interpretation*. New York, AMS Press.

Parsons, T. (2005 [1991]) *The Social System*. London, Routledge.

Parsons, T. (1970) "Some Considerations on Social Change". In: Eisenstadt, S.H. (ed.) *Readings in Social Evolution and Development*. New York, Pergamon, pp. 95–121.

Parsons, T. (1967) "Evolutionary Universal in Society". In: Parsons (ed.) *Sociological Theory and Modern Society*. New York, Free Press, pp. 490–520.

Savage, S.P. (1981) *The Theories of Talcott Parsons: The Social Relations of Action*. London, Palgrave Macmillan.

Schatzki, T.R. (2002) *The Site of the Social: A Philosophical Account of the Constitution of Social Life and Change*. University Park, Pennsylvania State University.

Strauss, L. (1965) *Natural Rights and History*. Chicago, University of Chicago.

Touraine, A. (1965) *Sociologie de l'action*. Paris, Le Seuil.

Wrong, D.H. (1999) *The Oversocialized Conception of Man*. New Brunswick, Transaction Publishers.

Chapter 10

Critical rationalism and the theory of society

A summary

Masoud Mohammadi Alamuti

Introduction

The central aim of this book is to liberate the theory of society from a justificationist concept of rationality involving infinite regress and to integrate the philosophy of critical rationalism into the theory of society through the theory of
human action. The implementation of critical rationalism to provide such a theory
of action requires reinvention of the non-justificationist concept of reason. The
first part of this book devotes itself to 'Epistemology and Critical Rationalism' in
order to show how a conjectural account of objective knowledge through the concept of unfalsified claims provides critical rationalism with a new epistemological
foundation for addressing the question of how to judge a claim of rationality as
true. The answer found in the first part is that the premises and inference forms of
such claims may be accounted as true if not shown to be false. The second part of
this volume, 'Towards a Critical Rationalist Theory of Society', uses a reinvented
philosophy of critical rationalism to explore how the ideal types of rational action
shaped by a new concept of rationality may alter our understanding of social order
and social change.

Summing up my answers to the question of how critical rationalism contributes
to the theory of society, Chapter 10 proceeds in three sections. The first section
shows how the non-justificationist concept of reason defines rational action. The
second offers a brief explanation of the critical rationalist theory of society, and
the third outlines the potential consequences of my theory of society for a sociology of the open society.

Section I: non-justificationism: rationality and human action

The main reason for posing the question of objective knowledge in Chapter 1 at
the starting point of this volume is to show the *inability* of justificationist epistemology, whether intellectualist or empiricist, to address the problem of objective
knowledge due to the involvement of infinite regress. This issue points out the

Critical rationalism and the theory of society   199

need for a new theory of knowledge to address the problem of objective knowledge. Before approaching such a theory and showing how it leads to a new conception of rationality, I have argued that Popper's critical rationalism and Bartley's pancritical rationalism rest on the justified true belief account of knowledge and hence cannot provide the theory of society with an ideal type of 'rational action' suitable for addressing the problem of social order.

With the defects in the theories of objective knowledge in mind, I have designed Chapters 2 and 3 to offer a new critique of the philosophy of critical rationalism to counter the justified true belief accounts of knowledge that Popper and Bartley apply to address the question of what rational beliefs are. In light of these critiques of Popper's and Bartley's critical rationalism, Chapter 4 has gone on to suggest a non-justificationist epistemology according to which Chapter 5 has aimed to reinvent critical rationalism through a non-justificationist theory of rationality.

In this way, the first part of my book 'Epistemology and Critical Rationalism' has provided the second part with a new philosophical basis for the development of an entirely new micro-foundation for the macro-theory of society. It becomes clear during my arguments in Chapter 6 that justificationism acts as an obstacle for an accurate reading of reason and subsequently for understanding the contribution of critical reason to the rise of social order and its change. In the framework of this background, Chapter 7 has shown how the non-justificationist concept of reason introduces a new theory of human action for the reformulation of the theory of society.

The non-justificationist concept of reason and human action

The central aim of Chapter 7 has been to use the non-justificationist concept of reason to return the human actor's autonomy to the theory of human action. I have argued that it is not possible to show how a peaceful and just social order comes into being and how to transform an existing social order into a new one without a fundamental change in the micro-foundations of macro-sociology.

The critical rationalist action theory is central for implementing the integration of critical rationalism into the theory of society due to its application of the concept of rationality in dealing with the question of how reason drives action without involving infinite regress. Moreover, the critical rationalist theory of action provides the theory of society with a micro-foundation by answering the question of how rational action makes a peaceful social order possible. For these reasons, I have tried to create a systemic link between epistemology and the theory of rationality, on the one hand, and the model of human action and the theory of society, on the other. This linkage has enabled me to infer key insights for the theory of society resulting from the replacement of justificationist epistemology with non-justificationist epistemology. This substitution allows us to base a new model of human action upon a concept of 'rationality' that does not involve infinite regress

200 Critical rationalism and the theory of society

and informs us how actors apply critical reason to reach the normative and institutional agreements that are necessary for understanding the rise of social order and explaining social change.

As argued in Chapter 6, the main problem with the justificationist models of rational action such as Kant's model of action is that the function of 'reason' cannot be addressed accurately by a concept of rationality built on a justified true belief account of knowledge. Let it suffice to say that justificationist accounts of knowledge are unable to provide a model of rational action on an epistemological basis that shows how the actor uses objective knowledge to drive action. In Chapter 4, I have argued that the conclusion of a rational argument cannot be *justified* as true since neither the premises nor the inferences may be infallible. For this reason, I argue that it is possible for the actors to avoid infinite regress by using objective knowledge in terms of unfalsified conjecture to rationalize their behaviours and that actors can utilize fallible premises or inferences to see whether the conclusion of a rational argument is refuted by argument or experience.

The novelty of my non-justificationist theory of knowledge lies in two key points. Firstly, the premises of a knowledge claim are to be regarded as criticizable rather than justifiable. Secondly, one falsifying premise can refute a claim of knowledge as the conclusion of a rational argument. These two points enable non-justificationist epistemology to imply that all claims of knowledge can be considered as objective if and only if their premises or inferences are not shown to be false. This new theory of knowledge leads to a general theory of critical rationalism in Chapter 5 that implies that claims of rationality, including the theory of rationality itself, can be subjected to rational scrutiny to determine whether their premises or inferences are shown to be false by argument or experience.

The infinite regress involved in justificationism implies that action theories defining their concepts of rationality based on the justified true belief account of knowledge cannot explain the role performed by reason in the actor's determination of his goals and means of action. Hence, the question of how reason governs action remains unexplained in a justificationist framework. Once we admit that the role of reason in shaping action has not been addressed properly, the need to replace the justificationist account of reason with non-justification becomes evident. Popper's critical rationalism and Bartley's pancritical rationalism, however, do not offer the non-justificationist concept of reason necessary for understanding that it is reason, not passion that drives action.

Popper's and Bartley's justificationism and the meaning of rational action

Chapter 2 has argued that Popper's notion of critical rationalism as a moral attitude of listening to criticism and learning from it does not suffice to show how the actor uses critical reason to guide his actions. While Popper argues that he

Critical rationalism and the theory of society 201

follows Kant in saying that being rational is a moral choice in favour of reason, Kant's argument that the actor can employ pure reason is aimed at showing that reason justifies the actor's moral actions, but not that the actor follows moral law because of irrational faith in it. Popper's critical rationalism involves justificationism through the erroneous premise that critical rationalism can be justified if and only if all the claims of rationality can be justified by argument or experience. However, the mistaken demand for justification poses the question of why critical rationalism should have to be justified to be considered true.

Chapter 3 has argued that Bartley, while recognizing the justificational nature of Popper's critical rationalism, presents the alternative theory of pancritical rationalism that involves the same problem. Bartley argues that a separation of justification and criticism enables theorization of critical rationalism. A critical rationalist is a person who admits a belief as a true belief if and only if he has held all of his beliefs open to criticism and then realized that the belief in question is not refuted by argument or experience. While Bartley has made a vital contribution to our understanding of critical rationalism by moving from an *irrational faith* in reason to a *rational faith* in reason, his pancritical rationalism does not show how actors apply deductive logic to explore whether a rational belief is actually a false conjecture. Chapter 4 has shown that the lack of a non-justificationist model of deduction prevents exploration of whether a claim of rationality is refuted upon demonstration that its premises are untrue.

In brief, Bartley's use of a justificational model of deduction prevents him from explaining how to refute a rational belief held open to criticism in practice. Therefore, pancritical rationalism does not inform us how critical reason works or answer the question of how human action is driven by reason. The novelty of my epistemological critiques of Popper's and Bartley's theories of critical rationalism lies in showing that their philosophies of critical rationalism rest on the justified true belief account of knowledge reflected mainly in the justificationist model of deductive inference. If Popper's critical rationalism and Bartley's pancritical rationalism are unable to show how reason works, how can they show that reason drives human action and contributes to the rise of the normative consensus necessary for a peaceful social order? Hence, I have argued in this book that the philosophy of critical rationalism ought to be reinvented according to a non-justificationist theory of knowledge for integration into the micro-foundations of macro-sociology.

Chapter 7 has used the notion of the separation of justification and criticism to formulate a model of rational action according to a non-justificationist theory of rationality. This new theory of rationality defines the function of reason as operating through conjecture and refutation. The faculty of reason proposes a set of premises to devise a claim of validity, and the non-justificationist model of deduction allows it to examine this claim. When even one of its premises of the claim are shown to be false, reason enables the actor to reach a rational conclusion concerning the truth or falsity of the claim in question.

202 Critical rationalism and the theory of society

The novelty of my philosophy of critical rationalism lies in the fundamental point that my theory explains how to refute a claim of rationality held open to criticism logically once even one of its premises has been shown to be false. This novel reading leads us to change our understanding of critical rationality from mere openness to criticism to critical rationality as the determination of all our beliefs through objective knowledge in terms of unfalsified conjectures. Therefore, Chapter 5 has introduced a general theory of critical rationalism to explain how reason works and becomes better through conjecture and refutation. However, through its non-justificationist theory of knowledge, my theory of rationality gives an entirely new content to the meaning of trial and error than that found in Popper's logic of scientific discovery. This non-justificationist concept of rationality has prepared the ground for addressing the question of how critical reason drives action for the creation of common values and social institutions to manage the unlimited pursuit of self-interest and enable collective cooperation for social good.

To define the model of human action according to the new theory of rationality, I have argued in Chapter 7 that allowing reason to perform through conjecture and refutation does not limit the role of reason in shaping human action to find effective means for given ends. Unlike the utilitarian action model, but similar to the Kantian model, human reason through conjecture and refutation has a more important role to play: this new theory does *not* view the goals of action as purely subjective and determined by passions, but as objective through unfalsified conjecture. Thus, the critical rationalist model of human action uses non-justificationist epistemology to show that action means *as well as* action ends may be objective due to the actors' unfalsified conjectures regarding the means and the ends.

It is worthy of note that Kant's theory of rational action, the doctrine of practical reason, follows the same spirit of showing that reason governs action due to the moral law that a rational being can give himself. However, Kant's moral philosophy is not successful in fulfilling its promise because the infinite regress involved in Kant's theory of knowledge prevents it from explaining how reason shapes moral law. In contrast, the non-justificationist theory of critical rationalism enables us to recognize the capacity of critical reason for making the ends of an action as well as the means *rational* by basing them on objective knowledge in the sense of unfalsified conjecture. Therefore, the critical rationalist model of action refutes a key distinction made by the sociological theories of action between the *action type of value rationality* and the *action type of instrumental rationality*. In both of these cases, the rationality of an action depends on unfalsified conjecture to support the actor's claims regarding the 'rationality' of the ends or the 'rationality' of the means.

Non-justificationism and emancipatory action

The non-justificational concept of reason has played a key role in proposing the critical rationalist models of action. Inspired by these models, the emancipatory action type is central for showing how 'rational beings' use their objective knowledge to discuss the meaning of the good life. This critical rationalist portrait of the actor does not refer to an oversocialized man in modern sociology who uses practical reason merely to respect a given system of values, but rather specifies an independent actor who, regardless of social conditions and personal interests, enters into a dialogue with others to create common values for building a peaceful and just social order. Chapter 7 has proposed the mechanism of *thinkers-social movements-masses* to express how the social dialogue between rational beings takes place. First, thinkers activate their critical reason to suggest a concept of the good life, and, once social movements have accepted that concept and provided a tangible reading of it, the masses join in to strive for respect of the notion of the good life. In this manner, the process of social dialogue leads society to reach a system of common values. Non-justificationist epistemology enables the critical rationalist theory of action to argue that independent actors apply objective knowledge to reach an agreement on common values and social institutions for controlling egoistic behaviours to make a peaceful social order possible.

Section II: critical rationalist sociology: an overview

Two main problems confront critical rationalist sociology. The first is the problem of social order, i.e. the question of how critical reason enables actors to *create* the common values and institutions necessary for managing the pursuit of self-interest. The second is the problem of social change, i.e. the question of how critical reason allows the actors to *revise* their common values and institutions in order to replace the existing social order with a new one.

Critical rationalist sociology and the problem of social order

By applying the proposed theory of action, Chapter 8 has attempted to comprehend the problem of social order from a new point of view. To this end, it has argued that the question of how the actors reach an agreement on ultimate values is central to the critical rationalist theory of society. Parsons's theory of social order does not address the question of how actors arrive at a moral consensus on the ultimate values because the theory regards the value system a given fact. The reason for Parsons's assumption is found in his justificationist critique of Kant's moral theory, which prevents him from exploring a non-justificational solution to the problem of ultimate values.

Kant argues that the actors can give themselves a universal moral law to provide a rational standard of behaviour for managing the pursuit of self-interest. Like Weber, Parsons reasons that Kant cannot *justify* his universal moral law due to premises that are self-evident for him. However, Chapter 8 reminds us that a non-justificational defence of the universal moral law is possible. Kant's

204   Critical rationalism and the theory of society

epistemology deals with infinite regress due to its justificationism, and the doctrine of practical reason cannot address the process of attaining common values. Acceptance of my critique of Kantian ethics reveals how the epistemology of critical rationalism enables the theory of social order to show that critical reason is the means by which actors give themselves universal moral law. Unlike Kant, critical rationalists regard moral law as criticizable, but not justifiable.

Critical rationalist sociology bases its explanation of social order upon a new epistemology of rational action. In spite of the assumption of the utilitarian model of action that the goals of action are subjective and cannot be rationalized, the critical rationalist model of action argues that the goals of action, just like the means, may be rationalized. Thus, the solution of critical rationalism for the problem of social order can be summarized as follows: the separation of justification and criticism enables the sociologist to argue that peaceful social order is possible among individuals pursuing their goals due to the critical reason the actors employ to agree on a system of moral values and social institutions. From this writer's perspective, what enables critical rationalist sociology to argue that individuals give themselves common values and social institutions is the non-justificational epistemology that shows that dialogue among individuals is possible without infinite regress. The central claim in this book is that the rise of social order through the creation of common values and institutions cannot be explained without recognition of such an *epistemological capacity* in rational beings. In other words, the novelty of my theory of social order lies in the argument that the critical rationalist theory of society provides an *epistemological solution* for the problem of how actors *agree* on common values and build social institutions of law, governance and market according to the value system they have given themselves.

Critical rationalist sociology introduces five mechanisms of social order. Through the metaphysical mechanism, the actors use critical reason to discover a shared view of the universe that defines the place of man within the universe. The moral mechanism refers to another dialogue on concept of the good life. These metaphysical-moral learning processes allow the actors to rationalize their 'validity claims' regarding the universe and the good life. In this sense, we can speak of actors creating common values that individuals give themselves for managing their individual behaviours to prevent conflicting goals and means. Based on these first two mechanisms, the actors initiate a set of legal, political and economic mechanisms as *institutional learning processes* with the aim of turning their normative consensus into the social institutions of law, governance and market that make a peaceful and just social order possible.

In addition, the critical rationalist theory of society analyzes social order according to a similar cognitive possibility that it recognizes for actors who are able to reach an agreement on the concept of equal rights to the good life and use that concept to discover a legitimate form of governance for enforcing the equal rights. The actors also use their concept of equal rights and legitimate governance to discover an efficient mechanism of resource allocation for mobilizing scarce

Critical rationalism and the theory of society   205

resources to meet the needs of the good life. Thus, I suggest that the *cognitive possibility of rational dialogue* enables actors to turn common values into a set of institutional agreements on human rights, legitimate governance and effective mechanisms for resource allocation.

Critical rationalist sociology and the problem of social change

Critical rationalist sociology applies its theory of human action to provide a solution for the problem of social change. Chapter 9 has used the epistemology of critical rationalism to answer the question of how actors can use critical reason to discover whether common values and social institutions suffer from mistaken premises and need revision. For social change as well as social order, the cognitive capacity of rational beings with access to critical reason is what lets the actors open the premises and inferences of their normative and institutional agreements to self-criticism. This epistemological self-criticism reveals the mechanism necessary for social change.

From a Kantian perspective, it is possible to see the reason why rational beings are capable of giving themselves a universal moral law and creating a moral community of rational beings according to the universal law. However, the Kantian theory of society faces two major problems. First, it cannot tell us how human actors who *cannot* justify the premises of their moral claims may use practical reason to reach a normative agreement on a universal moral law to regulate their actions towards a peaceful social order. Secondly, the Kantian theory of society does not explain how rational beings who have used practical reason to agree on a universal moral law can revise this law when they realize that the premises of this law are shown to be false. Hence, Kant's theory of society would not explain how rational beings change their society once they have realized that the universal moral law they have given themselves might actually be wrong. Kant's justificationist epistemology does not allow modelling human action to see how actors criticize the moral laws that cannot withstand rigorous logical examination.

However, it is the concept of *rational belief* as *unfalsified conjecture* that allows us to model rational action so that individuals can open their previous understandings of the universe, the good life, human rights, legitimate governance and economic efficiency to criticism. Thus, the critical rationalist sociology of social change can give actors the role of questioning an established social order from an independent position due to the general theory of critical rationalism that has already made it possible for reason to question whether its claim of rational belief is false due to its premises and forms of inference.

The novelty of my theory of social change lies in the cognitive capacity it specifies for human actors. This is what enables them to examine the established value consensus on the meaning of the universe and the good life and to use the power of their normative criticism to initiate institutional change in society in areas regarding human rights, political governance and economic order.

Section III: towards a sociology of the open society

Upon completion of this volume, I would like to note that the theory of society developed here through the reinvention of critical rationalist philosophy prepares the theoretical foundations for a sociology of the open society. In particular, the critical rationalist theory of social change prepares the ground for discovering the mechanisms of the transition from a closed to an open society.

The transition from a closed to an open society requires the model of a human actor who is not just an oversocialized individual adapting his behaviour to social conditions and reproducing social order, but who is also an independent actor behaving according to his objective knowledge, regardless of personal interests or social conditions. The relationship established in this volume between non-justificationist epistemology and the general theory of critical rationalism and the application of that relation to introduce a critical rationalist theory of society provide the sociology of the open society with new theoretical foundations, making it radically different from Popper's theory of the open society. This first volume has reinvented the philosophy of critical rationalism upon the basis of a conjectural-refutational account of knowledge in order to make the critical rationalist theory of society the new foundation for a sociology of the open society.

Index

academic scepticism 21
actors 163, 187; as agents of social
  evolution 156–159; beliefs regarding
  universe 7; critical reason 8;
  determination of actions 152–155; equal
  political power 173
Agassi, J. 41, 98
agents of social dialogue 158
Albert, H. 43, 61, 174–175
Alexander, J.C. 107
Andersson, G. 41
a priori knowledge 16–17, 23, 28, 31

Bacon, F. 18
Bartley, W. 2, 87, 201; criticism, non-
  justificational concept of 46–49, 51, 56,
  61–62; critique of justificational theory
  of knowledge 4, 48; justificational
  approach 23; justificationist conception
  of rationalism 49; limits of rationality
  52–54; non-justificational logic of
  science 51; pancritical rationalism
  46–52, 55–63, 89–91; on Popper's
  critical rationalism 52–57; on Popper's
  irrational faith in reason 54–55;
  rationality, non-justificational concept
  of 2–3, 57; *The Retreat to Commitment*
  48, 63n1; separation of justification and
  criticism 47–51; solution for problem of
  rational belief 59–60; theory of critical
  rationalism 44; theory of rationality 3,
  46, 49–51, 54–58, 61–63; uncritical
  rationalism 46–47
Beall, J.C. 78–79
Bendix, R. 119–120
bourgeois capitalism 118
Bourricaud, F. 127
Burnham, D. 15

Calvinism 119
Cartesian epistemology 19
cognitive developmental psychology
  138–139, 194
Collins, S.L. 186
communicative actions 132–136, 138,
  140, 194
communicative rationality 132–136, 173, 194
conjectural knowledge 3, 32–34, 70–71, 88
conjectures and refutations 6, 32, 37–38,
  43, 49–50, 71, 88, 152, 154, 157, 168,
  175, 201–202
consensual epistemology 130, 132–134,
  139–140, 144, 159
critical rationalism/critical rationalist
  theory 1–8, 18, 24–25, 27, 33, 35,
  38–44, 52, 60–62, 66, 71, 77, 80–81,
  84–85, 87, 169, 200–202; action
  theory 6, 146, 154–155; Albert's
  epistemological view of 43, 61;
  Bartley's pancritical rationalism 46–52,
  55–63, 89–91; concepts of value and
  instrumental reason 156–157; cultural
  change and 185; Diller's view of
  61; explanation of social order 204;
  formulations 94; growth of 95–103;
  irrationalism and 42; justificational
  perspective 40–41; market process 175;
  Miller's epistemological view of 42–43;
  as a moral attitude of openness 43, 53,
  55; as moral commitment 44; and moral
  dialogue for common values 103–105;
  and moral dialogue for social order
  159; moral philosophy 171; Popper's
  definition of 1; Popper's philosophy of
  38–44, 52–55, 88–89; Popper's view of
  39–42; rationality problem and 92; and
  rationalization of social order 157–158,

164–165; separation between justification and criticism 88–89; sociology 178–179, 188, 195, 203–206; in terms of unfalsified conjecture 7, 91–95; theory of politics 173; theory of social change 181–196; theory of social order 7, 165, 170–171, 177–178, 182; theory of society 170

critical rationalist sociology 178–179, 188, 195, 203–206

critical rationalist theory of social change 181–196

critical rationalist theory of social order 7, 165, 170, 177–178, 182

critical reason 3, 7–8, 52, 55, 62–63, 87–89, 95, 103–105, 148–159, 165, 168–174, 176–179, 181–183, 185, 187–193, 195, 199–205; rationalization of society and 157–158

critical theory 81

critical thinking 81, 91, 95, 195

cultural mechanism: of social change 182–189; social order 7

deductive inference 51, 73–74, 201; justificational model of 74–75; justificational versus non-justificational 77–80; modus ponens and modus tollens 74–76; non-justificational model of 76

deductive logic 14, 36, 63, 69, 73–77, 80, 85n3, 201

Descartes, R. 13–14; dogmatic epistemology 12–13, 18; 'I think, therefore I am' 14–15; *Rules for the Direction of the Mind* 14; self-evident principles 14–15, 17; theory of knowledge 15

Diller, A. 60–61

discursive ethics 134–135

dogmatic and sceptic theories of knowledge 3, 9, 12

dogmatic epistemology 12–13; challenges 13; of justified true belief 12–20; notions of 13

dogmatic intellectualism 19

dogmatic rationalism 15, 42, 97–102

dogmatist epistemology 3–4

driving forces of social change 6, 110–111, 128, 162

Durkheim, E. 5, 159; justificationism 111–112; model of human action 109–110; moral codes of behaviours and social order 110–111; social epistemology 108–109, 111; theory of society 111

economic mechanism: of social change 192–193; of social order 174–176

economic order in society 176, 178–179, 192–193, 195, 206

economic problem in society 174, 176–177

ego development 126

egoistic behaviour 7, 103, 136, 147, 161, 164–165, 170, 172, 174, 176, 182–183, 191, 203

emancipatory actions 165–178

emancipatory type of rational action 152–153

empiricism 13

empiricist theory of knowledge 17–20

ends-in-themselves 119, 166–167, 184

epistemological capacity 204

epistemological inquiries 5

epistemology of critical rationalism 42–44

epistemology of science 34–36, 43, 71

equal access of individuals 172

equal rights of rational beings 171–172

evolution of society 135, 137–140, 155–156, 158, 181, 193–194

fallibility of the premises 22–24, 84, 95

falsification principle 35, 66, 81–82

free labour 118

general theory of critical rationalism 5, 85, 88, 91, 94–95, 97–98, 102–103, 105, 143, 149, 152–153, 161, 178, 185, 195, 200, 202, 205–206

genuine knowledge 10

Gettier, E.L. 10–12

good life, concept of 187–189

Habermas, J. 5, 155, 159; communicative actions 132–135, 194; epistemology 130, 140; justificationism 139–140; moral consciousness 138–139; notion of justified consensus 130–134, 136, 139–140; rationality of actions 132–134, 136; rationalization of social systems 137; speech acts 131–134; theory of social evolution 135, 137–140, 155–156, 158, 181, 193–196; theory of society 130, 134–136; truth as justified consensus 130–131; validity claims 131–132; worldviews 138–139

Hobbes, T. 161; approach to problem of action 147; political order 186; portrait of human nature 162; problem of social order 124, 135, 146–147, 150, 161–164, 181

Hobbesian problem of social order 124, 135, 146, 150, 161–162, 164, 181

Index 209

human rights 7–8, 171–178, 181–182, 189–193, 195, 205–206
human society, evolution of 8
Hume, D. 15; critique of induction 16, 23, 28; justificationism 31, 49; problem of induction 28–29

ideal type of rational action 6, 112
inductive logic 19, 23
inductive reasoning 28, 31, 34, 60, 69
inference forms 13
infinite regress 48, 103; problem of 68
institutional learning processes 204
instrumental actions 132–134
instrumental rationality 132, 136, 151–152
intellectual certainty 14
intellectualism 13
intellectualist theory of knowledge 13–17
intuition 14
irrational faith in reason 1–2, 4, 40, 42–44, 46–49, 51–58, 60–61, 87, 89–90, 92, 104, 201; *see also* Popper, K.
irrationalism 2, 28, 31, 41–42, 46, 52–53, 87, 89, 91, 97–98; *see also* critical rationalism/critical rationalist theory

Jaegwon, K. 15
Jarvie, I.C. 35–36, 41, 98, 101; *The Republic of Science* 36
Joachim, H.H. 14
justificational concept of rationality 5, 39, 57, 156
justification/justificationism 5, 9, 11–12; Durkheim's 111–112; epistemology 11; forms of deduction 74–75, 77–80; justificationist critical rationalism 75, 98–100; model of rational dialogue 104; philosophy of good life 187; separation of justification and criticism 5, 47–51, 72–74, 79–80, 83–84, 88–91, 95, 143, 148; theories of action 143–145; theory of knowledge 27; theory of rationality 5, 103–104; theory of society 6
justified consensus 130–134, 136, 139–140
justified true belief: account of knowledge 9–12, 20, 25, 67–68; dogmatic epistemology of 12–20

Kant, I. 15, 134–135, 203; critique of empiricism 28; *Critique of Practical Reason* 149; critique of pure reason 16–17, 28, 112–113, 149; doctrine of practical reason 112, 114; epistemology 16, 23, 112–113, 166, 203–204;

intellectualist theory of knowledge 16–17; justificationism 16–17, 28–29, 31, 129–130, 148–149, 166; Kingdom of Ends 166–167; model of rational action 113–114; modern scientific knowledge 121; moral philosophy 113–114, 150, 157, 166, 168, 204; practical reason 6, 117, 121, 134, 147, 150–151, 167, 171; pre-modern scientific inquiry 16; principle of justice and notion of rationality 171; pure reason 15–17; rational beings 149; rationalism 17; solution for Humean problem 28, 112; solution to problem of action 149; theory of knowledge 28, 121, 149; theory of practical reason 148–150; theory of society 205; 'things-in-themselves' 23; 'uncaused cause' of action 149; Weber's critique of moral philosophy 116–117, 120
Kingdom of Ends 166–167
knowing process 9
knowledge 3–4; absolute true 19; a priori 28; conditions for 10–11; dogmatic theory of 13; empiricist theory of 17–20; genuine 10; as inner representation of outer reality 15; intellectualist theory of 13–17; intuition basis of 28; as justified true belief 9–12, 20, 25, 67–68, 149; objective 11; as unfalsified conjecture 83
Koertge, N. 58

Larson, M.A. 169, 186
law 171, 189–190
legal mechanism of social order 170–172
legitimate governance 7–8, 173–174, 189, 191–192, 204–205
limits of rationality 52–54, 57
Locke, J. 18, 99–100; epistemology 18; *An Essay Concerning Human Understanding* 18; notion of innate ideas 19; *Of Civil Government: Two Treatises* 164; solution to problem of social order 163–164; version of utilities 164
logical judgment 5
logic of social development 137–139

macro-theory of society 152
market process 175, 179n1, 192
masses 158
Mayhew, L. 164
metaphysical mechanism: of social change 185–187; of social order 7, 165–169

210 Index

metaphysical theory 4
micro-foundations of macro-sociology 87, 152, 157, 199
Miller, D. 42–43
modus ponens 74–76
modus tollens 39, 62, 74–76
moral consciousness 138–139
moral dialogue 103–105, 188–189; for common values 103–105; for social order 159
moral law 113, 116–117, 121, 123–124, 129, 143, 145–153, 156–158, 165–168, 172, 182–185, 188, 201–205
moral mechanism of social order 169–170
moral philosophy 148–150
Musgrave, A. 10–11, 13, 17, 20, 67–68, 100

non-justificational model of deduction 76
non-justificationism: concept of reason and human action 7, 199–200; criterion for falsifiability 81–82; critical rationalism 71, 97, 101–103; deductive inference 5, 73–74, 76, 79, 81–82; emancipatory actions and 202–203; epistemology 2, 4–5, 66, 94; formula for 84–85; instrumental rationality 151–152; moral philosophy 149; non-justificationist model of rational dialogue 104; theory of action 145–146, 150; theory of knowledge 4–5, 43, 77, 82–85, 96, 103, 150, 156, 181, 185, 200–202; theory of rationality 5, 93–94, 98–102, 199; value rationality 150–151
normative consensus 177, 182, 201, 204
normative development 138
normative model of action 6, 145
Notturno, M.A. 31

objective knowledge 3, 5, 9, 11, 13, 16, 19, 21, 48, 66–67; conditions for 72; dogmatic and sceptic epistemologies of 21–24, 69–70; as justificational concept 24–25; non-justificationist standard of 94; as unfalsified conjecture 70–73, 88, 93; *see also* knowledge
openness to criticism 3–4, 54, 57–60, 62–63, 66, 73, 78–81, 83–84, 87–88, 90, 93, 101–102, 105n1, 156, 188, 191, 201–202
open society 2, 1–2, 8, 39–40, 198, 206
ordinary actions 153–155, 178–179
ordinary type of rational action 153–155
oversocialized conception of man 147, 152–153, 155, 184, 203, 206

pancritical rationalism 2–4, 47, 51, 55–63, 87; comparison with uncritical rationalism 57–58; critical reflections on 58–61, 63n2; Diller's critique 60; logical critique of 61–63; rationality problem and 92; separation between justification and criticism 89–91; Watkins's critique 58–59
panrationalism 48, 56–57, 62, 90–93, 99
Parsons, T. 5, 118, 150, 154–155, 159, 161–163, 203; action theory 121–122; dimensions of action 128; on Durkheim's epistemology 111; functions of social system 128–129; justificationism 129–130; scheme of pattern variables 125–128; socialization process 126; sociology 120–121; solution to Hobbesian problem of social order 124–129, 135, 146, 150, 161–162, 164, 181; theory of social order 7, 166–167, 170; theory of society 120, 125–129, 162; unit act 121–122, 154; utilitarian model of action 122–123; view of social change 183–184; voluntaristic action theory 121–123, 125–126, 144, 152
pattern variables, scheme of 125–128
Petzall, A. 18, 99
pluralism 100–101
pluralistic liberal society 100
political governance 174, 178, 182, 191, 195, 206
political mechanism: of social change 190–192; of social order 172–174
Popper, K. 87, 201; *Conjectures and Refutations* 32, 50; critical rationalism 1–2, 4, 27, 38–44, 46, 52–54; critique of justificational theory of knowledge 32–33, 48–49; deductive inference 38; distinction between context of discovery and context of justification 32; epistemological problem 30–32; epistemology 4, 37–39; epistemology of science 34–36, 43, 71; idea of conjectural knowledge 32–34; 'intersubjective' testability of scientific claims 37; irrational faith 54–55; irrational faith in reason 1–2, 4, 40, 42–44, 46–49, 51–58, 60–61, 87, 89–90, 92, 104, 201; justificationism 2, 52–54; logic of scientific knowledge 36–37; *The Logic of Scientific Discovery* 36; modus tollens 39, 62, 74–76; non-justificational concept of criticism 38; notion of rational

Index 211

criticism 62; *The Open Society and Its Enemies* 39; principle of induction 29; problem of induction 4; question of objective knowledge 27; rationality of science 31; reading of epistemological problem 27–28; solution for induction problems 34–37; theory of knowledge 31; theory of open society 2, 206; theory of science 27–28, 32, 34–37, 44nn2–3; *The Two Fundamental Problems of the Theory of Knowledge* 34

postconventional pattern of problemsolving 138, 194

preconventional pattern of problemsolving 138, 194

predestination doctrine 119–120, 140n1

principle of justice 171–173

problem of action theory 146; critical rationalism and 147–148; Hobbes's approach to 147

problem of demarcation 34–35, 50, 81

problem of induction 4, 16, 27–36, 49, 58, 61, 69–71, 88, 112

problem of objective knowledge 3, 5, 9–25, 29–33, 37, 66, 68, 71–72, 82, 85, 93, 198–199

problem of social change 140, 181–182, 185, 203, 205–206; *see also* social change

problem of social order 161–165, 167, 170, 176, 182, 199, 203–204; critical rationalist formulation 164–165; solution to 161–164; *see also* social order/social ordering

problem-solving ability of theory 4, 49, 51, 55, 62, 71, 89–90

property rights 174

pure reason 15–17, 28, 113, 149

Pyrrhonian scepticism 21

Quine, W.V. 79

rational action 6

rational beings 7, 91, 112–118, 148–150, 157, 165–166, 170–177, 184, 188, 202–205

rationalist theory of human action: emancipatory type 152–153, 165–178; ordinary type 153–155, 178–179

rationality, problem of 91–93

rationalization of society 155, 157–159

Rawls, J. 100–101

reason, role of 6

Restall, G. 78–79

Rowbottom, D.P. 43–44

scepticism/sceptics: academic 21; critique of dogmatism 23; and critique of objective knowledge 21–24; dogmatism 48; epistemology 4, 20–24, 27; historical origin 21–22; irrationalism 2; Pyrrhonian 21; response to intellectualism 22; sense experiences 22

Sceski, J.H. 33

Schmid, M. 138

scientific inquiry 16

scientific knowledge 28; *see also* knowledge

self-evident principles 13–15, 17–18, 21–22, 24

sense experiences 13

separation of justification and criticism 5, 47–51, 72–74, 79–80, 83–84, 88–91, 95, 143, 148, 201

shared values and institutions 155–156, 178

social change 7–8, 129, 140, 155, 157–158, 181, 195, 198, 200, 203, 205–206; concept of the good life 187–189; in context of metaphysical beliefs 185–187; critical rationalist view 188; cultural mechanism of 182–189; economic mechanism of 192–193; emancipatory action and 181–182; governance and 189–192; governmental mechanism of 190–192; moral mechanism of 188; non-justificational perspective 156; Parsons's view of 183–184; political mechanism of 190–192

social dialogue 7

social evolution 135, 137–140, 155–156, 158, 181, 193–194

social institutions 7–8, 126, 153, 156–158, 178–179, 181–182, 195, 202–205

social integration 139, 194

social movements 7, 158, 187, 189–190, 203

social order/social ordering 7, 182, 203–205; critical rationalism and moral dialogue for 159; critical-rationalist theory of 7; cultural forces of 7; economic mechanism of 174–176; human action for 165–178; legal mechanism of 170–172; metaphysical aspect of 7; metaphysical mechanism of 165–169; moral mechanism of 169–170; political mechanism of 172–174; problem of 161–165, 167, 170, 176, 182, 199, 203–204; role of ordinary actions in 178–179; sociological analysis of 176–178

212   Index

social rationalization 137, 157
social systems 126, 128–129, 137
sociological analysis of social order 176–178
sociological theory 143, 147, 150, 159, 161
speech acts 131–134
superego 126
supply and demand mechanism 174–176, 193

temporal structuring 17
theory of human action 6, 150; 'emancipatory' ideal type 152–155; instrumental rationality 151–152; value rationality 150–151
theory of irrationality 97
theory of knowledge: Descartes, Rene 15; Kant, Immanuel 28, 121, 149; Popper, Karl 31
theory of society 1–3, 5–8, 44, 46, 85, 87, 103, 105, 107–112, 152, 155–157, 159, 161–162, 164, 166–167, 169–170, 182–183, 196, 198–199, 203–206; Durkheim, Emile 111; Kant, Immanuel 205; Parsons, Talcott 120, 125–129, 162; Weber, Max 112
theory of voluntaristic action 121–123, 126, 152–153
thinkers 158
thinkers-social movements-masses 7, 158, 187, 189–190, 203
Thorsrud, H.: *Ancient Scepticism* 20; sceptic epistemology 20–21
Tudor idea of order 186

uncritical rationalism 46–47, 56–58
unfalsified belief 5, 7

unfalsified conjecture 5, 66, 91, 205; objective knowledge as 70–73, 83
utilitarian and normative models of human action 143–145
utilitarian model of action 6

validity claims 100, 131–132, 134, 153, 204
value rationality 126, 132, 134, 145–146, 150–152, 157, 202
value system 7
voluntaristic action theory 121–123, 125–126, 144, 152

'war of all against all' 110–111, 124–125, 136, 147, 154, 158, 161, 163, 167, 183
Warren, M. 116–117
Watkins, J.W.N. 58–59
Weber, M. 5, 146, 150, 168, 203; concept of meaningful action 114–115; critique of Kantian practical reason 117–118; critique of Kant's moral philosophy 116–117, 120; justificationism 117–120, 168; models of rational action 114–117; *The Protestant Ethic and the Spirit of Capitalism* 118; role of Calvinism 119; *The Sociology of Religion* 118; theory of society 112; understanding of predestination 119–120; value rationality 112, 114–118, 120
worldviews 118, 120, 138–139, 158, 166, 168–169, 177, 186–187, 189, 195
Wrong, D.H. 124, 147, 161–162; 'The Oversocialized Conception of Man in Modern Sociology' 147

Young, H. 15

Printed in the United States
By Bookmasters